Fifty Sounds

FIFTY SOUNDS

A Memoir of Language,
Learning, and Longing

POLLY BARTON

Liveright Publishing Corporation
A DIVISION OF W. W. NORTON & COMPANY
Independent Publishers Since 1923

For information about permission to reproduce selections from this book,
write to Permissions, Liveright Publishing Corporation, a division of
W. W. Norton & Company, Inc., 500 Fifth Avenue, New York, NY 10110

For information about special discounts for bulk purchases,
please contact W. W. Norton Special Sales at
specialsales@wwnorton.com or 800-233-4830

Manufacturing by Lakeside Book Company
Production manager: Beth Steidle

ISBN 978-1-324-09131-8

Liveright Publishing Corporation
500 Fifth Avenue, New York, N.Y. 10110
www.wwnorton.com

W. W. Norton & Company Ltd.
15 Carlisle Street, London W1D 3BS

1 2 3 4 5 6 7 8 9 0

"Well, how do I know? If that means 'Have I reasons?' the answer is: my reasons will soon give out. And then I shall act, without reasons."
—LUDWIG WITTGENSTEIN,
Philosophical Investigations, tr. G. E. M. Anscombe

"The reach of desire is defined in action:
beautiful (in its object), foiled (in its attempt),
endless (in time)."
—ANNE CARSON,
Eros the Bittersweet

"(language experiences orgasm upon touching itself)"
—ROLAND BARTHES,
A Lover's Discourse, tr. Richard Howard

Contents

Preface

IT'S MY LUNCH BREAK AND I'm being serenaded by a lime-green owl. "Did you know!" the owl calls as it swaggers jauntily across my line of sight, "There are more people learning languages on Duolingo in the US than there are people learning foreign languages in the entire US public school system!"

The year is 2019, and I will soon be traveling to Italy for the summer, which is why I have found myself being taught Italian vocabulary and grammar, along with a variety of trivia, by this digital apparition, the mascot of the language-learning app Duolingo. I learned of Duolingo's existence only recently, but it transpires to be phenomenally popular, offering courses in 23 languages to 300 million users worldwide. Initially, there seems to me something faintly Japanese about the wing-gestures made by the mascot, Duo, but I check and discover that the company originated in the United States, as I suppose I should have guessed from the trivia-nugget above; it's the brainchild of Luis von Ahn and Severin Hacker, born out of the idea that "free education will really change the world."

Duo's screech is unvoiced but it sticks in my head nonetheless, whooping and half-demented, Disney-villainesque: *Did you know! Did you know! Did you know!* And no, as it happens, I didn't know. At least the first time big-eyed big-eyelashed Duo addressed me, I didn't know. By the tenth time it pops up on my screen I've begun to feel very familiar with this particular bit of trivia, and I also know something else: each run-in with it leaves me feeling a little unclean, in a way I can't really account for.

As the fact I am spending my lunchtimes with Duo reveals, I am not entirely skeptical of its methods, and I don't find the comparison drawn between public-school language education and the Duolingo model outrageous, at least prima facie. Unlike a lot of language-focused applications, Duolingo is not devoid of audio content; it has clips of real people talking, and invites its users to speak phrases into the microphone, so they are at least interacting with how the language actually sounds, and feels in the mouth. While its level-unlocking structure drawn from the world of gaming means that users might be focusing on strategies to pass rather than to truly master, the same accusation could be leveled at language education in schools: there is, in short, a lot of hoop-jumping. You learn the language the way that the exam boards or the green owl want you to, but it is, at least, a start. If it makes language education accessible and enjoyable to those who might not otherwise have access to it, then that is surely a good thing.

So why, then, does Duo's factoid bring me such a sense of unease, and why do I begrudge his hooting pride? It dawns on me that the source of my discomfort resides, utterly unreasonably, with his use of the word "learning." I say unreasonably, because I recognize that this word is used legitimately to cover a whole range of activities undertaken with varying degrees of intensity. The generous, rational part of me can see there is no cause to bar people from calling their five or twenty minutes a day on Duolingo "learning a language." But even as I have this thought, another part of me stamps its foot resentfully, the kind of foot-stamp that ends up hurting the stamper, and declares that the world has turned its eyes from what is real and true. This part wants to say its piece. It wants wider recognition that there is another, far less stable form of learning—a radium to Duolingo's lurid neon.

The language learning I want to talk about is a sensory bombardment. It is a possession, a bedevilment, a physical takeover; it is streams of sounds pouring in and striking off scattershot associations in a manner so chaotic and out of control that you are taken by the desire to block your ears—except that even when you do block your ears, your head remains an echo chamber. The language learning that fascinates me is not livening your commute and scoring a dopamine hit with another "5 in a row! Way to go!" Rather, it is never getting it right, hating yourself for never getting it right, staking your self-worth on getting it right next time. It is getting it right and feeling as if your entire existence has been validated. It is the kind of learning that makes you think: this is what I must have experienced in infancy except I have forgotten it, and at times it occurs to you that you have forgotten it not just because you were too young when it happened but because there is something so utterly destabilizing about the experience that we as dignified, shame-fearing humans are destined to repress it. It is a learning that doesn't know goals or boundaries, and which is commonly known as "immersive." The image that springs to mind is a lone figure wading

gallantly into the sea, naked, without a single swimming lesson behind them.

As you'll have inferred from my self-righteous tone, I
speak from experience. "Immersion" is exactly what I did
when I went to Japan, although probably it's more correct
to say that immersion is what happened to me. If I'd known
what I was getting myself into before I went out there I may
well not have had the nerve to go, and knowing this, I don't go
around patting myself on the back for having done it. At least,
I don't believe that I do, until I'm confronted with the pride of
a green owl, and then I realize that there is some part of me
that wants for this experience of mine to be recognized. Not
only is this part not rational—it's furious with all the goal-
driven rationality of the commute-friendly app.

In particular, what I'm burning to tell Duo is the following: Did you know! When you immerse yourself in a very different language as a total beginner, not only do you not have
goals! You also have no system within which to conceptualize
what those objectives could be—discounting, that is, over-
arching goals like "learning to read," or "becoming fluent,"
which themselves start to seem less and less meaningful the
more you poke around beneath their smooth surfaces!

Immersion in a foreign language is a bombardment of
sounds, until you decide that you are going to actually do
this thing and learn, and then it becomes a bombardment of
imperatives: learn this, learn this, learn this. *Just start from
the basics*, sings a voice in your head as you are tossed around
in the waves of incomprehensibility. Yet as you continue to live
in a language you don't know, it becomes increasingly obvious
to you how much this category of "basics" could theoretically

encompass. Greetings and everyday interactions are of course basic, and there is always something embarrassing about not knowing basic forms of verbs. Everyone knows numbers are incredibly basic, as are colors, clothes, the subjects you study at school, animals, anything to do with weather, and adjectives for describing people. In fact, we could go ahead and say that every object is also basic, and there is something particularly alarming when you don't know how to say the first words you would have learned in your language(s) as a child: teddy, buggy, shoelace. And then there is the most fundamental-seeming vocabulary of all: abstract nouns, like justice, friendship, pleasure, evil, and vanity.

If the language in question has a writing system different from that you know, then even mastering "the basics" of the spoken language isn't enough, because a whole new category of basics awaits you in the form of the written one. In particular, Japanese is the gift that keeps on giving in this regard, having as it does three different scripts: two phonetic ones, katakana and hiragana (collectively known as kana), with 46 characters apiece; and then the kanji, or characters of Chinese origin, 2,136 of which have been officially deemed "in common usage." Which means, there is never any shortage of basics to trip you up and convince you of how little you know.

Last week (this is true), I had to look up a kanji that turned out to mean "owl." It wasn't entirely new to me; I'd learned it somewhere down the line and then forgotten it, but the experience still brought me to my knees with shame. Yes, it's not a commonly used character, but then I'm supposed to be a translator. I should know something as basic as "owl."

As I sat staring down in despair at the owl kanji, wishing

my self from two minutes ago had only managed to remember it, wondering how I could have failed to recognize a legless bird on a tree, I recalled without warning an incident from long ago, back when I'd been learning Japanese for a little over two years and had just found a job at a small Japanese publishing company in London. One day I glanced up to see O, a senior employee, approaching my desk. In his hand were two of the slips that employees had to submit when requesting or reporting time off, and as he moved closer, I saw they were the ones I had recently filled in.

"Polly-chan," he said, pulling up a chair beside me, looking at me in a way that managed to be both conspiratorial and didactic, "Let's talk. Your kanji usage is all over the place."

"Oh," was all I had the wherewithal to reply. I felt simultaneously apprehensive about what was to come, and flattered that he was taking the time to school me individually.

"Sometimes you write them perfectly, and sometimes they're totally off."

As he spoke, O's eyes drifted to my computer monitor, around whose edge I'd stuck up a number of kanji written out on small post-it notes. I remember that one of them was "crow": the same as "bird," but with the stroke symbolizing the eye missing. This had cropped up during one of the translations I'd been asked to do the previous week, and I hadn't known it.

"You don't need that," O said, pointing at the crow. He began to hover his finger around the other post-its, informing me which I did and didn't need. Then, with hawk-like focus, his attention moved back to the offending slip.

"Look," he said, his finger thumping the desk. "Look what

you've written here. This is missing a radical. You can't just miss parts of kanji like that, because then they mean something else entirely. You're trying to write 'problem' and this says 'mon.'"

Maybe sensing that I was struggling a bit to keep up, he looked me right in the eye, and enunciated in English of a crispness that bordered on hostility, "'Mon' means 'gate.' You've written 'gate.'"

I looked down to see that he was, of course, right. My slip read something that might be rendered in English: "Unforeseen absence due to health gate."

Even ten years on, this episode feels as real and close as it ever did, and I can't resist the idea that, in some way, it still encapsulates my status in relation to Japan. To wit, I am always writing the gate. It's a huge, lofty gate of the kind found in temples; I stand by its posts, passing in and out momentarily, variously welcomed, frowned at, and ousted by its keepers. Even when I'm inside, I'm perpetually aware how quickly I could again be pushed out, that I could find some basic item inexplicably missing from my knowledge. Sometimes I ask myself if things would be different if I'd done my undergraduate degree in Japanese, or a proper language course, or a PhD—if I'd entrusted the responsibility for accumulating the basics to a system larger than myself in some way. The answer, I think, is *slightly*. I imagine I would feel at least slightly less liable to have the rug pulled from underneath me, to realize suddenly that I'm on the wrong side of the gate.

For when learning takes a primarily autodidactic form, mastering something is dependent on noticing it, or having it pointed out to you. To the extent that you're not consulting other sources, obtaining an accurate view of the inventory of items to be learned is all down to exposure, and your ability to perceive that exposure, which is particularly relevant when we're speaking about aspects of language and culture radically different from anything we've experienced before. We can notice them, be outraged or intrigued by them, exoticize them, and therefore hoover them up, bump them to the top of our rota—or, else, we can fail to see them really, fail to appreciate them in their fullness. We are too busy thrashing around in the waves, gulping, spitting, and trying to stay afloat.

———

When it comes to Japanese, another possible candidate for inclusion in a list of "basics" is its vast range of onomatopoeia—or mimetics, as this area of the language is often referred to. I say possible because the question of whether or not onomatopoeia should rightfully be seen as "basic" could be debated endlessly, but suffice for the moment to say that, as someone approaching the language with a profoundly English mindset, I didn't register it as such. Indeed, in a way I now find pretty embarrassing, it took an encounter with a dictionary to convince me of the prominent, and in some way fundamental role it plays in the language.

The dictionary, lying on the desk of a very stylish colleague, and one of the most attractively designed books I'd ever seen, was three fingers thick. At my colleague's encouragement, I opened it up to find it full of illustrations and, bizarrely enough, a lot of photographs of Western-looking children. These accounted for maybe a finger's worth of pages, but that still left two fingers' worth. Two fingers' worth, so maybe 250 pages, of Japanese mimetic language and its various usages for native speakers, laid out dictionary-style in the order of the Japanese syllabary.

I would like to pause for a moment here and spell out briefly for the unacquainted what this order consists in, because although culturally its function is analogous to that of the alphabet, the detailed picture is somewhat different—inevitably so, when we consider that its component parts, the kana, represent not individual consonants or vowels like the letters of the Greek or Roman alphabets, but longer, rhythmic units of speech called morae. The closest equivalent to morae we have in English are syllables—and indeed the kana are often referred to as syllabaries—but there is an important discrepancy, namely that a long Japanese syllable—tō or kyō—can be composed of two or three morae, so a two-syllable word such as "Tōkyō" or "happi" may be made up of three or four kana [to-u-kyo-u, ha-p-pi].

The system by which the kana are ordered—modeled on the phonology of another moraic language, Sanskrit—is known as the gojūon. This translates literally as "fifty sounds," and is a reference to the 5 × 10 grid used to display the characters that each symbolize a particular sound. The five vowel sounds found in the top row—a, i, u, e, o—are then transposed in the second "K" row to become ka, ki, ku, ke, ko; in the third "S" row to become sa, shi, su, se, so; and so on, for a total of ten rows. There is also an anomalous addition: the character "n," added significantly after the origin of the table, is the only kana that doesn't end in a vowel sound, and cannot be used to begin words. To complicate things even further, this late addition which floats freely at the bottom of the table is not the only deviation from the mathematical accuracy that a name like "fifty sounds" might suggest. In fact, the fifty sounds have never actually numbered fifty: the sounds "yi" or "wu" never existed; "ye" disappeared in the tenth century; and "wi" and "we" were made obsolete in the 1946 script reform, substituted by the sounds "i" and "e" from which they had become phonetically indistinguishable. In its current incarnation, the gojūon comprises forty-six elements, as follows:

	A	I	U	E	O
—	a	i	u	e	o
K	ka	ki	ku	ke	ko
S	sa	shi	su	se	so
T	ta	chi	tsu	te	to
N	na	ni	nu	ne	no
H	ha	hi	fu	he	ho
M	ma	mi	mu	me	mo
Y	ya		yu		yo
R	ra	ri	ru	re	ro
W	wa				wo
n					

To return, then, to the dictionary, the first page listed words in the order of the fifty sounds: aan, atafuta, a'kerakan, a'sari, anguri, a'pua'pu, ahaha . . . These days, I could tell you what most of these words mean; back then, I recognized one. What mattered, though, was not how much I did or didn't understand, but rather the realization this encounter brought about. *I'm not delusional after all*, it ran, *all those individual instances of onomatopoeia which have intrigued and niggled at me are part of some recognized holistic phenomenon.*

I have no intention of implying that sound-symbolism is in and of itself a unique feature of Japanese, or somehow incomprehensible to us as Anglophones; on the contrary, English has a healthy array of sound-symbolic vocabulary, ranging from words like "oink," "splash," and "boom," which conform to the dictionary definition of onomatopoeia as those words emulating the noise of sound-producing phenomena, to more indirect or borderline examples like "zig-zag," "trudge," and "dilly-dally," which emulate the qualities of things they represent, as opposed to their sounds. In the case of "dilly-dally," for example, the "d" sounds connote lethargy and heaviness, while the reduplicated structure suggests a drawn-out quality, both of which in some way prop up the word's meaning of dawdling. When we begin to tune in to this aspect of our language, we find that even verbs which would not commonly be registered as mimetic, like "trudge" and "slip," do in fact transpire to have sound-symbolic properties.

Nevertheless, the onomatopoeic landscape within Japanese differs from that of English in two main ways. Firstly, there is a discrepancy when it comes to numbers. Although exact quantities of mimetic vocabulary are hard to calculate and compare across languages, it is generally acknowledged that the size of the Japanese onomatopoeic vocabulary surpasses that of Indo-European languages by three to five times, and is by some reckonings the largest in the world after Korean. Secondly, and perhaps more crucially, is the difference in the way that mimetics are categorized; like many other languages, Japanese differs from English in acknowledging a specialized class of onomatopoeic words, and its mimetics take one of a number of several specific patterns, which for the most part make them immediately recognizable as such. As a result, in Japanese there is a far clearer sense of which words are and aren't onomatopoeic, and much more of a social precedent for verbally naming and acknowledging the use of mimetic language, which forms a marked contrast to the blurred and mostly undiscussed boundary lines of English onomatopoeia. There is also a clear and well-understood distinction between giongo, where words mimic sounds, and gitaigo, where words are mimicking non-auditory properties.

These factors go some way to explaining why it took me a while to focus in on Japanese onomatopoeia, and why I was predisposed to underestimate the importance of its place in the language. Yet the more I read about Japanese mimetics, the more I came to understand that I wasn't alone in this. Japanese mimetics have been largely overlooked in the field of linguistics and related scholarship, part of a pattern of marginalization that can be traced as far back as a declaration by Ferdinand de Saussure, the founder of modern linguistics and semiology, that onomatopoeic elements of language are "marginal phenomena" which are "never organic elements of a linguistic system," and "far fewer than is generally believed." Uncomfortably enough, my assumptions made me an unwitting part of a whole movement of

Westerners, striding boldly forth with their unchallenged assumptions that the unknown will conform to the pattern of what they are used to, and riding roughshod over any evidence to the contrary.

Indeed, it is really only in the last few decades that linguistics scholars have begun to kick back against this marginalization, mounting the case that, unfortunately, one cannot magic away the thornier elements of language simply because they do not conform to the neat rules upon which one has decided for one's system. Japanese linguistics scholars of recent years have provided an eloquent and impassioned argument for the affective, somatic aspects of Japanese mimetics, which means they cannot be analyzed purely in terms of their semantic dimension. For those who have grown up with them, argues Sotarō Kita, one such linguist, the ability of mimetics to evoke vivid, affect-rich "images" of an experience, to place listener and speaker alike immediately "at the scene," is beyond doubt. "The question," he adds, "is how to characterize this feeling."

Although admittedly not of a kind which would satisfy any linguistics scholar, we could hazard one characterization of this feeling by turning to the very mimetics whose effect we're trying to account for. Maza-maza, we might say in an attempt to describe the impressions they leave— the sound of something seeming very vivid. I could translate what my dictionary says about the word: "The state of a certain occurrence being distinctly perceived in the mind," or else give some examples of the English translations of sentences containing maza-maza which I find online: "a vivid reminder of the fact that," "clearly brought home to someone that," "graphic statement," etc. I could try and explain why it is that I hear the word in my best friend's voice, the voice of various characters in novels I have read and translated, the voices of a hundred different people, and why I can hear where the emphasis falls when it is to be especially emphasized. I could attempt to describe why it now feels to me that this sort of onomatopoeic language is where the beating heart of Japanese lies. Why, from a certain point in time, I ditched my previous ambition to master the bewilderingly complex web of honorifics that even native speakers routinely get wrong, and which always seemed to distinguish hardcore Japanophiles from those whom Japanese society merely humored, and set my sights instead on being able to use mimetic language properly, naturally. Why, to the extent that I still have a linguistic ambition, it is to speak the kind of Japanese which takes mimetics as its beacon: a Japanese of gesturing and storytelling, of searing description, of embodied reality.

Leafing through my first dictionary of onomatopoeia, identical to that of my colleague, I felt with a vivid certainty that my whole project of learning Japanese was doomed. I've misused mimetics and felt burning embarrassment; I've used them correctly and felt great satisfaction, and then later, a delayed sort of burning embarrassment, for being a smart-ass. I have found them ridiculous, adorable, intuitive, counterintuitive, enlightening, profound. Now when I look back at the course of my language learning, they lie there studding my path like waymarkers, tracing the course of my evolution. My relationship with the Japanese language has, in general, been an affect-driven one, but there is something about my journey with Japanese mimetics that feels unique.

Throughout what follows, Japanese mimetics will serve not only as a specific linguistic phenomenon, but also the symbol of a particular view of language. In this understanding, language is something we learn with our bodies, and through our body of experiences; where semantics are umbilically tied to somatics, where our experiences and our feelings form a memory palace; where words are linked to particular occasions, particular senses, which gradually fade the more practiced we become but remain there nonetheless in memory, forming a personal genealogy of the tongues we speak. In some way, it represents the opposite of the textbooks, memorized lists of verbs, and smartphone apps that come to many people's minds at the mention of the words "language learning."

Since it is inseparable from the bodies that speak it and the feelings that drive it, this form of language does not permit of a reductive semantic analysis. At the very least, such an analysis is bound to miss something, and it is to exactly this something that this book would like to attend. What follows, then, holds no aspirations to serve as a balanced or academically rigorous investigation, vowing instead to concern itself with felt experience; it positions itself less as interpretation, and more as erotics—as unscientific and unashamedly subjective celebration of the interpersonal dimension to taking up a language. Over time, I have come to believe that if language learning is anything, it is the always-bruised but ever-renewing desire to draw close: to a person, a territory, a culture, an idea, an indefinable feeling. These pages offer themselves as a paean to this act of devotion.

———

[A note: in what follows, I will be deviating from the strict dictionary definition of the English word "onomatopoeia" as that which refers exclusively to words imitating auditory phenomena, and rather using the words "onomatopoeia" and "mimetics" broadly and interchangeably to refer to any sound-symbolic vocabulary.]

Fifty Sounds

¶ giro': the sound of eyes riveting deep into holes in your self-belief, or vicariously visiting the Nocturama, or every party where you have to introduce yourself

SOMETIMES I THINK THAT IF I could telescope the last fifteen years into a single scene it would go like this. We begin with a wide shot, the camera skimming the lofty ceiling of a large, open-plan room. Sunset seeps in through the tall windows, picking out bright parallelograms of light on the walls, and we hear the gentle burble that marks out the early stages of a party. It's hard to pin down where this party is, because in truth it isn't one party but all of them, so for the sake of argument let's have it somewhere in Britain. The Japanese version plays out quite differently, anyway. So the odd snatch of recognizable English, then, as the camera begins to float its way down from the high ceiling, homing in on a corner where a woman is standing with a group, holding a glass of wine, introductions, let's say it's some kind of opening and they all have nice semi-creative careers: graphic designers, journalists, event coordinators. Everyone is politely fascinated and fascinating, but when the woman is asked what her job is and tells them she's a translator, is asked what languages and says, Japanese, you can feel even on screen a crevice opening up

in the air. It's not incredulity or aggression, not awe or surprise or defensiveness, but it's not unlike any of these things,
and there is some exhaling, some eyebrows raised in a way
that they weren't for the graphic designer. Some alert glances
and follow-up questions. And then the conversation moves
on, shifts away from the woman because her body-language
seems to indicate that she doesn't want to hold forth on what
it is that she does. The moment passes, conversation limps
along for a while and then the cluster starts to disintegrate.
The woman makes to move off, and a man who had been
standing opposite her reads her movements and breaks off
with her, two fish flitting away from the shoal. He says her
name, which he has remembered, and appends to it a question
mark. They come to a standstill facing each other, a little way
off from where the group was before. He reintroduces himself, maybe they shake hands, and then he leans in slightly,
his palm coming to rest against a partitioning wall, a lopsided
smile floating on his face, and he says, "So . . ."

We wonder, with the woman, what's coming, although
something in the woman's expression suggests to us that she
knows in her heart of hearts exactly what's coming.

"Why Japan?"

The camera freezes for a moment to take this in, catch the
incline of his torso, catch the look in his eye which, despite
the smile still suspended across his face, is strangely urgent.
Probing is a word you could use to describe this look, and
it feels more marked coming from someone you wouldn't
expect to show unveiled interest in another person—who you
might expect to view such behavior as a form of weakness.
And then we pan to the woman, and we're expecting this con-

versation to proceed in the intense yet witty way that conversations are supposed to go at these parties, particularly in films of these parties, but what comes over her face is instead a look of discomfort. Surely by now, we think, this woman will have formulated an answer to come out with in these situations, something pat, light, flirtatious, even if it isn't strictly accurate—but it seems that she hasn't. Instead, she visibly melts from the question, face scrunching up unphotogenically.

"I don't really know." She flashes him the hopeful smile of someone trying their pet once again with a food they know all too well it dislikes. "It just sort of happened."

The camera pans back to the man's face and we recognize the glint in his eyes from before, undiminished—in fact if anything augmented—and now, if we were not feeling it before, we start to feel uncomfortable. We confirm to ourselves that there was something about his previous expression that was oddly intent, that we hadn't just been imagining it. It dawns on us that this man is not going to accept this non-answer, and the first note of panic sounds in our chests. We're unclear why the woman is being so reticent, but what is clear is that the man will do everything in his power not to let her disappoint him. We don't know why, either—if it's some specific query he has, or some commonality he's felt between them: a darkness, a difference. Is he a Japanophile? Or has her uncalled-for coyness piqued something in him? In any case, the look is unmistakable, and it grows more so every micro-second the camera lingers on the glint in his eyes. The glint speaks.

Prove yourself, it says. *I'm serious, now. Don't let me down. You owe me this.*

———

Needless to say, of course, this woman is me. I am the woman who has been asked at a conservative estimate a thousand times over the last fifteen years why and how she found herself in Japan in the first place yet still doesn't have a decent answer to offer, and I am the woman who is naive enough to go on hoping that the next time she's put on the spot the response may miraculously come to her as it never has before, fully formed and universally accepted, as edifying to her as it is to her interlocutor. Or at least, I have been, in the past. As the years go by and no succinct answer surfaces, my belief that some new fact will reveal itself as the driving force behind the direction my life has taken inevitably diminishes. In fact, as time passes, something else happens; I've become more and more sure that what's brought me all this way is something verging on a feeling, or a darkness, or a cluster of interrelated feelings and darknesses—something which feels to me quite specific, but is almost impossible to pin down. Except right now, I feel like I might be able to do it. In this moment, the answer I feel to be the most truthful would be to point to that final shot of the man's glare, poised on a knife-edge between thinking the woman important and thinking her a waste of time, and say, this. This in the eyes right here, this is why I was in Japan.

It's hard to know what to name a look like that, so as to account for its force. Were this not a film but a manga, then the close-up of the man's eyes would be appended with a sound-effect in written form. Giro' it would say, in dark blocky strokes. Giro', where you drop sharply off the end of the "o" and leave a taut pause. This pause is known in Japanese as a sokuon. Preceding a consonant, as it usually does, a sokuon indicates the lengthening or gemination of that consonant, which is why in standard systems of romanization, it is symbolized by duplicating the subsequent consonant: girotto, for example, where "to" is the quotative particle frequently needed to integrate the mimetic into the sentence, enabling its transition to adverb and so on. Here, though, I've opted to symbolize the sokuon with an apostrophe, partly because there are some sounds, like this one, which end in a free-hanging pause, which I want to talk about without presupposing what comes next, and partly because I feel the apostrophe draws closer to summoning the spirit of what the Japanese symbol does, in opening up a hole, a gap, a pause. Shut up, the sokuon says, and allow the drama to play out.

Which is apposite here, because giro' is a sound very much concerned with drama. Giro' is a sound of utter attention on the part of the giro'ter, so you can almost hear the heart of the giro'tee skipping a mini-beat. A Google image search for giro' yields an array of animals—dogs, cats, bears, owls—glaring; this is the sound of not softening the ferocity of one's look for the sake of social nicety. Giro' is about letting your eyes fulfil their natural, most aquiline potential. It is about using the assets biology and society have granted you to make immodest demands of people.

———

To explain that I feel this giro'ting has been happening to me all my life, that it seems to me in some sense an archetype of social experience, seems both too much and not enough. I feel that I need to speak more about my response to it, although in a sense the fact that I'm perceiving it as a giro' already says all you need to know, namely: it works on me. It predated the reel of conscious memory, then it continued to work through childhood and take various guises, where it was feared and loathed and occasionally triumphantly overcome, and then it brought elation. And so it has become the site that is returned to again and again, becomes that which is chosen, even as it is still feared and loathed and uncomfortable.

I suspect, for example, that it was a similar kind of giro'ting that convinced me to do a philosophy degree, all because, at the age of seventeen, I went to visit an acquaintance of my mother's who tutored teenagers attempting to get into specific universities. I wasn't in need of tutoring, but I'd been encouraged to apply to Cambridge, and my mother had arranged for me to go and speak to this woman to help me make up my mind whether I should. Which was how I found myself in her front room, eyes roving her bookshelves and the wings of her armchair as she stood in front of me and asked me questions about the Cambridge philosophy course.

"What do you know about it?" she asked, as her eyes bit into me, full of a strange light. "I mean, presumably you know that it's the birthplace of analytic philosophy? Wittgenstein was there, of course, and the course very much still reflects his legacy. Nothing 'continental' permitted, it's all Germans." Unlike teachers at my school, unlike almost any other woman I'd encountered, this woman didn't smile when she spoke, or otherwise soften herself. She held her tall body perfectly erect. "I suppose the question is, does that sort of analytic rigor appeal to you? Because it's not for everyone."

In honesty, I didn't know what analytic rigor really meant. I wanted to study existentialism more than I did any Germans, I was still wondering whether I wouldn't be better suited to English literature than philosophy, and just standing in a room with this woman was enough to make me feel wholly inadequate, a grinning, blushing, placating, childish mess. And yet there was something in the way she leaned in and frowned slightly when I spoke, as though she were trying to locate something she'd dropped in a clouded stream, the way her light eyes latched onto me as if trying to see through to whether or not I was worth bothering with, which sent a shimmer of metallic excitement through my veins.

As it happened, this meeting proved a more or less accurate taste of everything that was to come, everything I would feel on a daily basis at Cambridge. I was giro'ted by my philosophy professors, by my supervisors, by other students in my discussion class, and I felt constantly and thoroughly inarticulate and girlish and inadequate. Then, in my third year I stumbled upon the ultimate pair of eyes to giro'te me like I'd never been giro'ted before: those of Ludwig Wittgenstein. They had saved him up—at least that was my understanding of it. You worked through the history of philosophy in your first and second years, tackled the major ideas and then finally, in your third year, when you were allowed to select your modules, you could, if you played your cards right, encounter him. You were ready to. Certainly I was ready to, and the draw felt immediate. Soon enough, my bilingual edition of the *Philo-sophical Investigations* became a permanent fixture on the desk in my student room, and often I would return to myself from a trance to find myself staring at the photograph on the cover, incapable of peeling myself away from the pull of Witt-genstein's gaze. There was something about it, even in a black-and-white photograph, that contained depths I couldn't begin to put into words.

In time, I would find out that it wasn't just me, that many have fixated on the wonder of Wittgenstein's eyes. Years later, to my great surprise, I would open up W. G. Sebald's *Aus-terlitz* to find a photograph of them, extracted from the rest of his face but unmistakable nonetheless, staring out at me alongside those of an owl and a bush baby clipped into iden-tically sized rectangles; the comparison illustrates the narra-tor's point that the inhabitants of the Antwerp Nocturama share a quality with "certain painters and philosophers who seek to penetrate the darkness which surrounds us purely by means of looking and thinking." But it was the words of Colin McGinn, who devotes several lines' worth of descrip-tion to Wittgenstein's eyes, that I found the most resonant: "Imploring," McGinn writes,

> yet with an intense rage flaring just behind the iris, send-ing off an unnerving blend of supplication and admo-nition. . . . The look is simultaneously delicate and military, tender and ferocious. If you stare hard at the face, it seems to shift aspect from one of these poles to the other. . . . You feel the excitement and peril of an encounter with the man.

Thanks to McGinn, I felt I could fully formulate what it was that drew me: as I stared down at the picture of Wittgenstein on the front of the *Investigations*, not a full-frontal photograph of the kind featured in *Austerlitz* but a side-angle shot with Wittgenstein looking pensively off into the mid-distance, I would feel not only a pull, but a familiarity that seemed to bubble up from somewhere deep; it was like he was requiring something of me. *Come over to my side*, those eyes seemed to be saying, as ridiculous as it was to admit. *Be in this with me. Don't let me down.*

I did go over to his side, or at least I tried. I saturated myself in his philosophy, and allowed it to rearrange the apparatus of my thinking. The whole of my degree, I'd been waiting for my chosen subject to affect me in this way, and now it was actually happening. I believed in what he was doing. My feelings of inadequacy didn't go away when I studied him, but at least I was sure he was worth feeling inadequate for. And meanwhile, I was preparing for an inadequacy of a different order of magnitude: I was applying to go teach in Japan, where my mind would be rearranged in a different yet similarly irreversible way.

Framing it like this, even I want to reach for the question: why Japan? How did I know that this country I knew nothing about would have the power to do it, that it would look unsmilingly at me, "simultaneously delicate and military, tender and ferocious," so that I craved to become the sort of person that might satisfy? That it would giro'te me, again and again? Maybe it was just self-evident: going somewhere so different, there was never any chance it wouldn't be that way. To my twenty-one-year-old self, who had a radar for such things, it was clear that there I would sit forever poised on the knife-edge, impaled by an ever-renewing need to prove myself. That there I would live, every day, "the excitement and peril of the encounter with the man."

¶ giza-giza: the sound of seeing what you thought was yours through the lens of an alternative system, or of having your cock incomprehensibly sucked

CHERRY-BLOSSOM PINK IS HOW YOU could describe the color of the book that I used to cram for my interview at the Japanese Embassy. Now I wonder if that connotation was intentional, although unlike almost every other book about Japan, the cover didn't actually feature any pictures of cherry blossoms. It featured instead the bewildering instruction: *Teach Yourself Japanese Language, Life and Culture*. I had plucked it off the bookshop shelf because that was precisely what I was trying to do, and I suppose that subconsciously I embraced the title's ambitious promise, even as a more discerning self informed me how inadequate a single volume could ever be in facilitating that kind of knowledge. I say that, and yet as I let my eyes fall down the index page now, it strikes me as surprisingly detailed and wide-reaching in scope, and not overly dominated by the standard clichés. If I had actually consumed its contents in their entirety, I might have been able to bluff a working knowledge of the country. As it was, I don't think I ingested 20 percent.

Uncomfortable as it is to remember, I had the arrogance

back then to believe that I would be accepted into the Japan Exchange and Teaching Programme regardless of what I knew or didn't know, and regardless of how I felt about the country. Though I was entitled in many ways, I don't think this brand of presumptuous confidence was characteristic of my general approach in life, and I'm still not entirely sure what made this time different: whether it was specifically Japan which I thought would be clamoring to have me, or whether I rather thought myself over-qualified for a position teaching English (having, let's be clear, no teaching qualifications or experience of any kind). In any case, I underestimated the program completely, in a way that only became fully clear to me with the announcement that I'd been put on the waiting list, and that A, my boyfriend, with whom I'd applied, had been rejected flat out. I wasn't scandalized and I didn't feel they were mistaken, at least as far as I was concerned. The sensation was rather that of having been put in my rightful place.

All of which begs the question of what my motivation was for applying in the first place. I don't find it easy to unpick this question, but maybe the simplest, most honest answer I can give is: because A talked me into it. I was certain that I wanted to leave the country, but I was thinking about going to Bologna, which I'd fallen for during a visit in the summer holiday of my first year. Then A found out about a nationwide government-sponsored teaching program in Japan, and somehow before I knew it, I'd agreed to his idea that we both apply. I think I found the structure of it all appealing, the almost total surrender of any autonomy. As for the idea of going to Japan itself, I wasn't really sold on it, either with him or alone.

In hindsight, I can find a pattern and a sense in this ambivalence, although I'm aware it might read like the over-generous interpretation of a parent, a "Johnny is very sensitive" reimagining of history when it couldn't be plainer that little Johnny is in fact a conceited, spoiled, imperialist little shit. But here we go: the truth is I had been captivated by Japan—or at least, by what I thought was Japan—in numerous ways, for numerous years. As a teenager, I bought a book of ukiyo-e prints from a bookshop near my house which I would spend hours poring over, making my own versions in watercolors. I was fascinated by the script, the looping threads of kana that ran down the sides of the paintings and the blockier Chinese characters, and I would make terrible attempts at copying them without having a clue what they were saying. Not long after, I took down *Confessions of a Mask* from my mother's bookshelf. I still remember the illicit delight I felt at reading about the evolution of Yukio Mishima's "bad habit," his insatiable appetite for pictures of wounded, melancholic, muscular men in the mold of St. Sebastian, and the abject horror he had felt, after swooning over a picture of what he thought was a strapping young knight, at discovering that it was in fact Jeanne d'Arc. I liked the extremity of it all, this whiff of austerity and bleakness that I sensed there, as in the Haruki Murakami and Kenzaburō Ōe novels I'd been reading at A's instigation. Japan seemed like a place where everything was a secret, until it very much wasn't, and that was attractive to me.

And yet, back when my senior school had begun offering optional after-school Japanese classes, which proved so popular that a waitlist formed, I'd been one of the few in my year who didn't sign up. Not only did I not want to participate; I found something faintly risible about my classmates who would come back from the classes waving little origami frogs, or slips of paper with their names written in katakana. It wasn't the culture that bored me, but very specifically the non-Japanese people who got excited about it. Even at that age, I found the idea of being a white person "learning" Japan embarrassing, and I wanted nothing to do with it. The Japan I wanted was not the cloying, fluorescent, high-pitched one that anime lovers dreamed about and which reached out its arms in welcome. It was muted, austere, monochrome, picked out in pale pink and red like an Utamaro print, and it didn't admit foreigners. In short, the Japan I wanted didn't want me. Thumbing the pink covers of *Teach Yourself Japanese Language, Life and Culture*, I remembered again my instinctive embarrassment towards being a learner, only now I was the one clutching the origami frog.

One evening, A brought round to my room a book that he'd found in his parents' house during the holidays: a guide to dirty Japanese. It had been left there for unknown reasons by his uncle, who was married to a Japanese woman. Our interview was impending, the serious pink book was at hand, and the plan for the evening had been to study Japanese politics and the names of the prefectures, but our attention was soon rerouted. The dirty book seemed to be aimed at a diverse spread of readers: those attempting to navigate their way through the world of casual or non-casual sex in Japan as residents or tourists, those interested from a more linguistic perspective, and those, like us, who were just looking for irresponsible titillation. I remember a chapter of insults (fun), and a graphic list of sexual instructions (eye-opening). The book also featured a relatively comprehensive explanation of Japan's different kinds of prostitution services, which had mostly been dreamed up in order to get around the law banning the selling of penetrative sex. I recall being fascinated and horrified in equal measure by the idea of Soapland, a bathhouse-style setup where the customers were, in the words of Wikipedia, "soaped up and serviced" by sex workers.

There was no question, though, about the part we were most drawn to. The page with which we would become obsessed reproduced a menu from one of the types of establishments styled as massage salons. Such places, the guide informed, had a variety of names of English origin, all somewhat disorienting in the way they seemed to sound conceivably like real phrases and yet to mean ostensibly nothing: "fashion health shop," "pink salon," "image club." All of the menu items, too, were clearly derived from English and written in katakana, which I knew from *Teach Yourself Japanese Language, Life and Culture,* was the alphabet principally used for writing words imported from English and other languages. But if these words had come from English, it was not English as I had ever known it.

The menu featured two columns: on the left was the original katakana notation, and beside it the romanized version in italics. Of course I could not make head nor tail of the katakana, but neither could I get my head around its romanization; A, on the other hand, who had been taking Japanese lessons for a couple of months and had been fascinated by the language for much longer, seemed far more able to navigate the page, to digest what was in front of him. And so it was A who found it, the menu item that was to become so legendary for us: kokku sakkingu geemu. His finger pointed to it on the page in front of me, its sudden urgent rigidity suggesting glee, or at least the certainty of an incredible find. What? I couldn't see from looking at those strange strings of letters how they were supposed to say what they were supposed to say, or in fact how they were supposed to say anything at all. And so A, strides ahead of me, read it aloud, and it was only then they slid into shape, that I could link the strings up with words that I understood: Cock Sucking Game.

The whole thing made my brain reel. "What actually *is* it, though?" I remember asking A over and over that night. I must have seemed like a suspicious child, trying to grill her parents for information on a sexual practice whose precise nature is still veiled in the murk of mystery. Actually, I felt like that child. It seemed to me like a secret the world was keeping from me, and wresting it into the open was a matter of pride, of proving that I was savvy enough—even if the process of coaxing out that information proved only the opposite. "Why game? What does that mean?"

A couldn't elucidate what exactly it would be that made the Cock Sucking Game a game, in the same way that my mother had once struggled to define, in response to my persistent questioning, what was so special about a Chicken Special that was often on the menu for school lunch. Yet the most puzzling aspect, the aspect which told me I was getting something wrong, was that neither of them seemed to feel my puzzlement. They were mature enough to know that these were just words occurring in a context where it was okay if not everything meant something definable: that they were functioning, more or less, as names.

I couldn't say with certainty back then that A was good at

katakana pronunciation (in hindsight: he was), but to me at the time it certainly had the ring of authenticity, of something to which I had no access and which seemed utterly other. "Say that one," I'd say, pointing to hooru bodii massaaji, and as he said it the sounds on the page would come to life: Whole Body Massage. "But it hasn't got a 'w'!" I'd object. "Do you think it's 'hole body,' as in they're massaging the holes?"

A linguist might explain my discombobulation as follows: I didn't understand yet the system by which Japanese was transliterated into English—especially this form of romanization, where elongated sounds are represented as double vowels (ee) rather than with macrons (ē), which can be very confusing when conflated with English pronunciation rules. To add to this, I didn't have an awareness of the prevalence of either gairaigo (foreign loan words) or what is known as wasei eigo (literally "Japan-made English"), where English words or morphemes have been used to create neologisms, of which "pink salon" is a prime example. Given all that, it was no wonder everything felt incredibly mysterious. But even that seems insufficient to me as an explanation. What slapped me in the face over and over was the sensory quality of it all: here was the sound of my own language, but passed through the filter of some utterly unimagined system. The logic of the system was unknown to me, and yet it was immediately, viscerally clear that it had one.

———

The Japanese mimetic word for jagged, serrated, saw-like, is giza-giza, and the first time I heard it said, in reference to pinking shears, I grinned inappropriately because it sounded to me like "geezer geezer." I grinned also because it seemed crazy and implausible that a word so unwieldy could mean something like jagged. Now, it feels obvious to me that this is plausibility incarnate. To be jagged, serrated, to veer from one extreme to another, is to be unwieldy almost by definition: of course the word for it should contort your mouth in that way. And giza-giza was how the first words I heard in katakana sounded to me, including kokku sakkingu geemu. It seemed so much more time-consuming to trace the ups and the downs of the minute particles into which everything seemed to be separated, rather than eliding everything as I was used to doing. I didn't know why it was happening, and it felt like an absurdist parody, like being confronted with a distorted mirror of oneself—disarming, intriguing, unsettling.

———

We were in the middle of revising for our finals when I got the call. I'd been in the university library that day, and had left my phone in the locker along with all my other possessions that wouldn't fit in the single transparent carrier bag you were allowed to take into the reading rooms, and so it was only when I went outside to accompany A on a cigarette break after lunch that I saw I had a voicemail message from an unrecognized number.

Standing there at the top of the steps outside the library entrance, my phone pressed to my ear, I listened to a woman from the embassy tell me that I had been granted a place on the program, departing on the first of August. It was fainter, but there was an aspect to her accent that I recognized from A's katakana pronunciation: the system. Her voice was neither warm nor cold, and it imparted only the necessary information. In what felt like a *Mission Impossible* touch, she told me that I had twenty-four hours to make my decision.

I remember standing still, looking down at the flight of steps, the trees, the concrete paving stones below, everything that made up this world which I had such muddled feelings about, and where I felt like such a terrible muddle myself. Nothing had changed; it wasn't even excitement that I felt, exactly. But now, out of nowhere, the scene contained within it the possibility of being only that: just one of many possibilities. I didn't feel special, validated, vindicated—it was oddly not about me. If you'd have asked me before that phone call whether or not I was going to be going to Japan, I would have said the likelihood was that I wouldn't. Now, I understood on some level that going to Japan was my fate. Which is just a way of saying, I had abnegated responsibility. By smashing through my arrogance, putting me on the waiting list, and telling A that they didn't want him, Japan had signaled to me in some fashion that they were in charge. Now it seemed very clear to me that they'd done this so they could accept me in this muted way: I was to be had, but with the minimal possible enthusiasm. I was to go, knowing that I wasn't really wanted. Which meant, I was to go.

¶ zara-zara: the sound of the rough ground

ONE OF THE FIRST THINGS I remember from my time as a philosophy undergraduate was a dawning sense of terror at the way people around me spoke. Sitting on the polished-wood benches in the lecture hall, I watched in astonishment as the mouths around me opened to release long, intricately structured sentences, unhalting and studded with all the right buzzwords. Even more noteworthy than these oratory skills was the burning desire to speak that I sensed running through their pronouncements, a desire that seemed the polar opposite of my wish to remain as quiet as possible. Where my peers appeared to see philosophy as an arena for dialogue, I conceived of it as something which I thought and felt too deeply about to be able to discuss it with just anyone, although it is impossible to say whether in fact that was just an excuse for avoiding the humiliation of doing it badly.

I was a mess at Cambridge, and thinking back to that time now still feels painful. Maybe as a response to this, I sometimes find myself wondering—impossibly, nonsensically, as if out of some instinct to solve and thereby heal the past—if my experience would be different if I had had then more of the confidence I do now. Particularly, I fixate on the question of whether I would be able to be more vocal in classes;

if I'd find it in me to express myself like someone for whom self-expression wasn't so torturous. I put meaningless questions like this one to myself, and generally come to the conclusion that I would, indeed, give it more of a go; I'd put myself through the shame of speaking out in that hard-edged male environment, and get good at talking the talk. Somehow this conclusion consoles me that I am not a total lost cause.

And yet fairly recently, for the first time in ages, I was given the opportunity to talk philosophy in a context that should have been totally unintimidating, and I messed it up in a way I still think about often. I was out with a friend on a long walk, with swathes of road ahead of us, when he came out and asked me to explain to him what exactly Wittgenstein had said, and what it was I liked about him. I've made it a policy in my life, more or less, not to talk about philosophy unbidden, because I've learned that the avenues it leads down are rarely satisfying for anybody involved, but here was an explicit invitation. There was no obvious excuse for me not to do the topic justice, and I felt, for a brief second, pretty optimistic. I girded my loins, opened my mouth to begin, and then down it rained on me: a premonition of total failure—the exact same premonition that I'd felt back in university which I'd found so paralyzing. I remembered, then, what it was like: the white sheet of total fear that seems to descend before the eyes, through which I can glimpse a stretch of infinite possibilities. I remembered how perfectly insurmountable it feels.

In fairness to myself, I would say that Wittgenstein is not an easy philosopher to give a brief introduction to, and the possibilities for where to begin are genuinely plentiful. Part of the problem is that really, there are two Wittgensteins; he produced two distinct and irreconcilable bodies of thought over the course of his life, as encapsulated by his two best-known works, the *Tractatus Logico-Philosophicus* and the *Philosophical Investigations*. The philosopher whom I credit with having shaped my way of conceptualizing language and whom I think about all the time is the later Wittgenstein, the *Investigations* Wittgenstein, so in a sense I would have been justified in diving straight into him, but I didn't feel comfortable with simplifying in this way. Maybe it's something to do with the way that I was taught at university, but I can't shake the feeling that the radicalness of the *Investigations* only truly makes sense within the context of what came before it, which reached its most extreme articulation with the *Tractatus*.

Given which, I see now with the clarity of hindsight, I should have seized the stage I'd been handed by my friend and headed assuredly and engagingly for the lengthy director's cut version of the Wittgenstein story, starting out with an account of what the *Tractatus* represented. I should have talked about how it developed from a near-ubiquitous view of language where words name objects in the world and "sentences are combinations of such names." More particularly, how it grew out of a quest to understand the relationship between mind, language and world that Wittgenstein had inherited from Bertrand Russell and Gottlob Frege, where the logical proposition was seen as the key to revealing the structure of both thought and the universe itself. I should have explained all of this in a way that didn't dwell too much on specifics, but still managed to establish the key point: the emphasis with this way of thinking lay not on the actual usage of language, which was an inevitably messy and changeable matter, but rather the eternal truths revealed by the laws of logic: as Frege put it, the "boundary stones set in an eternal foundation."

In actuality, feeling a strong sense of self-imposed pressure, I rushed through this part of the explanation, diving straight into the most bewildering elements of early Wittgensteinian thought out of some sense they would be the most attention-grabbing. I explained how when Wittgenstein drafted the latter parts of the *Tractatus* on the Eastern Front during the First World War, ethics and religion were much on his mind, and though these matters formed a late addition to the book's inventory of topics, Wittgenstein's way of dealing with them was to deem them literally meaningless to speak about, insisting that the only meaningful propositions were facts about worldly states of affairs. Indeed, one of the strangest aspects to the *Tractatus*, I told my friend, is that the propositions making it up themselves emerge as meaningless, precisely the sorts of things that can only be shown and not said. What surfaces from the terse numbered propositions making up the book, I continued, is a bleak, mystical, lonely landscape inhabited by these alien entities, where communication about anything of significance is technically impossible. And then, seeing my friend's look of understandable confusion, I tried immediately to rush on. I waved a hand and said never mind, nobody really gets the *Tractatus*. What really matters is the next bit, and the next bit goes like this.

———

There was a brief spell when Wittgenstein felt that with the schema he'd laid out in the *Tractatus*, he had cracked the central questions of philosophy as his cohort had understood them; as he wrote in a letter to his mentor Russell at the time, "I believe I've solved all our problems finally. This may sound arrogant but I can't help believing it." And yet before the *Tractatus* was even published, which admittedly took some years, its author had begun to grow dissatisfied. Neither was this dissatisfaction over just a few niggling, unresolved issues within the system he had laid out. Rather, the ideas that began crowding in upon Wittgenstein suggested a radically alternative way of construing our language.

Namely, what if our language was not in fact "a flawed, distorting mirror" of reality, but a complex, naturally evolved system to be taken on its own terms? What if, in order to attain a clear view of our interaction with the world, we had to train our eyes not on the idealized abstractions of logical representation, but rather the intricacies of the words we used on a daily basis? What if language assumes meaning through its usage in the community that gives birth to it, and its primary function is not the internal thought but the social interaction? What if unraveling the truth behind key concepts was not a question of isolating their form, but rather tracking the myriad ways they were used in the real world? If the true task of the philosopher was to put his or her ear to the ground? What if, ultimately, the path to untangling our linguistic reality lay not in idealization and abstraction and prescription, but observation and specificity and description?

History has it that as these questions became ever more irrepressible, Wittgenstein began to conceive of an entirely new approach to philosophy. "What *we* do," read the new mission statement from a man who had, until not so long ago, awarded a key role in his philosophical system to logical entities like "atomic facts," whose precise nature was obscure to him, "is to bring words back from their metaphysical to their every day use." From being at the vanguard of advocating a distinctly un-everyday approach to words, Wittgenstein became the philosopher who aimed to rescue people from the seductive pull of the "crystalline" ideal, which he knew from firsthand experience led only to bad philosophy, and to help them find clarity in a different form instead—a dirtier, realer, and more bottom-up one: "When I talk about language (words, sentences, etc.) I must speak the language of every day."

Except my real-time explanation was, of course, less coherent than this. Not only could I not quote directly from memory, but I couldn't paraphrase well either. I was torn between not wanting to use language that would alienate my friend, and not wanting to dumb down too much, yet I'm not enough of a speaker to be able to tread that line and explain the concepts in simple language which still conveys their radicalness. In fact, I remember being quite alarmed when I heard the words falling from my own mouth: how self-evident, how nothingy they sounded. And then I heard myself wrapping up: "So language is just, like, as we use it!"

"Oh, right," said my friend.

I don't know if it was his disappointment I felt in that moment or my own, but either way, I couldn't bear it. Sensing the prospect of both Wittgenstein's appeal and my own being consigned to the funeral pyre, my mouth started talking with the speed that until just a few seconds ago was unattainable:

"Maybe you can't understand how great it is without understanding the context," I gabbled. "Maybe it's impossible if you can't see what a real breath of fresh air it is in comparison to everything else that went before. Maybe if you haven't experienced the impulse to idealize language in the first place, it's just not going to be that revolutionary."

I would say that, of the entirety of my car-crash explanation, this is the part I regret the most—regretted it, in fact, even as it came out of my mouth. The worst thing about it was not that it was so obviously an excuse for my own inarticulacy, nor that it tried to shift the blame for the anticlimax onto my friend's lack of philosophical training. Rather, it was how it made out philosophy to be something that only rescues people from itself, and implied that idealizing and essentializing language is something that only philosophers would ever do, which is the opposite of what I believe to be the case. For sure, philosophers have thought and theorized about these topics more than the average layperson, and their idealization is more visible, more explicit, and often more ontologically fantastic, but I believe that for the most part, the mistakes of the philosophers largely reflect our inherited view of language, particularly as monolinguals—which is one reading of Wittgenstein's declaration that philosophy "is a battle against the bewitchment of our intelligence by means of our language." Our language is the lens through which the world is constituted for us, and as long as that remains for us a unitary default (as long as we are part of the linguistic majority) we never have the opportunity to question it, or at least to do so in a fundamental, world-shifting, ground-pulled-from-under-one's-feet way. We do not learn to define our context at all, because it is transparent to us; it is only a short step from this to a felt sense that *this is all that is possible*. Which means, necessary. And thus the contingencies of our very contingent reality—the sociocultural context into which we are born—take on an unshakeable aspect of profundity and permanence; we confuse the rules of our framework, which Wittgenstein calls "grammatical propositions," with deep, metaphysical truths. I strongly believe that even if we do not go so far as formulating intellectually the idea that the structure of our language in some deep sense mimics the structure of the world, this is the default understanding from which we work; that as Wittgenstein puts it, "It is like a pair of glasses on our nose through which we see whatever we look at. It never occurs to us to take them off." I believe this not only because I studied Wittgenstein and idolized him, but because it was corroborated by being in Japan, an experience I would describe in its most succinct form as having the glasses pulled off my face and sensing in acute detail the struggle my myopic monolingual eyes went through. I believe it because I have felt it to be true.

———

Of course, I didn't say any of this to my friend. Instead we changed topic, gladly putting Wittgenstein behind us. But almost as soon as my failed explanation was over, I started wondering what I would do if I had this opportunity over again. How could I have done better? Should I have ditched the attempt to speak about the philosophy itself, at least at first, and made it more of a narrative? I could have begun with the psychological aspect of Wittgenstein's big shift, and my admiration for the willingness he showed in exposing his previous flaws. It strikes me again and again that although people are for the most part very accepting of the idea that true creation necessitates destruction, that genius sweeps the path of old fogeys and outdated value systems and ruthlessly exposes weakness, there's not much talk of what to do when it is your own past ideas that are littering the path. What if you have published works you later realize are terribly flawed, privately subscribed to or publicly endorsed ideals you now find abhorrent? What if the work you need to destroy is your own? I think the answer generally modeled in the world, particularly in academic circles, is to remain sheepish, to attempt to sweep any misdemeanors under the carpet and pray they're not found out; if you absolutely have to change your beliefs, do it so gradually that it's possible people may not notice. At the very least, don't go out of your way to publicize your errors. I am fascinated by the way Wittgenstein ignored this precedent entirely, choosing to savage his past contributions with unstinting humility, taking swipes throughout the *Investigations* at "the author of the *Tractatus*." There are numerous extraordinary elements to Wittgenstein's biography, and one is the candidness with which he spoke to others of what he perceived as their failings, but more refreshing still is his openness about his own shortcomings, even within the context of his philosophical works. "A picture held us captive and we could not get outside it," he says, in reference to the so-called Picture Theory of Meaning at the heart of the *Tractatus*, "for it lay in our language and language seemed to repeat it to us inexorably." In part, it's this honesty about reckoning with the past which makes the *Investigations* feel to me not just human, but also urgent and believable—the same brand of urgency and believability you could imagine in a self-help book from someone who has devised a method of hauling himself from the depths of addiction. And in a sense it is an addiction, or at least an affliction, which is rife not just among philosophers but great swathes of the general populace.

I would have liked to have conveyed to my friend that, although it's the content of Wittgenstein's later work which is important to me, I feel his journey there gives it an added layer of meaning. It's fascinating to look at the transition between these two utterly different philosophical methodologies, to see the way that the *Tractatus*' rigor and quest for clarity are transfigured now into a radically new form. And from here, continues the fantasy, I could have gone on to talk about how this transition can be seen in the structure of the books—which I think, in retrospect, is what might have most excited my friend, who is amongst other things a visual artist. One of the reasons the *Tractatus* was and is such an esoteric wet dream for so many is that it is seen to have realized the fantasy of a total mathematical purism of language, with each sentence or paragraph numbered according to a unique system whereby the relationship of all the sentences to one another can be intuited by their numerical value. I find it amazing that while the *Investigations* ditches this complex classification system, it retains the broad structure of numbered Bemerkungen or "remarks," unusual in the context of philosophical treatises at that time. Yet if the look on the page is roughly comparable between the two books (even though the *Investigations*' remarks are often considerably longer) the significance of this structure has undergone a more or less complete shift. Far from the polished propositions we find in the *Tractatus*, like ball bearings lined up in immaculate rows, the *Investigations* is more like an assorted collection of rocks and pebbles of varying sizes. The fragmented structure evokes the notebook; indeed, much of what is published of late Wittgenstein outside of the *Investigations* was taken from his actual notebooks, blurring the distinction between manuscript and rough draft, and the title one of his other key works, *Zettel*, literally means "slips of paper." And yet this manner of presentation seems to stem from something more than sheer expediency—something that sits hand in glove with the whole methodology it aims to promote.

Rather than holding out bottled certainties in the form of categorical statements, the *Investigations* seeks to show itself in the act of groping for truth, so that the reader might also learn how to do the same. Specifically, Wittgenstein's shift from a didactic model to a therapeutic one is signaled not only by a more tentative style of writing, but also by the inclusion of excerpts in the style of reported conversations between unnamed parties, so that readers experience the sensation of putting their ear up to the door of Wittgenstein's rooms and catching a snatch of one of his infamously long discussions. The reader is left with the distinct impression that what matters is less the exact results being conveyed, and more the way of parsing the world that the book imparts. In the preface, Wittgenstein himself notes that "after several unsuccessful attempts to weld [his] results together" into a coherent whole, he accepted that "the best he could write would never be more than philosophical remarks"; that he realized at some point that this format was "connected with the very nature of the investigation," forcing us as it does "to travel over a wild field of thought criss-cross in every direction."

What does a "criss-cross" manuscript actually look like, we might legitimately ask. In this case, it looks like a profusion of questions, sometimes great paragraphs composed almost entirely of them. When there are statements, they are often clearly signaled as conversational gambits, beginning perhaps "I want to say:" or "Suppose I say:" or "One is inclined to say:" or "It will be possible to say:". There are em-dashes, illustrations, and more italics than seem feasible; there are heaps of brackets and symbols and double ellipses. The whole book is peppered with exclamation marks. All told, this is not what we think of as academic prose, especially not within the philosophical tradition. It's amped up, somehow feverish, like a fiercely precocious child tugging at you and demanding to be listened to. And yet, maybe exactly because it needs your attention, there is something compulsive to it also. Bizarre and unsettling, but each time I pick up my fat gray copy of the *Investigations* with Wittgenstein on the front and let my eyes fall across its pages, I feel a visceral comfort rippling out from my center. I feel like I'm talking to a person. Or, perhaps I should say: I *feel* as though I am talking to a person!

And indeed, we find an exclamation mark also rounding off what is perhaps the *Investigations*' most famous sentence: "Back to the rough ground!" With the charismatic nature of Wittgenstein's prose, there are any number of propositions that we could take as slogans for his overall project, but in terms of succinctness, this one is hard to beat. "We are talking about the spatial and temporal phenomenon of language, not about some non-spatial, non-temporal chimera," he reminds us. "We want to walk: so we need *friction*. Back to the rough ground!"

And now, in the next stage of this fantasy diatribe, I tell my friend that at the time I discovered Wittgenstein, I needed friction and rough ground, very badly. It would be an exaggeration to say that it was the *Philosophical Investigations* that sent me to Japan, but at the time that I encountered it, it was becoming clearer by the day that the rarefied air of Cambridge was not doing me well. Ever since I'd got there, all I'd done was wish myself different—maybe I'd always wished myself different, but now the wishing was an obsessive drone that filled my waking consciousness. Every day I would struggle to become sheer mind, my body a graceful cipher, and every day I would fail. Every day I would pray to wake up and be able to speak in perfect polished sentences like the people around me, and every day I'd find that, surprise surprise, I couldn't, and I still blushed horribly when I tried. There was therefore something about the *Investigations* which felt to me remarkably like self-acceptance. Reading it made me feel very sure that I wanted to get the hell out of the place, and go somewhere with plenty of grit.

And finally, in this imaginary encounter, I tell my friend about how, as I was first sitting down to write this book, a thought came to me. In the Japanese translation of the *Investigations*, "rough ground" would be rendered with an onomatopoeic word. It had to be so. It would be so, and this would prove the feasibility of this project, the coherence of my whole concept for writing this book. Suddenly, I was nauseated with excitement and nerves, as if the viability of everything I wanted to write about hung on the translation of this one phrase. Unable to wait, I asked a friend in Japan to check next time he found himself in the library. In a few hours, I had a text back from him: "Zara-zara shita jimen ni modorō!"

And like that, I had passed my own test: zara-zara was the mimetic word for "rough," and a word I knew very well. I could picture the gesture that people would make when they said it, moving their four fingers from side to side across a surface, actual or imagined. I was pretty sure that the man I'd been in love with had said it several times of my skin. I'd heard kids say it of the floor, the walls. Now it was there, translating Wittgenstein's "rauhen Boden," his earthy war cry.

It was just a tiny fact, a small serendipity of translation, and I could see that to get over-excited about it was fetishistic. But there was no disavowing that part of me wanted to scream for joy, and not purely because I'd had my project redeemed. It was also because I truly felt that, although Wittgenstein had doubtless never encountered the word zara-zara (or any other Japanese mimetic for that matter), it served as an encapsulation of much of his worldview. It was a word that had no pretensions to purity, whose affective dimension drew the attention back to the behavioral practices surrounding language. It was a word that wore its genealogy and its humanity on its sleeve, which felt perfectly of the soil. It was a word free of clear ideas, full of bodies, and rugged with friction.

¶ mushi-mushi: the sound of insects being forced from your body, or laughing as you vocalize an unthinkable situation, or being steamed alive

I ARRIVED IN JAPAN MIDWAY through summer, except this was not summer like any I'd experienced before. I'd been warned about the summers, the humidity, but like most other things, the words meant little to me until I was there and the heat was upon me, three-dimensional, wet and so dense that I found myself wading through it as if traversing a vat of hot jam. I remember the insult of it, the way the prickling sensation of the heat drawing the sweat from my skin felt like a swarm of microscopic insects were being drawn out through my pores, and this memory is inseparable from the utterly inescapability of how my first Japan felt. There was no retreating inside of my head to emerge when it suited me; everything conspired to ensure I had to be there constantly, fully sensate. There was only adjusting to the particulars of the situation assigned to me, watching those particulars unfold in total powerlessness.

My particulars unfolded thus. I was to be placed on the remote island of Sado in the Japan Sea, a two-and-a-half-hour ferry ride from mainland Niigata, on the northwest coast of Honshu. After being taken into school on the first afternoon on the island, I was driven back to the flat where I would be living. I remember walking in, looking around me in confusion. I was clearly indoors, an indoors whose floor was divided into shining laminate and tatami-matted sections, but this indoors was hotter than outside, which was already stifling. M, one of the teachers at my school, also looked around him. Maybe there is an air conditioner, he said, but there was no air conditioner. Finally he opened the sliding cabinet at the side of the room where my futon was housed and found in there a standing fan, which he pulled out and plugged in at the wall. A semicircle of lukewarm air half a meter in diameter issued from the fan. It seemed to me utterly inconceivable that I could live in a place like this, which was to say, not die in a place like this. I stood by the window staring out in disbelief. After a while, I opened it and stuck my hand out. It was hard to tell now which section of air was cooler. They were both like hot jam.

The sound for hot jam, I soon learned, was mushi-mushi. "Humid," read the definition in the electronic Japanese–English dictionary I soon acquired; "close"; "muggy." I found it extraordinary that a word which seemed to me both so infantile sounding and so evocative could be defined in this way—an equivalence posited between it and fragments of English which seemed so factual and bland in comparison.

And what about the connotations, I would think: mushi, by itself, meant insect. I didn't know enough at this stage to know that the two weren't connected etymologically—that mushi-mushi was rather related to musu, a verb meaning "to steam"—and in my head, the false linkage made total sense. The hot, wet insect heat pressed in on me, and it was disgusting, and I was sure that I would never and could never get used to it.

Nor could I get used to how cheerfully people pronounced the phrase, in endless conversations about the weather: mushi-mushi, they would say and smile, or wince in a performance of distaste, as if doing so would somehow make this extraordinary experience normal. I felt like a lobster thrust in the pot, screaming, while all the other lobsters around me stoically tolerated the experience.

¶ min-min: the sound of the air screaming,
or being saturated in sound

WITH THE HUMIDITY CAME THE sounds. In the morning, as the sun blazed through my curtainless windows, the
cicadas started up, thickening the air further. Min-min is how
Japanese renders this cry, the "i" a high, bright sound, better
approximated in English with "ee," and this description has
always seemed to me almost preternaturally evocative, probably because we don't have a word specifically for the cicada
cry in English. In fact, I'd never spent time in a place inhabited
by cicadas before, and I was astonished not only by their volume but also the omnipresence of their sound, which seemed
more like a feat of some unknown technology than anything
nature could have achieved: maybe some construction tool I'd
not encountered before, or a proliferation of futuristic sirens.
Clamoring, textured, impossible to ignore, the cicadas were a
constant reminder that I was in another country.

But really, that was the same for all sounds since I'd arrived
here. In Tokyo, where I'd spent a few days participating in
an induction course before embarking on the long journey to
the island, I'd been shocked by the people standing outside
drugstores shouting into loudspeakers, by the incessant jin-
gles and announcements both inside and outside the trains,

by the chirping of the lights at the pedestrian crossing—the way everything seemed loud except for people's actual conversations. At my new school, passing down the corridors still unknown to me with their white walls and sludge-colored laminate, I heard a noise that at first I took to be the rhythmical bleating of an unknown animal, maybe a Japanese variety of sheep. It took me weeks to discover that it was in fact the noise made by the baseball club, the white-costumed figures practicing on the rust-red sand, their mouths opening to emit a kind of sound I'd never heard humans make before.

Then there was the staffroom, where I sat for most of the day. I arrived on the island during the summer holidays, when the teachers were off in different parts of the school teaching club activities all day, and everything seemed to me remarkably quiet—and then term started. Now every day began with a staff meeting, all the teachers standing up to face in the direction of the three big heads—the head teacher, the deputy head, the head of staff—who sat at one end of the room right by where my desk was, so that I felt myself caught in the crossfire of their sounds. And what sounds they were. All around me, mouths opened to release apparently clauseless sentences lasting two minutes, three, five, which left me gasping for air just to listen to, and my head crammed with questions: How is any human brain able to understand a sentence of that length, let alone produce one spontaneously? Is it conceivable that I will ever understand what is being said, and how long will that take? Does this "deskeredomo" construction have anything to do with desks? When is this going to end?

Once it ended, there was more talk, the perpetual flow of students entering and leaving, all saying a particular phrase when they slid the door open and then the same phrase in the past tense when they left, the carrying of books, the signing of documents, the red-penning of homework, all of these transactions mediated through dense codes, unfamiliar rhythms which I could not process and could only watch, hear, absorb, absorb, absorb, until I was saturated in sound.

Saturated, so that even when I receded from it, it was there, ringing in my ears like nothing had ever done before: min-min min-min. It feels true to say that before I properly spoke or understood Japanese, certainly before I was properly fixated by it, it assumed the role of constant internal soundtrack. My body was alive with the sounds it had collected up throughout the day. When I shut my eyes in bed at night I was souped in them, sounds that hovered between known and unknown, as if comprehensibility were not in fact the currency in which my brain dealt anymore, and what was being processed was rather the rhythms. And then snatches of it found their way into my dreams, hovering there tersely, like life-rafts above the flow of images.

¶ sa'pari: the sound of a mind unblemished
by understanding

THERE WERE TEN OF US on the island—ten foreigners, as everyone cheerily referred to us. Except that wasn't even true; there were plenty more "foreigners" than that, who had come years previously, married, and then settled. Rather, there were ten of us English teachers employed through the Japanese government—Assistant Language Teachers, as the official title ran, because we were taken on without any qualifications and were therefore obliged always to assist a trained Japanese teacher of English—who all worked in several different schools, covering between us every middle and high school and some of the elementaries on the island, of which there were surprisingly many, given that so much of the place felt more or less uninhabited.

Inevitably, we spent quite a lot of time with each other, talking constantly about our schools, comparing our lots and the strange things that had happened to us: someone taught at a school with only two students; someone had been served whale curry at school lunch; a teacher at someone else's school had been locked in a cupboard by a student. I think each of us held the secret belief that our particular situation was both the worst and the best of the lot—certainly I felt that way. At one of my three schools, the atmosphere was out-and-out toxic for reasons I struggled to get my head around, for superficially the community where it was located seemed not that different from those of my other schools, yet the bad feeling was so unmistakable that even the teachers alluded to it. Whatever I said in English was ignored, and whatever I said in Japanese was mimicked in a silly foreign accent. On one memorable occasion, I was told to "Go die!" by a student. Towards the beginning, on a day when I'd been seated at a lunch table with the fourteen-year-old boys who made up the lowest of the three English sets, all seven of them made a show of air-humping the imaginary beings sat on their laps while I stared into my bowl of rice and tried to imagine what having an appetite felt like.

Meanwhile the school where I was placed from Wednesday through to Friday and all throughout the holidays, was, for all its impenetrability, something like heaven to me. Lessons were great fun—ultimately it came down to that. Y, the other English teacher aside from M, would often say that the children in that part of the island were "pure," and I could see what he meant; in comparison with the kids at my other schools, they seemed innocent, willing to participate, and retained sufficient vulnerability to laugh. Then there was Y himself, who also had a part to play in how much I liked being in the school. I found myself drawn to him, relatively immediately; unlike at my other schools where I felt I was floating untethered and somehow ghost-like, there was something about having Y around that gave me a sense of grounding. As well as being an English teacher, he occupied an additional role that I didn't fully understand, although I assumed from the fact that certain students were always coming to see him that it was semi-pastoral. As my desk was near to his, and because he made an effort to involve me, his students began to talk to me even when he wasn't around.

In particular, there was a girl in the third year, S, who was very frequently in the staffroom, lingering by Y's side, with whom he—and therefore generally I—would sit at lunch.

Although somewhat shy, S seemed like a bright, engaged, and studious kid. Like most of the children, her spoken English was very limited, but as soon as I began to learn a little Japanese, she was happy to talk to me. A lot of the time she, Y, and I would talk in a triangle, he occupying a role less of a standard interpreter than a linguistic matchmaker, a de-inhibitor, attempting to instill courage in both of us to attempt speaking.

One day, when Y was out of the room, S came up to me where I was sitting at my desk.

"I saw your friend," she said, "Caroline."

I was already used to this assumption people made that as foreigners on the island, we would not only necessarily know one another, but also be close. In this case, the assumption was true: Caroline was a friend, and she had told me she would be giving a speech at an event at her high school for prospective students.

"Oh yes," I said in English. "She gave a speech, right?"

"Yes. Speech."

"How was it?'

"Huh?"

"How was the speech?"

She paused for a while and then said, "Sa'pari."

"Sa'pari," I said.

"Sa'pari."

"Oh," I said, and she walked off. I noted it down in my notebook: sa'pari, written out in the Roman alphabet, and then, painstakingly, in hiragana: さっぱり.

Now, after a couple of months, I had developed the ability to actually parse the sounds that people said to me as words. This meant I now had a framework within which to understand or not understand things, and almost everything fell into the latter category. However limitless the supply of words I didn't understand might have been, I still played the eager detective, collecting up each of these unknown words like precious clues as if the next one might be the one that unlocked the entire mystery. I took copious notes, tried to remain alert and receptive, and did my best to ensure my electronic dictionary was always on hand. Sometimes the dictionary was very reticent; other times, like now, it yielded several solutions, which led me down different mental avenues, and whose various definitions I didn't have the ability to choose between.

Now, the first definition for "sa'pari" read: "feeling refreshed," "feeling relieved." Then there was: "neat," "tidy," "clean." The third definition was: "frank," "open-hearted," "plain." Through all of these, I felt, I could sense some kind of thread; vague, certainly, but still there. The fourth one was different: "completely," "entirely."

Hmm, I thought. None of them really seemed like adjectives you could apply to a speech, delivered from a lectern on stage to a sea of schoolchildren sat on the floor. Or maybe this was it: maybe none of them were adjectives you would apply to a speech *in English*. Maybe this was a Japanese sensibility, and there was something in Caroline's mode of delivery that S had responded to—which had given her a sense of relief.

Caroline came from near Glasgow, and she had told me that people had immense difficulty understanding her; she'd already learned to modify the way she said "girl," transmuting from *gerul* to *gaarl* so as to more closely approximate the US pronunciation that people here were trained in. It seemed therefore relatively unlikely that her speech would be read as "clean," but I for one appreciated her frankness, particularly when a few of the other ALTs were rather gushing Americans; maybe S had felt the same. Admittedly, to comment on this rather abstract quality of her delivery seemed a markedly sophisticated reaction for a schoolchild to have about a speech given in her second language, but perhaps this was proof of what I hoped; that there was far more going on inside my children than I saw evidence for. Perhaps, although very limited English came out of her mouth, S's mode of apprehension of the language bordered on the mystical.

That weekend, hanging out with Caroline, I asked her how the speech had gone. There were a few of your school's kids there, she said, and I told her that one of my students had seen her.

"Oh yeah? What did she say?"

"Well," I said. "She said that she found it very refreshing."

Caroline looked at me.

"I mean," I said. "She said this word, which I don't quite get. But it means like clean, or crisp, or refreshing, or something. It sounds positive."

Caroline made the noise which most foreigners living in Japan develop: not a Japanese noise, but a particular variety of hmm that means, *in the face of this total incomprehensibility, I am not going to cling to the necessity of understanding, or I will lose my mind.*

———

I think it was a few weeks later when I got round to asking Y; by then we were already doing things we should not have been.

"What does sa'pari mean?" I said, and when he didn't give me a straight-out answer, I explained the situation.

"I don't understand," he said in English. "I have absolutely no idea what you're talking about."

"What? Why?"

"That's what it means. Sa'pari, is short for, sa'pari wakaranai. I cleanly, perfectly do not understand."

I gazed fixedly into the space in front of me, looking dazed. What shocked me was not, in fact, the size of the drop from my esoteric interpretation to the banal reality, but rather the immediacy with which Y had intuited what S's word meant.

I knew it already, but it hit me particularly then: here, in the world of language, the hapless detective never has a hope of outsmarting anyone. Here, for the most part, is a place where expertise belongs not to the person who pontificates the hardest or comes up with the unusual angle, but rather the one who thinks the most ordinary thoughts, or who doesn't need to acknowledge their thinking but simply knows, as it were with their entire body, what someone is trying to say.

This ordinary person knows which of the routes is the right one, without having to deliberate like an idiot, because they know how the land of the language is trodden. "A multitude of familiar paths lead off from these words in every direction," I could hear Wittgenstein's voice proclaim in my head; it was the person who had trodden each of these familiar paths countless times who would be able to tell, instantly, instinctively, which was the right one to take.

¶ nobi-nobi: the sound of space

EVEN FOURTEEN YEARS LATER, THINKING back to that
first year I can remember how the freedom felt: the looseness
in my limbs, the singing in my chest. When I make to describe
it, I want to reach for elements of the island's landscape—the
sea air, the wide open roads, the endless coastline, the huge
blue of the sky—and in fact, I'm certain that physical spaciousness did contribute a lot to the sense I had of being able
to slip off the edge of artifice and fall straight into eternity, but
that wasn't all it was. It was also freedom from the known.

I was aware at the time that speaking of freedom in the
context of foreign escape is a sticky notion, particularly as a
white person from a dominant culture with a colonialist legacy, and these days I'm even more aware of it. It's all too easy
to conceptualize the rural paradise you move into as a blank
canvas for your personal growth, and ignore the existing community; to feel yourself free from the tug of social conscience
as you trample across the needs of others, flout social mores,
and cause those around you discomfort and labor that you are
perfectly unaware of. I tried my best not to act in those ways;
at times I succeeded, and at others I failed. But whatever my
intentions, the intense feeling of liberation I began to feel was
undeniable, and the liberation was mostly from judgment. No

longer surrounded by pronouncements that I understood, I let the critic in my head float away and suddenly I found I could do and say things simply because I wanted to. More, as if the obligations clouding my vision washed away, I was far clearer on what the things I wanted to do actually were. It was as if what had been watching me all the time was my language; I had clung to it as the thing that shaped me, but now I was finding that a looser relationship with the language, perhaps having a looser shape altogether, was profoundly healing.

This development was surprising to me, but perhaps it's nothing to wonder at when we consider that the languages with which we grew up, most particularly if we have grown up with just one, are the building material through which our very selves are constructed. "Language is not only the medium through which existence is transacted," writes Rachel Cusk; "it constitutes our central experiences of social and moral content, of such concepts as freedom and truth, and, most importantly, of individuality and the self; it is also a system of lies, evasions, propaganda, misrepresentation and conformity."

There is very little which doesn't lie within language's scope of influence; as Wittgenstein spelled out time and time again, language is inextricably intertwined with behavioral practices and social codes. Our engagement in a particular linguistic culture is a performance in an improvisational play whose rules are pre-defined for us, and those practices deemed to lie the closest to honest, unmasked expression are no exception in this; in other words, the patterns of behavior that make up "being real," "telling the truth," and "expressing oneself" are as bound by social codes and conventions as any other. This doesn't mean that we as individuals can't be truthful, or light upon modes of self-expression that resonate with us or feel like our own, but we can equally learn to present an appearance of being open and authentic that doesn't feel that way inside. Depending on its intensity and context, the awareness of ourselves as "fake" can induce or be tied up with feelings of great despair, existential angst and depression. It can also serve as an impetus for change or recalibration.

Such recalibrations can theoretically take place from within the linguistic context in question. In practice, though, the idea of learning to recalibrate one's ideas of authentic expression from within the everyday realm of the culture where one learned those norms can for many feel bewildering or impossible; it can feel like the web of "lies, evasions, propaganda, misrepresentation and conformity" is too deeply tied up with everything simply to step away from. So people turn to other outlets, one such being the written word: "Very often a desire to write is a desire to live more honestly through language," notes Cusk. In writing, one can be at a remove not only from the observing eye of society, but also from the somatic memories attached to conversation.

Another place where people burdened by a sense of the inescapable mire of inauthenticity might seek refuge is in the bosom of another culture. Your own language is irrevocably sullied, you feel; there is too much irony, fraudulence, and you have been too deeply steeped in it. You need a new start. You need a retreat—which, as Barthes characterizes, the foreign environment obligingly provides:

The murmuring mass of an unknown language constitutes a delicious protection, envelops the foreigner (provided the country is not hostile to him) in an auditory film
which halts at his ears all the alienations of the mother
tongue: the regional and social origins of whoever is
speaking, his degree of culture, of intelligence, of taste,
the image by which he constitutes himself as a person
and which he asks you to recognize. Hence, in foreign
countries, what a respite! Here I am protected against
stupidity, vulgarity, worldliness, nationality, normality.

Immersed in the world of a different language, the subtle
alienations are gone, leaving only the huge, obvious, undeniable ones—and even those feel tolerable, because we know
them to be utterly beyond our control. To begin with. Then,
of course, the language-learning begins, the start of the gradual acclimatization process, the dissatisfactions and frustra-
tions. But amidst them, also, we catch glimpses of something
so magical we wish it could last forever. Barthes again:

The dream: to know a foreign (alien) language and yet
not to understand it: to perceive the difference in it without that difference ever being recuperated by the superficial sociality of discourse, communication, or vulgarity;
to know, positively reacted in a new language, the impos-
sibilities of our own; to learn the systematics of the
inconceivable; to undo our own "reality" under the effect
of other formulations, other syntaxes; to discover certain
unsuspected positions of the subject in utterance, to dis-
place the subject's topology; in a word, to descend into

the untranslatable, to experience its shock without ever muffling it, until everything Occidental in us totters and the rights of the "father tongue" vacillate—that tongue which comes to us from our fathers and which makes us, in our turn, fathers and proprietors of a culture which, precisely, history transforms into "nature."

Evidently, this is not a dream of the sort we can hope might one day come true, but a dream destined to remain a fantasy: knowledge without understanding is impossible because understanding is not, as it were, looking out dispassionately through the thick porthole of a ship at the scenery passing by outside. To understand is to be affected. To know a form of fakery specific to a language is to have been angered or hurt or betrayed once, twice, thirty times, by disingenuity of that kind. It is to have once been without that thick layer of glass—which is why, perhaps, we have found such a myriad of ways to construct glass windows within language. We cannot remain unaffected forever, which is why turning to a new language as a way of remaining unclouded and perfectly sincere is a doomed project in the long run.

For all that, I want to say that there is a hallowed period, in our first stretch of learning a foreign language, when we can feel that the spell of our dreamlike desire is working somehow—that our situation is not exactly as Barthes describes, but perhaps draws close. I think of the Japanese word for the time immediately after a man orgasms, kenja-taimu ("wise-man-period" or "sage time"); the idea being that this is the period when a man is able to be rational, disimpassioned, wise, free of the temptations that plague him at other

times, and it strikes me that in some way this is a good analogy for what happens when a person enters a new language.

Of course, in many ways, such a person is anything but
a sage—they understand almost nothing, there are more
embarrassments than previously seemed possible, and there
is the morbid frustration of not being able to express oneself
properly. But there is also, paradoxically, a sense of the cloud
lifting, and human discourse suddenly revealing itself to be
remarkably straightforward and pure. You are on holiday
from the disingenuity of language. You cannot express yourself except in the most basic terms, but through that infantile mode of expression you glimpse what could have been.
It seems to you that you can express yourself, plainly, with
terrible grammar, and a kind of deep profundity, forever and
ever. You have become Yoda, and you embrace the transition.
Your very incompetence, it seems, has liberated you.

————

Years after I left the island, in a different part of Japan, I
came to know a young girl who was being home-schooled, a
highly intelligent and headstrong eight-year-old who seemed
to me to belong to a different species to the diligent conform-
ists that the Japanese education system usually churned out.
The girl's mother and I stayed in touch for a while, and once,
after returning to the UK for a holiday, I sent her a photo of
myself standing in a Yorkshire field dotted with sheep. The
girl's response to the photo, reported to me over email, was:
"Those sheep are so lucky, being able to live so freely in a
place that spacious. I feel sorry for the sheep in the zoo."

Nobi-nobi was the phrase she used for "freely." It can also be rendered as "unhampered," "unobstructed," and has the same stem as nobiru, a verb meaning "to stretch," "to grow," "to elongate." It's worth saying that sheep are not a common animal in Japan, and so she had likely only ever seen them in zoos before. But when I got the email, and read it out loud to my boyfriend, G, the two of us stood there for a while, basking in the sense of how wise, how almost prophetic this pronouncement made her seem. "Nobi-nobi," I remember him mouthing—feeling, I imagine, the delight of the sound, and perhaps the same sense of wonder I had so often: that a word so particular and contextually specific could emerge so naturally from the mouth of someone so young. And maybe feeling also the visceral spaciousness that the word seemed to hold, that same loosening that I had experienced on the island. Having space to grow, having space to move forward—it feels to me that this is related to not just freedom, but almost every other good. To joy, certainly, but also to love—at least if we follow bell hooks in defining it as "the will to extend oneself for the purpose of nurturing one's own or another's spiritual growth."

¶ moja-moja: the sound of electric hair

EARLY ON, "MOJA-MOJA" ANNOUNCES ITSELF as the adjective for my hair. The kids come up and pat my head and say it, and at first, because I don't really understand anything, I don't know even what realm of utterance it belongs to. Once I've heard it from a few of them, though, I start to figure out that they must be talking about a specific quality of my hair, which marks it out from theirs. I know what the more usual word for curly is—kuru-kuru—and I say this in self-description, and sometimes I'll be almost corrected: no, moja-moja. I think to myself that I must look into what the classic use of this phrase is—what is it used for when not my hair—but then I forget, and it's years later when it comes up naturally in conversation, describing sheep's wool. I take this new fact with me to my boyfriend at the time, and say to him in something of an accusatory fashion: "This word that everyone says about me, that you say about my hair, why didn't you tell me it was for sheep!" He looks at me for a little while, blinking. "Not only sheep, though. Other things too." "Like what," I say. He looks away, either in thought or in diffidence. "Like . . . Struwwelpeter? You know, that German character with hair like this. Like he's been electrocuted." His hands form an excited arc of moja-moja around his head.

¶ yochi-yochi: the sound of tottering (at last)

EARLY ON DURING MY TIME on the island, my supervisor, M, asks if I can teach a private English class on Saturday mornings to a group of preschool children, one of whom is his son. I don't feel I can really say no, so I say yes and then regret my compliancy and lack of foresight for the rest of the year.

The children are of assorted ages with a median of three, and mostly they are gorgeous, but I find the lessons stressful in the extreme. This will turn out to be the case whenever I teach this age group in Japan, not because I struggle with the children per se, but because even when it seems patently clear that using the same results-oriented teaching model in teaching toddlers as is employed for school-age children and adults is futile, and it would be better for all concerned just to play in English, Japanese society and Japanese mothers unfailingly require recognizable proof of progress. The impossible demands this places on me as teacher inevitably leave me frustrated, and, unable to control the children to the extent that this style of teaching requires, I find I soon become overly disciplinarian in a way that disgusts me even as it is happening. In this particular case, the demanded proof of progress is a Christmas show; the children wear headbands with different animal ears stapled on, allowing them to transform into assorted animals from a Ukrainian folktale called *The Mitten*. I crouch in the "wings" of the "stage" mouthing the words, feeling irritated that the kids are not getting it right despite practicing more times than seemed bearable to me, and wondering to myself when it was that I became such a miserable bastard.

This specific type of stress is not the only one I experience; there is a more everyday tension too. I find just being at the grand, sumptuously decorated house of the family who hosts the classes and interacting with the mothers before and after the lessons, frequently with a steaming hangover, inexplicably exhausting. The host couple both speak excellent English, but the other mothers don't really have a word, and so I hover there like a lemon, trying to seem receptive and friendly while also teacherly, trying to communicate whenever that seems doable.

The wife of M, my supervisor, is often there too, accompanied by their little boy's even younger sibling. With his mass of black curly hair, he looks like a miniature professor and is one of the most adorable children I have ever seen. He is also a total rogue, and his mother seems not to feel inclined to restrain him in any way. When he turns eighteen months, it is said over and over, then he will join the class! This prospect is simultaneously appealing and dreadful to me. Today, as we stand around in the spacious entranceway with its parquet floors, he is having a well-behaved day. He pads between the people standing there in a haphazard way, occasionally shrieking with delight.

"Sooooo cute," I say, turning to one of the mothers next to me. "Kawaii, kawaii."

"Kawaii," she agrees, and then, as we watch him pad off toward the door where the lesson has been, she says,

"Yochi-yochi." She performs the gesture, her arms bent like robot arms, shoulders moving from side to side, imitating the toddler's way of walking. "Yochi-yochi."

"Yochi-yochi," I repeat, awkwardly.

Another mother close by hears us and laughs a peal of bright, self-conscious laughter. "Yochi-yochi," she joins in, and does the gesture, and nods. "Yochi-yochi."

At times like these, I feel that I am not dissimilar to a toddler myself, a being at which people repeat words and which repeats them back in an inept fashion, and this sense feels particularly acute when the word in question is a mimetic, like yochi-yochi. I should reiterate that in Japanese, a surfeit of onomatopoeic language in an adult context does not necessarily connote infantilism as it would do in English, but nonetheless, in mothers' speech to infants, mimetic language is particularly prevalent, and sometimes I sense that the toddler treatment of ramping up the mimetic content is being extended to me also. If this is true, I think the tendency comes less from any desire to educate me, and more from the instinct that a word like yochi-yochi derives some of its communicative power from a more affective, gestural dimension of language; that its sound-symbolic quality means it serves a better chance of transcending linguistic borders than anything else in the repertoire. And yet, even if the intention is improved communication, I am, also, being educated: babied and educated in one. In not very much time at all, the novelty of these sorts of encounters will wear off and I will start to feel permanently patronized, but right now I am still grateful for these inane interactions.

———

Something that strikes me in these moments is that I am not only the toddler speaking its first words but simultaneously its attentive parent, in that I am ever so conscious of what it has taken me to get to the stage where I can have even this kind of interaction—an interaction which might, to the untrained eye, seem like an entry-level conversation, but of which I was incapable at the time of my arrival. I am acutely aware that it is only with time, and certain forms of learning, that I have begun to stagger forward into the territory of the very minimally conversant, and what is astonishing is how little of this progress consists in my ability to spontaneously produce comprehensible sentences, which are still mostly beyond me.

Instead, the majority of this "ability" relates to learning how to read conversational cues, to tuning in to the rhythms of speech, to sensing and mimicking nonverbal behavior, and to knowing when and when not to try to speak. In a sense, this realization is Wittgenstein felt on the skin: "I should like to say you regard it too much as a matter of course that one can tell anything to anyone," he writes in the *Investigations*.

> That is to say: we are so much accustomed to communication through languages in conversation, that it looks to us as though the whole point of communication lay in

this: someone else grasps the sense of my words—which is something mental: he as it were takes it into his own mind. If he then does something further with it as well, that is no part of the immediate purpose of language.

In other words, familiarization itself can encourage us towards a view of conversation as trading perfectly formed, pearl-like ideas between one mind and another. Past a certain level of communicational competency, the enmeshed relationship that exists between behavior and language is concealed from us; familiarity encourages us to see spoken language as an impartial conveyer of meaning, standing discrete from the realm of behavioral practices, or indeed anything that has anything to do with real-life people.

In a way, it is hardly surprising that we underestimate the role played by our incredibly sophisticated codes of nonverbal and sociolinguistic behavior—the multitude of rules and practices which frame and facilitate our verbal communication—because they are so rarely the subject of discussion; we learn them through mimicry, as we imbibe the rest of our codes of conduct, and then, finding them everywhere we turn, easily cease to notice them. Which is why it is usually only when we experience a drastic change to our environment that the scales begin to fall from our eyes. As we are forced to become conscious of our unconscious competences or lack thereof, it becomes clear to us for the first time that "doing something further with" language—responding in certain ways, be they linguistic, paralinguistic, with direct action, or most likely a combination of these—is really part of what it means to mean anything at all. Understanding is not an internal switch flicked that nobody else can see; if you don't act upon an instruction, if you don't behave in the required way, you are not yet understanding. To comprehend within a particular culture means to act upon that culture's rules for comprehending—in the absence of some admissible reason for not doing so. And in a parallel way, to mean something by what one says is not to have a particular intention, or to perform a freestanding act of mind, but is, in a broad sense, to be participating in a community-wide game governed by rules, and in the more narrow sense, to be anticipating or expecting a certain response: "Yes: meaning something is like going up to someone."

If the best way to apprehend this quality of language is to be in a place where one's learned behaviors don't apply, and one has to learn new ones, then plausibly the greater the disjunct there is between this place and the culture perceived as "transparent," the harder and faster the revelations will hit. Certainly I was stunned by the sheer number of differences in paralanguage between English and Japanese, which I perceived more the more I learned: rules about repetition, about set phrases, about the gestures that accompanied words, about "back-channeling," i.e., interjections made while one's interlocutor is speaking. It's easy enough to provide anecdote-friendly examples—the Japanese way of beckoning, as demonstrated by the welcoming cat, is what we would see as shooing someone away in the West, for instance—yet what really floored me was no one particular discrepancy, and rather the comprehensiveness of the difference.

Similarly overwhelming is the slow-dawning under-standing of what it looks like to try and master this new system. How somatic it is as a form of learning, as you use every part of your body to read the cues of other bodies. The innate vulnerability of this, the intimate quality of the attention demanded to read people so physically and thor-oughly, and to hang on to their every tiny movement—an attention I occasionally find uncomfortable when directed at me by children. When I try to find the word to describe this act, I come up with "parroting," "apeing"; I'm intrigued by the way that English turns to animal imagery to convey the mindlessness, which here is to say, the totality of the mim-icry, when really it's our children who are the unrivalled champions. Yochi-yochi, yochi-yochi, they totter and stag-ger their way towards mastery.

————

Whenever I think about this form of mimicry, I remember a particular outing with a British colleague, and his Japanese girlfriend I was meeting for the first time. Despite my col-league and I working together as translators, I'd never before heard him speak Japanese; that night it turned out that he did so with a strong Lancashire twang and a notably British intonation. "Your Japanese is amazing," the girlfriend told me almost the second I opened my mouth, although it wasn't, and I think she was mostly persuaded by my accent. As I bat-ted off the compliments—a Japanese textbook I'd owned had instructed that while you definitely shouldn't accept compli-ments straight away, you are permitted at the third insistence to say thank you, because holding out for longer than that is considered ungracious in a different way—he turned to face the two of us and said,

"I don't think foreign people should imitate Japanese accents."

"What?" I said.

"I just think it's gross, to mimic people like that. I'd feel like I was acting all the time."

I felt like I'd been thrust out of the room where we'd been amiably conversing into a huge zero-gravity chamber, where I was now bouncing off the walls. So pure, so white was my feeling of disagreement, I didn't know where to start formulating a response.

I could see that the obvious response to most people who would make a pronouncement of this caliber would be to point out that learning a language can only be a form of mimesis. For sure, you can do it via a textbook, but that's merely putting the act at a remove; what is written in there is, at least nominally, taken from the language that people use "on the ground," which means you're still mimicking, only in a less accurate and a more easily digestible way. The strange thing was, though, that this colleague didn't come across like someone who had learned his language purely from a book; his phraseology was relatively natural, compared with many Japanese-speakers I'd encountered. I didn't understand. Was it that semantic forms of mimicry were permitted in his schema, while paralinguistic ones weren't? I knew that there were people who were more comfortable affecting tones of voices and

rhythms than others, and I sensed that for whatever reason this comfort seemed to go hand in hand with ability;
I could see that it wasn't easy for people who didn't have
"a good ear." I would even admit that I had also had the
experience of finding something uncanny and slightly nau-
seating at the sight of white people on the television or in
public speaking Japanese with all of the native speech patterns and the most fawning gestures from the repertoire,
so the "gross" accusation wasn't totally incomprehensible
to me. Yet nevertheless, to draw a line between imitating
the words that people said and the way that they said them
seemed to me not only arbitrary, but fundamentally untenable as a division.

Strangely, even though my colleague had in a roundabout
way just called me gross, I didn't feel insulted so much as I
felt slightly sorry for him. This wasn't just because I guessed
there was a sour-grapes element to this response of his, after
having been dealt a backhand slight by his girlfriend; nor was
it just because I really liked the way Japanese sounded, and
listening closely to and imitating (I felt these two actions to
be intimately intertwined) the profile of Japanese sounds and
people was one of the greatest joys that I had. I think more
than any of that, I felt sorry for my colleague because I knew
full well that my accent had come from undergoing a second infancy, which had been nerve-wracking, full of irritation, and necessitated making myself vulnerable, and I felt
like I saw through his words to a simple declaration that he
wasn't prepared to make an idiot of himself like that. That
he couldn't bring himself to pad around, yochi-yochi, while

everyone watched; wasn't prepared to crash into a wall now and then, and to risk the uncanniness of being a semi-professional parrot.

Back on the island, being simultaneously embarrassing and embarrassed had been grim at times, but I could also feel very intuitively that it was only because I'd been capable of going there that Japanese had been able to slip under my skin.

¶ zu': the sound of always and never having been like this

FOR THE FIRST TIME, I'M watching Y doing what I think of as "properly teaching." Clearly this isn't a fair description, because he teaches properly every day, but now he is introducing a new grammar point whose concept needs explicating, and it seems particularly "proper" to me because he's speaking in Japanese. Of all the teachers I work with across my various schools, Y is the one who uses the most English in the classroom—some older-generation teachers scarcely utter a word—but for an explanation like this one, the Japanese is necessary. The students are second-years, and they are learning the present-perfect for the first time, a tense which has no close correlate in Japanese. We started by introducing the topic with a role play in English, but that's now over, and I'm standing at the side of the classroom by the window, observing as he does the conceptual heavy lifting. He writes the last sentence of the role play large across the top of the board—not his usual looping cursive, but blackboard-friendly letters that still manage to look uniquely his: "I have lived in Japan for five years."

Underneath this sentence, he draws two circles and a long line spanning the distance between them. The circle on the left he labels "5 years ago," the one on the right "now." I miss much of the first part of the explanation because the Japanese is too complex for me, but I tune back in as he goes over to the "5 years ago" dot.

He's recapping how we use the simple past, which the children have already learned, to talk about a specific point in time. "I lived in Japan five years ago," he says, and jabs at the 5. "When someone uses the simple past like this, we know they were living in Japan *at a certain point in time*, but we don't know how long they were there for. If they say just, 'I lived in Japan,' without specifying when, then they could have lived there at this time, or this time, or this." His arm jabs away randomly, leaving little flecks of chalk along the line to show the possibilities of all the different temporal points at which this imaginary person could theoretically have lived in Japan, if they used just the simple past.

"But if we say, I have lived in Japan for five years, then what we mean is that from five years ago, I am living—"

With this he goes over to the 5 years ago point and hunches himself down sideways, the end of his stick of chalk pressed onto the point, and then begins to move himself along the timeline, arm outstretched, saying:

"Zuuuuuuuuuuuuuuuuuu'to."

Zu'to—I know this word, I think. I have seen it in textbooks and caught snatches of it in conversation. I remember that it means something like "the whole time." But I have never heard it played with, molded like this. I have only ever thought of it as a singular word, "zutto"—not a zu' with a quotative particle at the end, and I have never thought of the "zu'" part as meaning something like stretching on and on. I didn't know it could become an elastic band like this.

The kids titter slightly, exchange glances. Y's teaching strategy is to offer himself up as the village idiot so that the village can come together and learn. Also, I sense, to offer himself up as the village idiot because he knows deep down that this is the best, or only, way of getting the villagers to love him.

"When we use the present perfect," he goes on, reiterating, "we are saying that from a certain point on, we have been doing something continuously. *All the time.*"

He wipes the "for five years" from the sentence, then erases the 5 years ago from beside the little dot and writes Birth in its place.

"Or how about this? If we'd been doing something all this time?" He gestures between the beginning and the end of the line. "Any ideas what we'd put here?" He taps at the empty space in the sentence.

Someone from the class pipes up, "Always?"

"Exactly!" He's on form now. I can feel it in the air, as if the molecules have begun to move. There's a conviction to his way of speaking that keeps the kids hanging on his words, even if they think he's goofy. "Always! Exactly." He erases more of the sentence, so that he can fit always in the correct place.

"And so when we say, I have always lived in Japan, what you are saying is the point of your birth onwards, you are living—"

He goes right over to the birth point and again hunches himself down sideways like a little fetus, and then does it again with his chalk, his mouth stuck out like a bellflower, a little trumpet: "Zuuuuuuuuuuuuuuuuu'to."

———

Standing there with my bum pressed into the window ledge, I can see perfectly well what he's doing. I understand instinctively this technique of using his comfort and his ease to prove the safety of this scary foreign language to the kids, because it is about the only technique I have up my own sleeve. What's funny, though, is that this understanding doesn't prevent the technique from working on me. It does its magic even though I can see its mechanism—more crucially, even though the language in which he's safe-making is to me, and to me only in this classroom, the forbidding one.

Or was the forbidding one, I should probably say, because it's around this point that I slip inside. Zu'to—not only does the word come alive in his lopsided mouth, so that I now know I won't ever forget it, but something else takes place. For the first time, the possibility of being inside this language takes shape in front of me—or better put, takes sound, because it's as if the cymbal of what has always been collides with another, that of what has never been, and the two momentarily press the entirety of their surfaces into each other in a spilling crash. The crash says: you can be a part of this if you want to be. The crash seems to fill both my body and the classroom beyond.

Then it dies down, and I'm left with a different, calmer feeling of—what? Affection, attachment, communion: it could be called any of these things. I ask myself what it's directed towards. Is this affection for this man with the lop-sided mouth, crouching down before the blackboard? There is no doubt in my mind that it is for him. But it's also, insepa-rably, affection for this language he speaks, this form of life which I feel through him. *As if he were a medium channel-ing it*, I make to write, but really it's nothing as mysterious as that. He is just a person, an expressive, charismatic per-son from a different culture to mine, and his words lead off towards a thousand different practices, a million different experiences of which I have no grasp. This is the first time of heavens knows how many to come when I will notice this inextricable comingling of person and language, this affec-tion which can't decide which one of the two it's bonded with. At this stage, I'm not yet berating myself for not being able to separate out these things, not yet worrying that there's something fundamentally wrong with me. Instead, I'm just feeling this rush for the first time, which is close, and gripping, which brings our worlds together even as it holds them apart.

The other notable aspect of the cymbal feeling and its aftermath is how right and known it feels to have my world upturned like this. It's as if, without warning, I can feel the inevitability of contingency written into my own language, can feel that it had only ever been one of many possibilities, and a space for the other had always been there. Despite knowing rationally that everything I can feasibly claim to call myself has developed in, around, and through English, it feels as though on a subcutaneous level I am remembering a pre-linguistic self, a self prior to cultural training, who has no particular attachment to any particular set of rules. And this discovery is not surprising, because it feels somehow like the rightful order of things. In Toni Morrison's words: "No gasp at a miracle that is truly miraculous because the magic lies in the fact that you knew it was there for you all along."

¶ mecha-kucha: the sound of a truly mixed tool-bag

ONE IMAGE FROM THE *Investigations* which has always stuck with me is language-as-toolbox. "Think of the tools in a tool-box," Wittgenstein instructs us early on in the book. "There is a hammer, pliers, a saw, a screw-driver, a rule, glue-pot, glue, nails, and screws.—The functions are as diverse as the functions of these objects. (And in both cases there are similarities.)" It seems safe to say that Wittgenstein's principal point in drawing this analogy is to illustrate that, belying the superficial uniformity in the "appearance of words when we hear them spoken or meet them in script and print," there exists a diverse range of functionality. If we want an accurate picture of how language functions, we must be prepared to examine, patiently and unglamorously, each and every word in order to understand its precise mechanism, rather than lapsing back upon a referential view of meaning whereby each word in a language is similar because it "signifies something"—a claim which, Wittgenstein is clear, has "so far said *nothing whatever.*"

Aside from its specific aim, the analogy also forms part of a wider tonal picture. It is only a few pages into the *Investigations* that the toolbox surfaces, and we the reader may still have no idea where this book is taking us, but by this point the kinds of examples used will already have made it clear that we are reading no standard work of philosophy. Rather, with the influx of builders, slabs, locomotives, and so on that fill the first few pages, we will have noticed that the work locates itself firmly in the real world, even if the reasons for this choice are still obscure. This comes not simply from a personal preference on Wittgenstein's part, although his fascination with all things mechanical is well recorded, but coheres with the overall project of his philosophy, which stresses that the meaning of words lies in their everyday usages, rather than some hidden application which only philosophers can divine. In fact, one way of conceiving of the late-Wittgensteinian project is that of wresting the power over language from the hands of the philosophical elite and returning it to the everyday speaker, the seasoned user: hence, we could say, we see a surfeit of practical, proletarian imagery.

For me, there has always been something particularly evocative about the toolbox metaphor in this vein, because of the aura of chaos it carries. I've no doubt that, especially these days, there are plenty of households with a toolbox purchased from the DIY shop as a pristine set, its identically colored components all branded with the same logo, but the one that springs to my mind is modeled after that my father had: a great unfolding metal container housing an extraordinary range of tools of varied provenances, all of differing ages and states of disrepair, whose most noticeable feature was its hodgepodge quality. To my mind, Wittgenstein's toolbox metaphor seems to draw the mind not only to the diversity of linguistic functions, but also, by virtue of its scruffy, worldly associations, to the way that languages develop in real time, being added to and expanded, undergoing culls and replacements, and so on. Even the most organized toolboxes are bound to be a little rough around the edges; even utterly jumbled versions like my father's could get the job done very well indeed. Similarly, any language evolves over time, and the tasks it is called on to perform are perpetually shifting: it stands to reason that it will be at least a little bit of a mishmash.

To me, there is something about Japanese that seems to showcase this mishmash quality of language very clearly. Of course, there is a subjective element to this perception; it is always the learner-outsider, rather than the acclimatized speaker, who notices the inconsistencies of any specific tongue. The hellish unpredictability of English pronunciation, for example, is something we forget about as native speakers; it takes a learner lamenting that "bough" and "bow" are sometimes but not always homophones while "cough" and "cow" never are for us to remember that, not only is this objectively confusing, but that we ourselves struggled with it, back in the age before time. Yet to the extent one can usefully speak objectively of those qualities of languages necessarily perceived subjectively, it seems to me that there is an aspect to the Japanese writing system which brings this into relief. For while English sneakily veils its varied origins under the cover of twenty-six relatively similar-looking letters, Japanese boasts three discrete scripts, of which a typical sentence comprises at least two, and in most cases all three. Naturally, this feeds into the overall complexity of the writing system, which is "routinely acknowledged as the modern world's most complex"; it also seems to serve another, arguably more Wittgensteinian function in acknowledging, on a visual level, its assorted provenance.

This is clearest with katakana, the script reserved mostly but not exclusively for gairaigo, or words of a foreign origin. "Foreign" here should be understood as defined in a specific sense, for swathes of Japanese vocabulary, not to mention all three of its writing systems, have their origins in Chinese and are therefore also indubitably "foreign" by some definition, but within Japanese these are included in a different category to gairaigo; Sino-Japanese words derive from Old or Middle Chinese, while foreign-imported vocabulary displayed in katakana is primarily European, and of modern inclusion. Some of the earliest examples of gairaigo date back to the sixteenth and seventeenth centuries when the Dutch and Portuguese were the foreign nations with which Japan had the most contact; for example, the present-day Japanese words "tabako" and "pan" for "cigarettes" and "bread" come from Portuguese, while "histerii" and "randoseru" for "hysteria" and "satchel" are from Dutch. There are also some foundational items of French and German vocabulary adopted around the turn of the nineteenth century, particularly in the realms of science and philosophy; but since the Second World War, the ever-growing range of foreign-imported vocabulary has been derived overwhelmingly from English. And rather than sneaking these imports in unnoticed (as if they could pass unnoticed, being for the most part so different in their construction from Japanese or Sino-Japanese vocabulary), the Japanese toolbox marks them out as such:

as if a meticulous owner has thought to color-code its tools, the section acquired from the West is painted in the cherry red of katakana.

————

And what a shock this cherry-red section was set to cause me. However forewarned I believed myself to be for the Japanese treatment of English, nothing prepared me for the strength of what I felt when actually confronted by it. *What was it specifically?* I ask myself, and I struggle to answer, because it seemed to be everything.

It was, first and foremost, the sheer quantity of English words, and how different they sounded—the way that even those which were pronounced the most similarly to how I pronounced them were still markedly other, and those that were dissimilar were nearly unrecognizable. It was how, in some cases, the constituent parts of words were ostensibly English, mimicked English construction, but were simply neologisms; sometimes this was obviously and startlingly the case—"virgin road" for bridal aisle, "handle keeper" for designated driver—and sometimes they assumed the air of plausibility, so I would question myself—was "skinship" for physical contact just a word that I hadn't encountered yet? Was "paper driver" an Americanism? Then there was the unpredictability of it all, the way that "glass" was spelled differently depending on whether it was window glass or a cup for water: garasu and gurasu, respectively. The way everything that had once been English was abbreviated, constantly, so pineapple juice was pain jūsu, and sandwich was shortened to "sand":

sandwich cookie wrappers read, in Roman script, "Raisin Sand" and "Butter Sand," while strawberry sandwiches were "Fruits Sand." The seeming randomness of whether words were cast as plural or singular, and how this had no relevance to whether the words being described were plural or singular. While most things were irredeemably singular and never pluralized, nuts, beans, sports, suits, sheets, doughnuts and peas were always plural, giving "peanuts butter" and "suitscase" and countless pencil cases and T-shirts declaring "The favorite fruits is strawberry!"

Then there was the unflatteringness: even if some katakana renditions were endearing to me, many made me recoil in distaste, not only from their pronunciations but from what they seemed to represent about my language. In them, and in the kinds of objects and concepts they were used to describe—new things, artificial things, everything which globalism and capitalism had brought to Japan and taught it to value—I felt I could see a representation of the West through Japanese eyes, where it was crass and materialistic and spoke only of objects: manē for money, with a big flat drawn out "e" sound; naisu badē and guramarasu (glamorous) for a big-chested woman, and so on.

What was perhaps, in the final analysis, the most difficult to deal with was that the English-inspired elements of Japanese were not a temporary, makeshift insertion, but a legitimate, rule-bound part of the language. Embarrassingly, this fact took a while to fully sink in, and in my first few weeks I sustained the belief that if, while speaking Japanese, I said English words in my normal accent I would be understood, and would in some sense be "righter," because those were the "real" pronunciations. Eventually, of course, I reached the realization that gairaigo were a bona fide part of the Japanese language, and were spoken with authority as such; if I wanted to communicate properly in Japanese, that was how I would have to speak. I would have to say howaitobōdo instead of whiteboard, and shītoberuto for seatbelt, and if I didn't then I'd be wrong. If I wanted to talk about a film star, I would have to know how to say their name in the correct katakana pronunciation, otherwise I'd be met with incomprehension. That was just how things were.

———

Even in the midst of my fixation with katakana, I sensed there was something boringly predictable about dwelling on this aspect of Japanese. Certainly I feel it now. I think about all of those people from Anglophone cultures who have visited Japan and have regaled me endlessly with examples of the nonsense English they've seen splashed across T-shirts, pencil cases, and signs; similarly, I've conversed with any number of Japanese people whose first comment on their adventures abroad, before any reflections on how the country or the people were, was about the sushi restaurant where the lantern reading irrashaimasse was hanging upside down, or where all the employees were Chinese or Korean. Come on, I want to say, what about all the other stuff? Surely the ways in which your language or your culinary culture has been used or misused is less interesting than almost everything else about that nation, and the experience you had there? Whoever was doing it, this cultural navel-gazing seemed to me to reveal an inner miserliness, a horrible pedantry of the soul.

Yet evidently I too was a miser and a horrible pedant, because I was interested by it—although really, that's the wrong word. It wasn't that I felt any actual desire to think about this stuff; I would just find my mind ineluctably drawn to it, as if through a species of instinct. I was preoccupied by the deviant use of the language I'd grown up with going on all around me, and the more days I put behind me in the country, the more my feelings moved along the spectrum from a tourist's titillation to serious feelings of outrage, and anger, and exclusion. It's hard to write about those reactions without sounding like a whining, entitled child, and that is no coincidence, because, I see now, such reactions are indeed the tantrums of a child on whom the rules have changed unannounced, who is having trouble adjusting to an environment where they no longer know the lay of the land. My outrage at seeing English distorted was essentially a cultural King Baby syndrome made worse by the fact that, growing up as a member of the dominant cultural hegemony, I had rarely had to deal with a sense of marginalization pertaining to my language.

As undignified as they may be, I believe it's important to write about these feelings, because for many I think they are an unavoidable stage in the process of integration. I would often wonder if this whole experience was exposing me as a kind of linguistic tyrant, who went around waving the flag of multilingualism and multiculturalism while an inner brat fumed away about people breaking the rules. It appeared that it wasn't just me, either; almost every Anglophone I spoke with in Japan would either have similar feelings to mine, or at least feelings of some kind on the matter. An Australian friend told me that in his early days living in Japan, when getting on the plane in Brisbane after a trip home, hearing Japanese people using "katakana English words" would instantly give him "a sick feeling." "It immediately put me in the head-space of 'you're not with people who know you anymore,'" he said. "It was like being dunked in water."

For some reason, I link up the particular feeling of chaos which the Japanese treatment of English induced in me to a word Y used to use a lot: mecha-kucha. The more I got to know Y, the more I glimpsed in him flashes of something different from the other Japanese people I encountered—he was less reined in, in a way I found appealing. There I would be, sitting in the staffroom, reading in my textbook how when you wanted to turn down an engagement in Japan you mustn't say "No" but rather a phrase that translated as "That's a little bit . . ." and trail off, and there Y would be at the desk close to me, periodically exclaiming "Shimatta-aaa!"—"Shit, I screwed up!"—and pulling an exaggerated grimace. When something was bad he called it bad, and one of his favorite ways of doing that was this phrase: mecha-kucha. Looking it up in the Japanese–English dictionary now I find it defined as "the state of being disarrayed without any order," of "being mangled," of "being utterly without rhyme or reason." A student would make a disastrous attempt to do something, and this would be Y's response; it wasn't mean-spirited, but it was making no attempt to hide how flabbergasted he was at what a state the item in question was in. I found it dry and warm, both qualities that I craved back then, and it would make me smile whenever I heard it.

This was the word, in my affronted moments, that I wanted to level at Japanese. I wanted to shout it, in outrage; I wanted to stamp my feet, and tell the world how unacceptable this state of affairs was. Gradually, I realized consciously where this brattishness came from: that what is most repulsive or infuriating to us is not that which is truly other, but that about which we have rules, which are now being stomped all over. It's not a dissimilar feeling to seeing your siblings getting away with transgressions that you did not. I wanted to lie on the floor, pummel it with my feet and scream: *No! You can't call a cheese-filled burger patty "Cheese in Hamburg" because it MAKES NO SENSE!*

If I'd learned anything from Wittgenstein, it was that context was everything: the way that words were used in particular settings, the particular games played with language. You couldn't see a tool that looked roughly the same as one in your box and assume it functioned the exact same way, or was used to perform all the same tasks when the makeup of the rest of the toolbox was so wildly different. But it was one thing to know this and another to live it fully. It transpired that it required a considerable largeness of spirit to accept the way that these imported words were wielded with little consideration for their original usage and belonged to an utterly different web of associations to those they had in English. It was not the commandeering of the words that was painful, but rather the lack of knowledge around it; as my friend had pointed out, it seemed to signal very clearly that subtleties which had made up your world were lost, and you now had to abide by a different set. Nobody understood you, or had any interest in understanding you.

As time went on, I began to have flashes of understanding that felt nearly spiritual. I would be walking down a street, wondering for the umpteenth time how it could be that *so many* people could create a signboard for their shop or restaurant using an English word written in English script without thinking to check the spelling, when it would suddenly strike me that I was quite possibly the first person to ever notice this particular mistake—at the very most, only the tenth or twentieth. And with this came the understanding that the standards of correctness I had been brought up with literally did not apply here—to all intents and purposes, *these weren't mistakes anymore*, even when they were written in the Roman alphabet. What I was looking at and pointing out and obsessing over was not English in the way that I had previously understood the word; English itself had to be given a different definition here, to be governed by a different set of rules. And as I had that thought, I would feel an expansive sense of grace descending over me, and with it a feeling of immense relief. I had been manning a watchtower for a crumbling empire, I realized, desperately trying to do the duty that had been subconsciously instilled in me. Now came the news that the empire had fallen, and all I felt was peace. But I could only keep this understanding in focus for a short while before it would slip from view.

¶ chira-chira: the sound of the mighty loner and the caress of ten thousand ownerless looks

TO BE STARED AT, ALL the time, everywhere. Except to describe it as staring is already to misrepresent it, to conjure up an image of a long, fixed, open-eyed sort of look with a discernible owner, and while there are some of those, like the man who waits in the road outside your flat and stands still and solid as a rock as you pass, glaring at you with hatred in his eyes, it mostly does not feel that way. Rather, it is the glance thrown furtively, a move performed less with the whites of the eyes and more the dark of the eyelashes, so that en masse, the sensation is that of being caressed by a hundred feathered wings, or cut by a hundred tiny blades. Chira-chira is the word for it, this scattered, stolen look, the same word used for the soft twinkling of the stars, a light fall of snow, the fluttering of candlelight. Also broken down and used in the making of the word "pan-chira," the love of glancing up girls' skirts to catch a glimpse of their pants, a word which to me always sounds like some kind of superhero: the Mighty Panchira! And indeed, this perpetual snowfall of glances can make you feel like a superhero, caressed and carried aloft, and also irredeemably alone.

¶ jin-jin: the sound of being touched for the very first time

A MUSICAL INTERLUDE. IT STARTS with a voice, a sole raspy voice emerging from the silence, intimate and slightly unnerving:

Jin jin jin jin, the voice goes—*chi ga jin jin*

Hearing this song as someone who doesn't understand Japanese, it might occur to you to doubt whether or not this is, in fact, language. You may think it feels too sonically evocative to be real language: too creepy, too insectual. As it happens, it is both: it is language, and it is perfect sound. Jin-jin, reads the dictionary; the state of feeling pain in part of your body each time your blood pulses there. So let's hazard a translation for these lyrics, although it will be a bad one, for there is no word in English that can work like jin, can carry this meaning and yet buzz like an instrument when sung. Nonetheless:

Throb throb throb throb my blood is throbbing

Now the verse continues, a cappella and sinister as holy hell, as the singer describes her sense of seclusion from a world that is moving on without her. Both the plum and the cherry blossom have perished, the sheltered princess cannot get a wink of sleep. What, she wonders, will her first taste of dawn coffee be like? Now the singer reveals that despite her pressing sense of solitude, she understands that, factually speaking, she is not alone in her sensory deprivation: *you're a virgin, I'm a virgin too*, she sings. And then the brass band handsprings in, billowing with sardonic jubilation. *We're all yearning to be touched!* the trumpets seem to scream ecstatically.

Entitled "Virgin Blues," the track is a cover performed by a beloved singer named Jun Togawa. In the video, Togawa is walking alone down a train track, wearing a heavy over-coat and surgical mask and carrying a briefcase, when she encounters a high-school couple apparently in the throes of a budding romance coming the other way. These themes of isolation and difference, which the video brings out with almost comical clarity, are very much of a piece with the rest of her oeuvre; indeed, I think it is the way she deals with these themes so intelligently, and with such humor, strangeness, and self-awareness, that gave me such a strong reaction to her music when I discovered it five or so years ago. It was a reaction that I almost want to call a homecoming. Her work felt profoundly relevant to my life as it was then, and it continues to resonate now. And yet there is something about this partic-ular song that, from the moment I first heard it, has made me cast my mind back to a past me: it puts me immediately back to being back on the island. Specifically, it puts me back to being on my black swivel chair in the staffroom, learning Jap-anese and planning lessons, surrounded by a school's worth of hustle and bustle, feeling like I'm going out of my mind with a kind of longing that seems too all-encompassing, too holistic to tolerate any succinct description.

———

If someone were to approach the chair of this person and ask her if she was happy or miserable, she wouldn't have an answer. If asked what exactly she desired she wouldn't know that either, although she might try and get away with a response like "everything, everyone." What she does know is that she feels like this song feels: shivery and half-deranged with longing. She feels as though she's perched on the edge of a world, and what she wants more than anything is for that world to take her into itself. This perpetually renewed lack is like being suspended, acrobatic, mid-air, in the act of reaching towards something which lies just beyond the grasp.

It's only reading Anne Carson's *Eros the Bittersweet*, years later, that I can truly understand this feeling for the first time, and give it its rightful name: eros. It's through Carson, also, that I understand for the first time that the geometry of eros is, by necessity, triangular:

> its activation calls for three structural components— lover, beloved and that which comes between them. They are three points of transformation on a circuit of possible relationship, electrified by desire so that they touch not touching. Conjoined they are held apart. The third component plays a paradoxical role for it both connects and separates, marking that two are not one, irradiating the absence whose presence is demanded by eros.

In this geometric sketch of eros, the distance that prevails between us and the object of our affection is not a bug but a defining feature of what it means to desire—and so, too, is our permanent awareness of that distance, which takes the form of a moment-by-moment re-measuring of it. The separation needed to create the hole of longing has its ultimate root in the brute fact of "the boundary of flesh and self between you and me," but to the language learner, this third element in the triangle can assume a concrete form, a specific costume: distance takes to the stage dressed as language.

Your language is what is missing in me, that tantalizing body of knowledge which I do not have, which keeps me from what it is that I want. Namely, you. Namely, intimacy. Namely, the other, and the impossible merging of my self with theirs. That which prevents whole, unadulterated attachment is no more than language—or so we tell ourselves. Ultimately, it is this lack in us upon which we fixate. "Who is the real subject of most love poems? Not the beloved. It is that hole."

To be clear, I am not (only) talking about falling in love with a person who speaks a different language. What I want to suggest is something more controversial, more wide reaching: that things can also work the other way round. That learning a language, particularly when done in an immoderate, drowning, gulping sort of a way, sets us up very well indeed to become sensitized to the boundaries between people, where eros resides. Immersion begets desire, then continues to fuel it. "It is nothing new to say that all utterance is erotic in some sense, that all language shows the structure of desire at some level." Equally, I think, it is nothing new to say that we do not really notice this, until we fall in love—or until we start learning a language. Or both, at the same time.

Seen through this lens, making the commitment to learn a language is not solely a practical, rational, commendable choice, a way of improving communication, although it can evidently be all of those. It is also a doomed response to the desperation and the urgency and the thrill of adrenaline that the continued perception of this distance instills in us: it is an almost wilful misunderstanding of the distance, an attempt to grasp hold of it by identifying it—*the language barrier*—and in the same breath, resolving to do away with it—*I will surmount it.*

Which is not to imply the irreality of the language barrier, or to propose that learning language does not bring us closer to understanding one another. I suggest not that the distance which language poses is untraversable but that, as Carson notes, once it is sealed, we either rub up against a different kind of boundary—"the boundary of flesh and self"—or else, the triangle collapses and we are no longer in eros. Without its third component, the triangle cannot hold. To speak specifically of language, we are now in a place of familiarity. Perhaps one of comfort, of boredom, of frustration, joy, self-expression, oppression, resentment, maybe even a blend of all of these, but not of desire.

Never mind that, though, for the moment. I am still irredeemably there, held aloft in the world of eros. Surfaces hum, edges are blades, and everything is crying out at the fundamental tragedy of being separated in space. I know this because I too am throbbing, in a way that feels both regressive and also like a return to a fundamental truth: "Infants begin to see by noticing the edges of things. How do they know an edge is an edge? By passionately not wanting it to be."

Every interaction is a brush-up against these edges, an improvisational performance around the fundamental crevice that separates us, which stirs up the hope of our union as it spotlights our great distance. Yes, every conversation is a dance: if this isn't eros, I do not know what is. It is not that this dance is only available to the learner; the problem is rather that the seasoned dancer has forgotten what it is they are doing. "Language is a skin," says Barthes. "I rub my language against the other. It is as if I had words instead of fingers, or fingers at the tip of my words. My language trembles with desire."

———

One day I am on my swivel chair in the staffroom, playing a game to teach me the Japanese scripts. The game is called Slime Forest Adventure, and features a spiky ginger-headed boy with a bandanna who navigates his way around a neon-green island, sporadically venturing into the wooded areas. To help him fight off the slimeballs that leap out in his path, the player has to type out the phonetic reading of the characters splashed across the slimes' stomachs. The game is more absorbing than I imagined a language-learning game could be, and I am thoroughly engrossed in slime battle when I feel someone pause behind me. This is not a rarity: often kids entering the staffroom slow their pace when passing my desk as their eyes are sucked to the screen, less, I think, out of conscious curiosity and more through some sort of electronic bloodlust. Mostly they scuttle away as soon as they notice me noticing, but there are a couple of kids who come in regularly, and who have begun to interact with me, standing behind me and helping me with the answers. Today, I look around and see that the lingering shape is S, who is already well acquainted with Slime Forest.

It's lunchtime, she apparently has nowhere pressing to go, and there are few people around in the staffroom, so she leans in to look at the screen, helping me. And then, after a little while, she places her hands on my shoulders. It's hard to explain how unexpected this is. Human contact. For reasons I struggle to articulate, what springs to mind in this moment, fully formed as if it were the result of a neurological malfunction, is the phrase, *no man is an island*. I can only guess that my struggling brain is attempting to reassure itself that this is in fact normal, for people to touch one another; to acknowledge that I had, in fact, been feeling myself like an island, for months, something like a mute teenager tapping away at computer games at the epicenter of a functioning institution, and that it made sense that the unexpected lifting of this isolation would feel somehow right.

Because it does feel right, but also overwhelming, a burst of sensation that hurricanes through my body with an intensity I find hard to account for. Is this what happens when nobody has laid a hand on you for months? I don't know, but it feels utterly new, as if I have understood for the first time what human touch is, experienced it for the first time without the barrier of desensitization, and tears prick the back of my eyes with the sheer miracle of it.

"You're getting better," S says, still watching my character thwacking the slimeballs with his hoe, her hands still resting unmentioned on my shoulders. And though what I'm feeling is so all-consuming that it's hard to focus on anything else, I manage to engage in a way that is superficially normal, although it takes me everything that I have:

"What's this one, though? Is it 'nu' or 'me'?"

" 'Me,' 'me.' It's 'me.' "

And maybe, as we are talking, as I am doing my best to pretend I am feeling nothing, she senses in the way my shoulders relax how much my body is singing out to be touched, because she starts then to massage me with her thumbs, as we talk on, talking through even the ones I feel confident enough to answer alone: "This means eye, right?"

"Yes, eye."

And when she finally says she has to go and takes her hands away, I can feel their absence there like an ache, like a hole, like I was the first person ever to be touched, and now the tears come to my eyes uncontrollably and I try and blink them away until she's left the room.

¶ pota-pota: the sound of red dripping onto asphalt

IT WAS A MORNING IN early November. Like most school mornings, I'd woken at dawn and before setting out to work, had made my way down the assortment of tiny alleys, peppered with sunakku bars where men went to drink, to find the sea a plate of gray glass, broken up only by the bank of concrete tetrapods that lay at a little distance from the shore as if they'd been aiming for the beach but collapsed in neatly coordinated exhaustion before they reached it. There was the yellow wooden fishing boat lying in its usual place and the smell of bonfires in the air. I didn't always do this, but that particular day, I'd gone down onto the strand and walked along the stones, watching the sea fizz and foam in generous loops not far from my feet.

These walks brought me a kind of magical solace, which that day I found myself particularly in need of: it had been an unprecedentedly strange couple of weeks. The weekend before last, I'd been out for a party with the teachers from school, which had moved on to karaoke. I had been very drunk, as I would usually get at these all-you-can-drink parties, which would start at five in the evening and where none of the food contained any carbohydrates, and where the person next to you would continually top up your glass, and where the school janitor would be collected by his wife ninety minutes into the two-hour slot because if he stayed any longer then he "made mistakes," but in the limited period he was there he liked to sit next to me and drink sake continuously and talk—and so I had ended up falling asleep in the karaoke box, as was my tendency at those times. I didn't remember many of the particulars, but I remembered with some almost unearthly clarity being woken up by Y.

"Moshi-moshi?" he'd said as he gently shook my shoulder, his body leant over my supine one so that our faces were just a couple of inches apart, "Moshi-moshi?"

And that was how I learned that moshi-moshi wasn't just something that you said on the phone, but also when reviving the unconscious.

The following morning, I had woken again to a vision of his face, exceptionally close, where closeness didn't just signify physical proximity. He felt to me known in some way I found hard to account for, like a person who lived in my dream world as well as the world outside. It was nice, it was alarming, and I had a sick suspicion that I had in fact kissed him, and that the way in which that kissing had happened had been a bad thing in the eyes of the world. But the suspicion had no memory associated with it, was just a looming sense of certainty that could also have been the aftermath of a dream. Throughout the weekend, I imagined over and over arriving into school the following week, being called to the headmaster's office and summarily dismissed. I could cope with that, I thought; but what if he was summarily dismissed also—what if I had brought him down? I had no concrete examples to provide myself of how I might have done that, only a clenching in my guts. After a couple of days during which my adrenaline levels had reached new heights, I had gone into that school the following week to discover everything as normal. The first day, Y barely spoke to me. I was redeemed, maybe—there were times when it felt that every statement in Japan was tempered with "maybe," and after a while this began to leach into the way that I perceived reality, that I formulated thoughts to myself. Yet this maybe-redemption brought its own discovery, its own loneliness: I didn't want to be redeemed. I wanted to kiss him, I wanted to have kissed him. I wanted something to tie us together.

I was dealing with this revelation by walking all the time, as though I had a worm that kept my limbs moving. It was around this point that I started sometimes walking to school, a two-and-a-half-hour walk in either direction, which I would begin at sunrise and finish after sunset. But that morning I hadn't. I had been for a beach walk and now I was in the car, and to convince myself that I was full of fighting spirit I'd put on a reggae tape. I was oddly excited about the day ahead, in fact, because my supervisor was away, which meant that I would have more time talking with Y than usual, but also slightly nervous, because Y was still something of an unknown quantity to me, however close he sometimes felt in my head.

It wasn't a long drive. I went straight down the main road that ran between the island's two biggest towns, and then right at the lights by the petrol station. The logo for the petrol station was a woman's face in red and white which looked like a Greek goddess, and though I went by several times a week, it still seemed to me a lucky omen, as if I was being blessed at each passing.

Now I saw the goddess in the distance, saw the lights were green, put on my indicator to turn right and cranked up the volume of the tape deck, then started in on my right turn.

The traffic lights had a pedestrian crossing; to my mind, they were the kind of traffic lights where I should have had right of way, but it turned out that here in Japan, I didn't. Too late, I realized the white truck coming towards me wasn't going to stop. Time stretched itself, the track blasting across the stereo opened itself out to reveal fractal multitudes in yellows and oranges and greens and reds, and then we crashed, splendidly, the front of the oncoming truck catching my blue car on its left headlight. It was apparent to me, wrapped in that blanket of distended time, that I was probably going to die, and then it was apparent to me that I hadn't died, but it wasn't relief that I felt so much as simply the shift of adjusting to a new reality. The world went on. Now I would have to deal with the aftermath of a car crash in Japanese.

———

Inside the small white truck were two construction workers, wearing towels wrapped around their foreheads and the trousers I was so in awe of, which flared out at their shins only to taper right in at the ankle. Theirs were lilac, and they had lilac jackets to match. Their faces, tanned to a luminous brown-gold, did not look friendly.

"Who can we call?" they asked. I told them I didn't have a mobile phone, and they roared with laughter. I retrieved from my trunk my diary, a standard issue JET notebook that I'd decorated with pictures, ripped from a fashion magazine, of people dressed as animals, where I'd noted down the number of my school. I told them Y's surname, and watched as they dialed the number to the school, switching immediately to polite phone voices.

The rest feels blurry. I don't remember how my car got over to the side of the road—I'm guessing that someone else drove it. After a while, Y pulled up, but he didn't really speak to me: he dealt with the men. By then the police were there, examining my international driving license. I remember them scrutinizing it, trying, ever so earnestly, to pronounce the word "Basingstoke," where the driving license had apparently been issued, as if that were an important piece of information in this particular scenario. I remember thinking very clearly how funny this would have been if I was in a state for finding things funny, and also understanding on some level that so long as I was in this country, there was going to be no serious situation that wasn't tinged with traces of absurdity.

Then, at some point, I recall being at the side of the road, while Y talked to the others, looking at my car. The radiator must have been crushed, because from its front it was slowly dripping red fluid onto the gravel, the drips very faintly audible above the sound of the road, of the policemen, of my heart pounding.

Sometimes words are applied to memories retroactively. Ever since learning the word pota-pota it has put me in mind of that scene. Pota-pota: the sound of water dripping, droplets falling on the floor, of crying, of flowers, fruit or other small objects falling continually. "Drip" is not a desperately melancholy word in English, and nor is pota-pota in Japanese, but for me it has always seemed to carry with it the sadness of this moment. The sadness of my car crying red tears onto the gravel, and all the other sadnesses which that stood for in that moment. The sadness of being laughed at. The sadness, and the shock, maybe more than anything, of realizing what a child I was in this society, of not really feeling part even of this car crash which I had caused, participated in, been given minor whiplash by. The sadness of this life that I was living which was driven by adrenaline and sometimes reggae but had nothing to say for itself when the real world came to call, when it plied the physical world with tremendous clumsiness and was held to account. *What did kissing matter when you couldn't even drive, or have a phone, or speak Japanese?* I could practically hear the policeman's voice asking me, beneath the layer of friendly banter. *Being pathetic is one thing, but why are you actively rejoicing in it?*

¶ kyuki-kyuki: the sound of writing your obsession on a steamy tile, or the miracle becoming transparent

BEFORE I KNEW IT, I was in the grip of an obsession. The more that I could read Japanese, the more, and the faster, I wanted to.

In the supermarket I turned products over and over in my hands, my gaze digesting their labels into sounds, and not only to check if they were products I wanted, but because I loved tracing my eyes over their lines: the calligraphic swoops of hiragana, the blocky bars of katakana. I wanted those shapes to be a part of me, so much I could scarcely bear it. I say this from the position of one who reads Japanese largely fluently, and now I don't feel that its forms are mine any more than those making up the Roman alphabet are, and in fact don't find them remotely special; but before I could run my eyes over them and see just sound or meaning, while I still saw them for the shapes that they were, I wanted to possess them, with a mighty avarice.

When I was in the classroom attempting to teach the children how to pronounce English words in my English way, the Japanese phonological system drove me to distraction: how could it be that the concept of a sole consonant didn't exist, that there was no way of vocalizing a sound which wasn't followed by one of the five vowel sounds? Why was a word like "stage" broken down into four morae: su-te-e-ji? More and more, I was developing a Japanese brain, and from inside that brain, I could adore how each kana represented a self-contained sonic unit, of which occasionally a single one sufficed to make a word. "Ka" was mosquito, "me" was eye, and "te" was hand. "Ga" was moth and "hi" was fire. When you strung two together, the list of possibilities already felt endless.

Now, in addition to all the sounds, my head became crammed full of letters. I would dance my finger through their moves, sometimes leisurely, sometimes frenziedly, on every available surface. Like every other newcomer to the country, I had hiragana and katakana charts on my wall and at home my eyes wandered over them constantly, busily tracing their contours as if they were not solid figures but animated dance routines. When I stood in the shower, I would carve out the characters in the steam that had formed on the tiles—ろ、る、ら—and my mouth sang them. My mind played over and over the English-based mnemonics I had, which I now can't remember if I invented or I'd read somewhere: *ro is rocking a baby, ru carries a ruby.* Once again I was the good girl learning to read, and it didn't seem to matter that I was twenty-one years old, and not two: it was hard to remember anything in which I'd taken such simple, unembarrassed pleasure for a long time.

It helped that I had a visceral sense that learning brought me closer to people. On the bus, with its under-seat heaters pumping out warmth that steamed up the windows and obscured the snowy mountains from view, a small boy in the seat behind me lunged into my field of vision, encroaching on my section of window to complete his drawing of a monster in the condensation on the glass. Underneath, he wrote its name, in the same letters I was writing out in the shower on a daily basis. It seemed to me in this moment like a strange yet wonderful coincidence that he and I were part of the same club—a club that required of all its members the same undertaking of learning to form exactly the same fleet of shapes. "We read too much, write too poorly, and remember too little about the delightful discomfort of learning these skills for the first time," writes Carson. "Think how much energy, time and emotion goes into that effort of learning: it absorbs years of your life and dominates your self-esteem; it informs much of your subsequent endeavor to grasp and communicate with the world. Think of the beauty of letters, and of how it feels to come to know them."

I would add to this only: think of what a huge body of shared experience it is, to learn the same script (the same three scripts) as someone, the hours that your fingers have spent making the same shapes. I sat there, glimpses of the outside now visible through the lines of monster and monster name, smiling like I'd witnessed some kind of miracle.

———————

Many years later, I was talking onomatopoeia with a high-school student of mine at the language school where I worked. Her spoken English was extraordinarily good in comparison to most people of her age, but although she'd requested "free conversation" lessons, the principle of having spontaneous conversation with someone older than her and in a position of authority was mostly beyond her, and it fell to me to ask her an endless list of questions. I liked her, I enjoyed talking to her and listening to what she had to say, and it made me sad that what went through my mind with each question I posed was a prayer that this one would buy me some time to think up the next, or even spark off the kind of conversation I could engage in without worrying about what was coming after. If only I was the lecturing type, I would sometimes think, the sort of person who could hold forth on various subjects unselfconsciously, and not feel pangs of guilt about not doing my teacherly duty in maximizing her speaking time, then she would probably have preferred that, but that wasn't who I was. And now I asked her what her favorite onomatopoeic word was in Japanese, and she fell into silence. I was just starting to think that maybe she wasn't going to come up with anything when she looked up at me.

"Kyuki-kyuki," she said. "The sound of a pen writing on a whiteboard."

"Kyuki-kyuki," I repeated after her dumbly. "Kyuki-kyuki."

The word was new to me. In fact, this was my first experience of hearing a new onomatopoeic word in Japanese and absolutely getting it. In that moment, it seemed to me that that was, in fact, the sound of a pen moving across a whiteboard, as expressed in language—the same sound that those tiles in the bathroom had made under my finger, as I wrote the first letters in the language. The sound too of the boy's finger on the bus window, and the kanji I'd spent years writing out in the steam on the glass during my morning shower.

When I thought on it, I could see how if someone had told me at the beginning of my time in Japan that the sound of a whiteboard was kyuki-kyuki, I would probably have thought how strange and cute it was—which is to say, how other, and how unrelatable; now, after years of amassing all of the peripheral information about Japanese and how it worked, after subconsciously tuning in at least in part to the system of sound symbolization that went with the language—where, for example, the k sound had associations with "hard sur-faces" and "light, small, and fine" objects, while the X-ki-X-ki structure represented "brisk or dynamic action"—the sound felt to me transparent. Just like, in fact, how I now struggled to see the shapes of the characters I had once traced over and over—how they had become interchangeable with the sound that they signified. The signifier had become see-through, and yet, unlike with English, I could remember a time when that wasn't the case. I could, albeit with effort, evoke a hint of the feeling, of what it was like to be on the outside of that, where to be on the outside meant, simply, often, to notice. To feel something, to struggle, to sense an obstacle; to admire, or to rage.

¶ muka-muka: the sound of nights with a
dictionary, and the thrill of drawing close
to someone's real feelings

SOMETIMES I WONDER HOW I ever thought I'd survive,
setting out for a rural island with just a handful of Japanese
words to my name. I suspect that the answer to this is that,
mostly, I didn't think—I didn't have the time or the space to,
and I trusted the premise of the program I was placed on—
but there was one actual thought that I drew comfort from,
and that was the idea that there were interpersonal dynamics
which transcended words, as manifested in body language. I
was good at body language, my reasoning ran, so I'd probably
be alright. Today, I still think this line of thought has limited
elements of truth to it: I do believe that people who are sensitive to this aspect of human behavior, albeit subconsciously,
are primed to fare better, even though nonverbal cues shift
across cultures. I also sense that people who are attuned to
body language are also more likely to be attuned to paralinguistic elements of language—tone, stress, rhythm, pitch,
volume, intonation, and so on—which modulate basic verbal
messages, and are hugely important in generating nuance. But
there's another element to this which strikes me as fundamentally mistaken, which is to conceive of the dynamic between

people as a layer floating separately to their language, instead of the reality, which is a whole body of straightforward verbal messages, paralinguistic features, and nonverbal cues, all thrown into the melting pot of conversation. Put plainly, when you understand everything going on between two individuals it is easy to speak of a "vibe" between them as if it were some gaseous substance rising off their conversation, but really this is just being tuned in to every level of their interaction. Understanding almost nothing, I found that I was often totally unable to read these dynamics between people—and when I did, my readings often turned out to be wrong. It was only with the formation of what I would call real relationships in Japan—relationships where people would break sentences down for me which I hadn't understood when they were said at natural speed in the wild—that I began to see how even very obvious things had remained obscure to me thanks to the paucity of my language abilities.

The train of events that demonstrated this most clearly to me was that surrounding the rift which existed between the two English teachers at my school: M, my allocated supervisor, and Y, with whom I was having an affair. It was amazing how long it took for the existence of this estrangement to dawn on me, when it seemed like the sort of dynamic that in an English-speaking context I would have latched onto very quickly. More, the discovery wasn't a single event, but a realization that kept on growing, like a great sea-creature rising in slow-motion from the waves, until the fact that I had initially doubted its existence seemed frankly extraordinary. Because after several months, it had come to me in full certainty that what lay between these two could be categorized without too much exaggeration as a silent, burning hatred of each other. Or maybe that's a misrepresentation. M's feelings were impossible to decipher, and there were times towards the end when I started to suspect him quite genuinely of having none. But at the very least, Y loathed M with a strength of feeling that I found as irresistible as any scab. I remember very potently the first time I picked at it, because it was the first time that Y and I went for dinner alone.

————

The day after the car crash, I was cycling along the main road at lunchtime, when I heard someone beeping at me, insistently. I looked up to see Y's huge white cube of a car, with Y in sunglasses behind the wheel. That was how I came to accompany him to the driving range near my flat, the same driving range that I would stare up at on my beach walks like it was something not of this world, its green netting lit up from below with a spectral light. We spent the afternoon hitting balls, and when we were done, he asked me if I'd like to have dinner at the yakiniku place close by.

"I don't force," he added immediately, with extreme gravity.

Everything was surreal and laced with comedy—for a start I had just spent the last three hours playing golf—but it was also thrilling, in a way that felt slightly new. How to navigate this gulf between us, the space that crackled with prohibition and attraction and wariness? In the lessons we taught together I had felt—and hoped that he had also felt—how well we worked in tandem, how we seemed to slot into each other's timing, but the only world that we shared was the world of school. And so that was what we talked about, as we fried little pieces of meat over an open grill set into the table between us.

Specifically, I began to ask him about S, the girl for whom he had become something of an unofficial chaperone. Thinking back, there was so much of the functioning of the school I didn't understand, so many systems in place that were utterly opaque to me and which the linguistic gulf prevented me from getting my head around, but of all the mysteries, this seemed the strangest, the most potentially scandalous. I'd gathered that S didn't like M, but was that the only reason that she avoided him? She also had some unusual requirements around eating lunch which I sensed might be tied up with this, but when I phrased that idea to myself it seemed hopelessly far-fetched. The sensation that came of spinning these wild theories reminded me of how it had felt to be the suspicious child that I had been.

It turned out that my theories were not only true, but they weren't as wild as the reality. Y informed me calmly that S had a phobia (he didn't use this word) of M, who was her form tutor; that she brought in her own dishes and chopsticks because she couldn't stand the idea of eating from tableware that he'd used.

"Wow," I said.

We talked about it for a little longer and then, in a way that seemed perfectly natural to me at the time, I gave my opinion—as though this matter, about which I understood approximately nothing, was something about which it was right and natural for me to pass judgment.

"It just seems a bit extreme," I said. "Not to wanting to eat from the school plates in case he's used them, it feels a bit . . . bizarre or something. Don't you think?"

Y looked up from his plate at me. I could see that his eyes were searching me out, though I didn't know what I was being searched for. Finally he spoke. His voice was heavy, a heaviness I already knew meant complexity, where complexity in turn meant emotion.

"I understand her feeling."

He looked at me again, his eyes big and moon-like, and I could see that I wasn't going to get any more—he was not going to talk about his feelings. It was only later, when I had a fuller understanding of the situation, and him, and Japan, that I could look back at this and see it for what it was: in some ways, the plainest expression of his feeling that there was. Its length was inversely proportional to its strength. Rather than connoting a stiff-upper-lip sort of concealment as I imagined, the brevity of the statement served to express the depth of the agreement, and the complexity and profundity of the feelings involved, which would make an easy off-the-cuff diatribe impossible. It was a confession, a marker of intimacy, which I only appreciated retroactively. Like with most of the retroactive understandings I experienced, I believed at the time that I had the correct interpretation, because none other suggested itself to me; and yet, there was something about the conversation that made it lodge itself with me, as if it possessed an intensity that couldn't be entirely explained when you understood it in the way that I had. It was that which kept me thinking about it, I suppose, which meant that eventually I could solve it in a better way.

The evening marked the start of me and Y as a real thing, but it was also the start of my fixation with the two of them: him and M. I'd confirmed that there was a real darkness there—that the den of intrigue extended back much further than I had ever thought—but I also sensed that I was being prevented from fully entering, which made me want to enter all the more.

———

A few months later, Y and I were sitting at the kidney-shaped table in his flat. It was a low table, so we had to sit either on the floor or on the low floppy sofa behind, which looked like it had seen better days but was comfortable in a way that felt almost illicit. That day it was the floor. Dinner was done, and we were drinking red wine, and talking.

That day for whatever reason, I brought up M again. Something had happened at school; he'd said something that annoyed me. He was frequently saying things that annoyed me, and sometimes I told him so. Sometimes I thought he was a truly awful person; sometimes I suspected that the awful person was me. After my rant had drawn to a close, Y nodded in sympathy, and said,

"Muka-muka suru ne."

By then, our evenings in his flat had converged upon an established format: we drank red wine and looked up endless words on my electronic dictionary, nominally in a bid to have a decent conversation, but somewhere along the way, the having of a decent conversation would cease to be important, or rather, it became clear that the best and most enjoyable form of conversation of all was to ditch any preconceived notions about how a conversation should be, and embark on this joint quest towards understanding together. So out came my squat silver dictionary, which had orange and blue buttons and a hologram sticker of a whale on the front, and I typed it in laboriously: mu ka mu ka.

As occasionally happened with more idiomatic words and phrases, the dictionary refused to give a definition, providing only an example sentence. It always seemed to me slightly shocking that it would do this, as if it had thoroughly imbibed Wittgenstein's dictum that "the meaning of a word is its use in the language." It also felt like a bit of a cop-out. But stronger than either of these impressions was a sense of sneaky delight, as if unearthing one of these contextual definitions was proof that I was wading into the deepest waters of the language. Now, as my eyes passed over the sample sentence, this sense was joined by a different kind of shock:

"The insects crawling about the garbage can are disgusting."

I looked up at Y and found superimposed on his body an image of a large black garbage bag, with oversized beetles and cockroaches scampering across its surface. I didn't know where to begin with the questions. Was muka-muka always associated with insects? Was this garbage bag image a standard one? Was this what he saw, and felt, when he looked at M? Did it always connote nausea, or could you use it more colloquially to mean just irritation, as this situation seemed to suggest?

Hanging above all of the mystification and the questions, the sense of being entirely without a roadmap, was a sense of delight at this darkness into which I'd been plunged. It was like I had stumbled into the recesses of language where language and imagery and feeling all came together—and they were, at least in part, his feelings, imagery, and language.

From that day on I became unable to look at M without thinking about a garbage can crawling with insects, or to hear the word muka-muka without thinking of Y. It was also from around this time that I became unable to conceive of ever not speaking Japanese.

¶ hiya-hiya: the sound of recalling your past misdemeanors

THERE IS A MOVE COMMON amongst Westerners in Japan referred to as "playing the gaijin card": excusing your ignorance, genuine or feigned, by your foreignness. "Foreignness" is here understood as what passes visually for foreignness: it's easier to play this card the more you fit the image of the blond-haired blue-eyed prince or princess, and those of Asian heritage who could be taken for for Japanese are less likely to be let off the hook for their incompetence. The idea of behaving in that way made me feel very uncomfortable, even before I'd consciously appreciated the kind of privilege it was premised on. I remember an American friend telling me of acquaintances of his who'd gone to a kaiten-zushi restaurant in Kyoto and played around with placing all kinds of objects on the conveyor belt—ten-thousand-yen notes, I want to say a shoe although I don't know if that can be true—and got off scot-free; I remember how my friend related this anecdote not exactly approvingly but not with disdain either, and I felt very clearly that his reaction wasn't horrified enough. This was not an acceptable way to go on.

And yet, I had still been in Japan and learning Japanese less than a year, and in terms of my linguistic development I was still a child; although most of the time I was polite and ingratiating, there would be the odd occasion when I found myself transgressing, testing the waters, without ever having planned to do so. I remember being in the staffroom of one of the schools I visited less frequently, and being posed a question by the headmaster, whom I violently disliked. He was short and stocky, there was something about his bulky torso that reminded me of a transformer toy. All of his conversations were designed to make him and his seem big.

"Are there bullet trains in your country?" he had asked me across the staffroom, in standard-level polite Japanese. I felt sure he knew the answer to this, and just wanted to gloat over his country's technological brilliance. Before I could stop myself, I replied, in the plainest, least polite form of Japanese that there is: "Nai."

I did know, by that point, that to use this form in this situation was seriously bad, but I also knew that the headmaster wouldn't know that I knew. To go further, I knew that he didn't in fact expect me to understand his question—expected someone to leap in and translate for him. And shit, I can remember the thrill of it, being there in the staffroom and sensing the air turn cold around me as I pronounced the word, with a defiant confidence: *Nai.*

I remember, too, being at a party, sitting next to the deputy head of the same school—a timorous and trudging but good-hearted man, who went tramping around after the transformer-headmaster—and when he turned to me, raising his glass of beer, and said "Kanpai!" I replied, "Chin-chin!" And I did this although, which is really to say, precisely because I knew that "chin-chin" meant "cock" in Japanese, and then went on to explain with a straight face that that was what most people said for cheers in the UK these days, not even really knowing anymore if what I was saying was passably true or not. And as I did, I scanned his face for signs of—what? Of discomfort, or consternation, or laughter, but there was none of that, and the twenty-one-year-old me got a kick from this, thought to herself, *how spineless!* and, *what a weed!*

————

To think about these transgressions now makes me feel very strange. In terms of linguistic development, the current me is not a Japanese adult, but she is closer than she was—perhaps she's in her late teens or early twenties, when there's still a lot to prove, and infractions of the social code feel at their worst. Indeed, the reaction I have on recollecting my misdemeanors is a physical one. I think of the beloved word of a beloved friend, hiya-hiya: the "feeling of cold or chill on the skin," the "feeling of anxiety that comes of thinking that something bad is going to happen, that the situation is going to proceed in a direction that is unbeneficial for you." More idiomatically translated, it's the feeling of breaking out into a cold sweat.

T, the hiya-hiya friend, is a highly compassionate, considerate man who tends to surround himself with more direct and outrageous people; almost every time we speak on Skype, he will relate an episode whereby a hiya-hiya attack is brought on by the antics of his boyfriend, or his friends, or his colleagues. The way his boyfriend addresses shop assistants; the way his friends say risky stuff in bars, or confront their partners, and so on and so forth. He uses it also as an adjective—things are hiya-hiya-inducing. He and I have spent a lot of time talking about our childhoods, about the perpetual fear we had of the adults around us doing audacious things, and he's used it in that context also. In fact by now, it's so much his in my mind that I can make out the contours of his feelings, his fear, his face in its syllables.

When I think about my naughtiness now, hiya-hiya is exactly what happens to me. Despite knowing rationally that the transgressions from my early Japan memories are not going to "proceed in a direction that is unbeneficial" for me—knowing that they are not going to progress in any direction at all, because they are more than twelve years in the past—I feel, whenever I summon them to mind, the hiya-hiya chill work its way through my blood. The other thing I feel is a kind of surprise that these occasions actually happened; feel, simultaneously, respect and terror for my past self. How ballsy and reckless she was, how little she gave a fuck.

Years later, I took my mother to dinner with my friends while she was visiting, and when the drinks were set down on the table, she lifted hers up and proudly and unsuspectingly pronounced the words, "Chin-chin!"

Even though I knew T and his boyfriend very well, and even though I knew the story would be a very tasty one to pick over with them at a later date, I still felt the hiya-hiya creep over me, and my thoughts turned to the people around us, and what they would think about my mother pronouncing the word "cock" so gleefully. And so all-consuming was the embarrassment that flooded through me that it didn't at that moment occur to me that I had, in the past, done the same, and worse because it was on purpose. In unwittingly re-performing one of my past transgressions, my mother had perfectly demonstrated how much more socially conformist I had become.

It's that evolution, which one could see as the development of a culturally located conscience, which makes me feel more sure that those early impulses of mine were not just recklessness—that they had a function. To the extent that we are children in a new language, we need to transgress in it. Not just to make mistakes, but actually to be naughty, to act with the suspicion that what you are doing is wrong. To force the adults around us sometimes to be our parents, so that we can learn for ourselves what it means to be an adult.

Another memory, then: here I am, sitting on the floppy sofa, with Y, transgressing. I am coming to grips with Japanese pronouns, of which there are many. Famously, there are many different first-person ones—watashi, watakushi, boku, ore, atashi, jibun, and so on—but there is also a range for the second person, despite the fact that these are used far less frequently than in English conversation, with people referred to instead by their names or nicknames even in one-on-one conversations.

Incidentally, the go-to Japanese insult is not about calling someone something—you're a douchebag, etc.—but instead opting for a second-person pronoun from low down the scale. "Don't you think that's interesting, and profound," an old Japanese man once said to me. His implication was, I believe, that Japanese was a far deeper language than English. "In English, the other person has to be degraded by being identified with something sordid. But in Japanese, that whole move can be performed by a single word. We choose a form of 'you' that is already degrading." I nodded, but in truth I found it hard to see how that immediately made Japanese a superior language, even if it did make it a more lexically concise one.

But anyway, for now my studies are concentrated higher up the spectrum. The learner starts by learning that the second-person pronoun is anata, which is polite, and they may also be told about its contraction, anta, which is more familiar. That day, I had been reading something in my textbook about kimi, which, the book said, is used by older men when speaking to subordinates at work or younger men, and also by men to women.

"Is it true?" I ask Y now of the above, and he nods. I actually end up asking him this question about a lot of things I've read in the textbook, like an idiot: *is it really true?* "But you don't ever say kimi," I say. "I've never heard you say it."

"I could do," he says. "It's kind of cute." And then he says, *kimi, your hair is hanging in front of your face*, and tucks it behind my ear.

And so, though I sense that I am not allowed, I try it back. I call him kimi.

"No," he shakes his head. "You can't say it to me."

"Why?" I say, in a way that is aiming to be cheeky and a little bit kittenish, but in fact makes me seem like a child. "Because you're a man? Because you're older than me?"

"Yes," he says, serious. "It's rude."

"But it's not rude if you say it to me?"

"No." He seems utterly unapologetic in a way that surprises me. I think I make a noise, some form of pff sound, and we get onto another conversation.

A day or a week later, I can't exactly remember, I call him kimi again. And I see it in his eyes, the genuine outrage and anger. It takes me back to transgressing in front of my own father as a child, although now I'm an adult I don't feel threatened in the way I did back then. But I see Y's seriousness, the flash of *don't mess with me* across his eyes, and I know that it comes from society.

Two things hit me in that moment. The first is the realization that to fall in love with someone in another culture is like finding a language parent. It is to reproduce something like the relationship that most people have in early childhood with their parents, not just in terms of the time spent with the person or people who first taught us language, but the intensity, the physicality, and maybe above everything the need for approval that is likely to make the endeavor succeed. I had relied on my parents and they had taught me to speak; now I had found someone else upon whom I relied, in various senses, albeit to a lesser degree. I had not consciously taken up with Y for that reason, and when I talk now about the chronology of my Japanese learning I tend to cast this the other way round, saying that one of the reasons I kept going was because I happened to fall in love with a Japanese man. And yet when I think about how much I hung on his words, how much the thought of irritating him bothered me even if I pretended otherwise, and how much that encouraged me to ingest not just his words but also the cultural obligations surrounding them, I can't help but think that maybe I, like goodness-knows-how-many other people, had hit unwittingly, almost as if through biological reflex, upon a strategy that would see me into something approaching fluency.

The other thing to strike me was just how patriarchal this society into which I was being inducted was. I too came from a patriarchal society, there was no doubt in my mind about that. But to have it written into the language so deeply seemed a step further—seemed to point to a gendered power balance which topped that I'd grown up with. People had asked me before I went to Japan whether I was worried about going there as a woman, and I'd said truthfully that I wasn't—I wasn't well-enough informed to be worried, and I believed that my foreignness would protect me, which indeed it did for a while. In fact, it might even be correct to say that this kimi exchange was my first sense of it encroaching into discourse in a way that felt markedly different from what I'd encountered before. With this sense came a faint premonition of how I would one day struggle to be in Japan, both as a woman, and as someone who rejected "because you're a woman" and "because you're a man" as a decent explanation for pretty much anything. For now, I was accepting the message he was passing on, but there would in the future come a linguistic adolescence when I was no longer able to do that. He was parenting me, and I loved to be parented by him, yet I knew this wasn't going to be sustainable forever.

Now, to imagine myself sitting there on the sofa with an

older Japanese man and calling him kimi makes me feel very strange indeed. I can imagine, also, telling the story on Skype to my friend, in response to him telling me a tale of some blunder that he's made in English, and him replying: *man, that's a hiya-hiya story*, and us laughing and laughing, and me saying, *god, I know, isn't it?*

¶ bin-bin: the sound of having lots of sex of dubitable quality

THE SEX I HAD BEFORE going to Japan was British, and it didn't involve many words. Of course language paved the way, in both long- and short-term senses, and I suppose the deed was punctuated by certain phrases, but my memory of it is of bodies speaking in the place of mouths, a silent communing of skins. There are two ways of reading this wordlessness, which pull in opposite directions: speaking drew attention to what was going on, and brought up feelings of embarrassment so it was therefore avoided; and speaking mediated the experience, made it a less sensual one. The silence never seemed to me like a conscious choice—it was just how things were. Speaking about sex while doing it meant in some important way connecting what I was doing with the outside world, making it visible, which was instantly shameful. I was bad at talking about sex, and I felt no desire to get better at it.

With Y, I quickly find myself in a different situation. Suddenly, there is a surfeit of language, what feels like a constant stream of adjectives functioning as statements: *you're sexy*, *you're pale*, *you're wet*, and the absolute favorite, *you're dirty*. This I am told over and over, and it is said with a tone of surprise, as if it really were a good thing, and it doesn't diminish his respect for me. This goes on for a little while, and then, after maybe the third time, there is a new statement:

"You don't say much."

"No," I agree. "I don't."

There's a little pause and then he says, "Why don't you talk like they do in porn films?" There's a hangdog expression on his face. "Why don't you say, oh yeah, or oh my god, you're so good?"

"Because we're not *in* a porn film," I say, in as dismissive a tone as I can muster. At this time, as so many other times, it passes through my head that I am doing a crazy thing, allying myself with a man more than twice my age, and so dissimilar to me. It occurs to me I am having sex with the kind of person I vehemently dislike, who believes out of unexamined male privilege and a sheer lack of imagination and inability to be present in the moment that life should imitate porn. I have only a vague idea of what sex in another language and culture should be like, but I know at least that it should be sexy and sensual and feel immediately right, despite all of the "superficial" differences. It certainly doesn't have any of this inanity. Why am I tolerating it? But then, as usually happens, I look at him again, and remember exactly what it is that I like about him—or maybe more accurately, remember very simply that I do like him, however bizarre the situations I find myself in with him.

To satisfy his linguistic cravings, I start teaching him phrases, which feels better. For reasons obscure to me he likes the word "erect," loves to use it in what he thinks is the right way, even though I've corrected him a number of times; likes to say it first in Japanese and then translate himself proudly into English, in almost a singsong: "I have erected."

Still, it turns out that that isn't enough, that my reticence isn't an issue he is going to drop just like that, and it becomes a long-standing issue between us: *Why don't you speak, why don't you speak?* I can't bring myself to say anything designed to arouse him in English, so as a compromise, I learn to say some of the right words in Japanese. A friend had told me before all this began that what you say in sex is kimochi ga ii (it feels good)—the same words that the girls at school said to me when they touched my hair in the lunch hall. The phrase undergoes a quick transformation in my eyes from feeling unwieldy—overly long and suspiciously structural—to seeming totally reasonable. Very possibly, this transformation takes place in the face of the alternative scenario of being entreated again to say *you're so good*, or *you're so big*. But this new addition to my vocabulary proves to satisfy only for a short time. A few moments in, it's met with a question in Japanese, which I understand: "Where?"

"What?" At first I'm genuinely bewildered.

"Where does it feel good?" he says. There's a sleazy note to his voice I don't like.

I look down at him in horror. You have got to be kidding me, I think. I never knew this was part of the deal.

"Where does it feel good?" he asks again, and I look away and say in my best Japanese, "My body."

He laughs. I hadn't been trying to be funny, but even in this situation—or maybe particularly in this situation—it still feels like a triumph to make him laugh. Because I like his face when he smiles, and also because I've realized that every second I can divert him, every second I can put off naming my genitals in English or Japanese or Icelandic is, in fact, a victory. And because when he smiles we are instantly people, and not wannabe bilingual porn actors again.

Over time, it gets better between us. I'm not sure if the references to porn were just there out of embarrassment or if the corporeal desires are taking on a more affectionate cast or what, but in any case they gradually grow less frequent. I come to know more about him, and in some ways to trust him. And yet his way of thinking about sex in general is still mysterious to me. We shouldn't have too much sex, he tells me, because he will perform less well at work. When I probe him about the truth of this he admits that this is just something that people say, and he has no idea whether it's really true.

One night, when we're lying hugging on his sofa, he says to me, "Do people in England think sex is a sport?"

I feel myself frowning. "What do you mean by that?"

"In America, people think of sex as a sport. So they say. We Japanese people don't see it like that."

"I don't really even know what that means," I say. "What does it mean, for sex to be a sport?"

"Well, you know," he says. "They do it with lots of people, they get good at it. There's no shame."

"But Japanese people watch loads of porn, and they're really unembarrassed about that," and he says, very simply, "Yes," and I think instantly of his closet, and the huge pile of porn magazines in there—which I found by accident when I went in there to touch his clothes when he was out, running my fingers along the row of his jacket-arms—and how miraculous it felt to me at that moment that I didn't feel that horrible shrinking-inside feeling I usually did when I came up against the fact that people I was interested in consumed porn in vast quantities, but oddly accepting of this crazy thing called society in which we were brought up. I also wondered to myself what it would be like to have this conversation if we could have spoken each other's languages any better—if it would have taken us any closer to understanding each other, or if the "sex as a sport" comments would have remained just as mysterious to me as if they came from another world.

Sometimes the words still come, and sometimes I now like them. Other times they are ridiculous. Occasionally, they are ridiculous and I still like them.

———

We are having sex in his room, up against the pillar that divides the kitchen from the living room, my cheek pressed into its cold whiteness. His olive-colored trousers are in a pool around his ankles. We are silent, until he says without warning, in English, "We are like wild beast." I smile, but only the pillar feels it. "We are fucking like wild beast."

There is a softness to his voice when he speaks English, an occasional high swoop that seems calculated to mimic American intonation, but joining that now is also a growl, so that the beast I imagine is a bear. I think of us as two bears in the forest, fucking up against a tree—a scene that I'm fairly sure has never occurred in the natural world.

Maybe now, for the first time, I understand what he's trying to do. Now when the fantasy is being evoked to intensify the reality, when it doesn't pull us away into some commoditized territory in which I feel alienated and uncomfortable, now that it's bears, and it's so patently ridiculous, all that I can feel is the intention: to turn on, to be turned on. Though it's hardly the sexiest thing that's ever happened to me, it feels like it's about us, and that is kind of sexy. It feels about desire, in its full stupidity—as if the secret of the erotic is that it is in fact ridiculous, bawdy, silly, and human. I think of how I once thought having sex in a foreign language might be like something from a nouvelle vague film. I think of how crazy the reality is, how unexpected and how utterly, mind-expandingly nuts, and how mostly what I feel towards that fact is overpowering affection. The craziest thing he can throw at me, I think, I am ready to take.

A few weeks later, I find the word on which to hang my conflicted thoughts. Our thing, because he works all hours and is often either working or away at the weekend, is weekday dinner. Even when he gets home really late we'll cook together, lay out the dishes on his kidney-shaped table and have a beer, say kanpai. Once a week or so, at the weekend if he's around, we will make a special meal. There are days when we have shabu-shabu, a table-top pot of broth in which pieces of thinly sliced meat are "swished" (for which "shabu-shabu" is the sound) for a few seconds until they're just done, then dipped in one of a selection of sauces. One day towards the end, he buys us horsehair crabs, one each, enormous orange pincushions with six plump old-lady arms, just about fitting into their polystyrene trays and wrapped in clingfilm, and we eat them with good sake that he's bought to go with them.

But this is before that. He asks me one day what is my favorite Japanese food, and I tell him that I think it's eel.

"Oh," he says. "You like bin-bin food." It's not said like the English "garbage bin"; the "i" is longer, more pointed.

"Huh?" I spin round and look at him. "What's bean-bean food?"

"Food that makes you powerful," he says. "Like red wine."

"Red wine makes you powerful?" I say, but I don't say anything more, and then we get caught up talking about something else, and I don't think much more about it, except by the end of the night we've hatched a plan to eat eel together at the weekend.

That weekend I go over to his place with some eel marinated in teriyaki sauce I've bought for a handsome price from the supermarket, along with a nice bottle of red wine. We're making the salad, the rice is cooking, the wine already breathing on the cabinet. We move around each other in silence, and I'm thinking about how I feel more strangely and happily domestic than I can remember ever doing before, when suddenly, as he begins to set the table, he says,

"Oooooh, today we can have lots of sex."

I look at him in utter astonishment. "What are you talking about?"

"I told you, eel is bin-bin foods," he says. "Makes you very powerful for sex."

"What!?" I say. It's hard for me to know why I feel quite so scandalized by this, but I do. "You mean it's like an aphrodisiac?"

"An afrogeniemac?"

"It makes you want to have sex."

He looks at me, and nods, very solemnly.

"It makes you erected," he says. "Like red wine."

I feel the breath flow out of me and then I am laughing, leaning down and grabbing my knees because I feel like I might collapse, not from hysteria as much as from just not being able to cope with anything anymore. What the actual hell, I want to say. What kind of a belief system is that, what kind of a word is that? This is long before I know that "pin" and "bin" suggest stretched out things, long, hard, flat things, and yet the idea that the concept of sexual virility could be expressed by something that sounds to me so infantile, so unsexy seems so very mad that it doesn't feel like there's space in my head to accommodate this new information.

Still, I know in some way that bin-bin may as well be the word that symbolizes my Japanese sex life, and maybe also my Japanese life in general: glorious in its specificity, its humanity, its absurdity. I want it to continue, and I cannot change it. And so, until the point where I decide I can't tolerate it anymore, the only thing to do is to embrace it.

I look up at him.

"Erect," I say weakly, from where I'm holding on to my knees. I don't even know who I'm saying it for.

¶ bare-bare: the sound of being so invested in something that it leaks into everything you do, or abandoning hope of appearing cool, or insidious paranoia

I SUPPOSE THE TIME THAT most adults venture closest to inhabiting a prolonged state of wonderment is when they are head over heels in love. This rapid vault into a state of ecstasy has been portrayed time and time again across every art form imaginable, but the specific depiction my mind reaches for is that in the novels of Iris Murdoch: the way love falls bolt-like upon her characters, and from one second to the next, the world as they experience it is transformed. In this new, heightened state, everything is wondrous and everything connected, feelings explode out of us like fireworks, and if we notice that everything we do or say is a cliché, it doesn't really matter to us because it strikes us that, fundamentally, this is a mode of life that is not only more pleasurable but also in some sense truer, righter, better. As Nabokov puts it:

> This capacity to wonder at trifles—no matter the imminent peril—these asides of the spirit, these footnotes in the volume of life are the highest forms of consciousness,

and it is in this childishly speculative state of mind, so different from common sense and its logic, that we know the world to be good.

This is an accurate description of the headspace at which I arrived after half a year in Japan, and, outside of experiments with psychedelics, it was as close as I'd come to feeling rapture towards the entire world, but I genuinely didn't know whether it should or could be categorized as the side effect of being in love with a person. What was happening, after all, was not just a case of suddenly seeing the familiar with fresh eyes; rather, everything in the world around me was, objectively speaking, substantially different from what I was used to, which only intensified the sense that my rapture was entirely reasonable—that everything around me was a feat of sheer imagination and the deep, wild, vertiginous sort of love I felt for every part of it was in fact a justified response. If other people didn't feel that love, it was because they were immunized in some way, but luckily, wondrously, I was not, which was why I could feel it in spades: for the kids, for their haircuts and their faces and the neon blue polyester of their sports kits, for the rituals and the architecture of the school, for the rice fields and the beach, and the outrageous synth covers of Eurythmics and Blondie and Stevie Wonder they played in the supermarket. And in a thousand different ways, for the language. For I was now learning to read kanji, and the world was opening up to me. One day, driving a section of road I'd driven and walked at least two hundred times, I watched as a cloth banner fluttering in the wind came to life, saw its meaning rear up and leap out of what I had previously computed as some form of geometrical design. *Car, it says car!* my head screamed inside. How, outside a car dealership, could it have said anything else? But that was common sense speaking, and common sense mattered little in the headspace I inhabited. What mattered was that kanji had been there all along, and today I'd read it, and that was a straight-up marvel. I had come into possession of a key to unlock the world around me. Not only was I in love with the sensation as the doors opened, but just sitting still with the key in my hand gave me an intense sense of connectedness with the world.

Looking back at myself then, I can't help feeling that I had come down with a type of connection-fever, and maybe what I was in love with above anything was the glimmers of togetherness glimpsed across the lakes of difference. In this vein, I remember teaching a class on prepositions where I handed out photocopies of the outline of a room, and asked the children to draw in the detailed layout as I described it: *There is a table by the window. There is a vase on the table. There are three dogs under the chair.* Some took to the task immediately, others needed a bit more coaxing, and a good few performed their reluctance by sinking into comatose immobility, their arms flopped out wide across the desk and their eyes pinned to the floor. And so I roamed between the desks, placed to stand separately from one another, repeating each sentence what felt like far too many times, occasionally tapping their pieces of paper and saying the most relevant command I could muster in Japanese—*draw, draw, please draw.* After a while I passed by the desk of one of the baseball players, a quiet boy I didn't have much of a relationship with, and who was one of the slumpers. Leaning over to look at his page, I saw that under his chair had appeared three baby circles, with the character for dog, 犬, penciled inside each one.

I knew that character. I had seen pictures of it in my kanji book, showing how in ancient Chinese it had moved through various stages of simplification from a detailed representation of a dog to the form it took now, and I also remembered the way that Slime Forest counseled learners to memorize it by picturing the dash as a woof coming out of the big dog's mouth (without the dash, the character meant "big"). I knew one of its readings, "inu," but as with most kanji for me then, I couldn't make an immediate connection to its sound: it was still more like a picture or a symbol, and this only heightened the impression that the baseball boy writing it was a creative genius, engaging in a practice that sat on the cusp of art and language. That he had produced, with his row of dogs, a work of impromptu concrete poetry. I pointed at them and laughed delightedly, as if he'd shared with me a private joke, and he looked utterly flummoxed.

It's evident now that, not only was the boy's response little more imaginative than drawing a circle and writing dog inside, but there was also no way he was intending it as a way of communicating with me. If anything, it was a retreat from communication, a sulky avoidance of anything English or artistic—but I was so crazy in connection that I couldn't see it like that. Like the very uncoolest of people, I was certain that I was included in everything, and everything was great.

———

I saved some of my most ecstatic feelings for Y, and the strange argot that we spoke. This hybrid of English and Japanese seemed to me like an invention of dazzling brilliance, from which originality came off like a volatile gas; I think much of this impression ensued from the way that mostly our grammatical framework was borrowed from Japanese, enabling constructions I would not have thought possible a few months ago. Even regular English expressions now took on Japanese sentence-final particles, and within not too long I found myself voicing constructions like "I think so da yo"— "da yo" being a sentence-ending that indicated the conveying of information not known to the speaker—because that seemed to me more expressive and emotive than a regular "I think so," even if I knew that that impression was limited to this space, this context. Which was the other crucial thing about mine and Y's language: it felt intensely personal. It was like a house we had built ourselves, each brick laid with a backward glance that says, *See? I did this for you. I did this for us.* Obviously, as time went on and I encountered other mixed Japanese/English-speaking couples, was part of them myself, I would come to see that really there wasn't anything that desperately unusual about the mishmash that Y and I spoke, particularly for two people with limited abilities in the other's native language, yet that didn't diminish the feeling in my memory, of turning to each other and trying with everything we had to touch our languages together, in a way that was special precisely because there was no rulebook.

Another grand prix for inventiveness I awarded to our attempts at clandestine conversation and arranging our secret rendezvous, while keeping up a public pretense of being just moderately good friends. This creative enterprise, which was comprised of feigning distance and impartiality in public, and all the other ways we had of keeping our connection secret, was thrilling and intoxicating, and it gave us a shared project to work on, and maybe more crucially, to speak about. So it was perhaps inevitable that over time we would develop set conversational patterns around said enterprise, a special subset of vocabulary. Early on, I remember Y told me that he was talking to his relatives about something which had happened while we were together. "Wait, did you tell them about me?" I asked, half shocked and half flattered.

"Of course not," he said, with great composure. "You're classified."

Later on, when we were closer and he used this expression for the third or fourth time, I asked him where he'd learned it and made the discovery it was lifted from *Top Gun*, which I found something of a let-down. But even that couldn't kill the aura of momentousness that lingered from the first time, when I found it endearing and sexy and somehow shocking. I suppose behind all that was the effect I assumed was the intended one: it made me feel special, and hidden in the right way, the way that precious things were hidden.

Other words that came up over and over again in our conversations were the Japanese verb bareru, meaning "for news to get out" or "for someone to be found out," and its mimetic version, bare-bare, used when a lie is blatant, when something is blindingly obvious, a secret is badly kept, and so on. Y was an expressive speaker at the best of times, but when he spoke this word he was almost a caricature. He was also very much a man, snarling, his Rs rolled. He would not fuck up, he would not lose control, would not be bare-bare: this was what his tone seemed to say. I, on the other hand, was laughably so. I didn't resent or dispute this characterization; I knew it to be true. This was part of the whole setup; I was an exploding thing. In fact, it was often me who offered up the evidence of my hopelessness, to be deemed by him laughably bare-bare. Like how the children had to ask me a question as part of each term's oral examinations, and some of them would ask about him: *Who do you love, we or Y? Do you love Y? Which do you take, love or money?* And each time I answered, I told Y, I blushed furiously. We talked about this over and over, laughed and laughed and laughed.

Looking back now, I find it odd that I could have joked around about all of this, because I was not half as unconcerned by the ethical dimension of our relationship as these conversations made me appear—was, in fact, plagued by a sense of guilt and paranoia about what we were doing. What I really wanted was to ask, in full seriousness, "Please will you tell me if what we're doing is really terrible?" Being unable to do that, though, I settled instead for these comical conversations which danced around the source of the concern. I felt, in a way I couldn't remember ever feeling since being a young child, as if my ethical radar was wholly out of range, and when I tried to make judgments about how bad what I was doing was, it felt like I was reaching into darkness. I found myself reliant on Y to tell me the truth, both about his family situation and the wider context of how marriage and infidelity and divorce were perceived in Japan. He had informed me that his marriage had been defunct for a long time, and his wife was pleased they were now living separately, but he feared the repercussions if he got a divorce because teachers were supposed to be role models, and thus to have unbreachable marriages. I didn't doubt that this narrative was one-sided, but I didn't distrust it in essence, and the more I thought on the situation thus defined, the more I came to feel like we were actually not doing any harm so long as we didn't get found out—that in some sense, it was only the exposure of our affair and the disruption that exposure would cause which would make our relationship morally suspect. So long as we were careful, we were doing no wrong; it seemed to me that possibly, that was a more Japanese way of thinking about things, and it certainly seemed to approximate Y's take on the matter, as far as I could get a handle on it. I could only assume it was that take that permitted him the calm around it that I wasn't able to have.

There was just one time I saw him freak out. The two of us were in the staffroom, having a conversation that wasn't so different from the kind that we'd have in his flat, except we were surrounded by teachers who appeared to be engrossed in their work but were almost certainly listening in. Our English protected us, or so we thought, but then out of the blue he switched. I'd outraged him in some way, and although he wasn't properly angry, he needed to let off the feeling, so he addressed me using a pronoun for "you" that is familiar, even derogatory. There was nothing radically bare-bare about this, in and of itself—I'd heard him use it with the kids in his sports team whom he knew well—but as language to adopt to a foreign teacher who one theoretically has little contact with, it was markedly inappropriate. I saw it flash across his face then: not only the realization that he had gone and done it, but also, I think, a sense of danger—the understanding that it was within his power to let himself down. That what we had somehow made self-control more difficult. "That was bare-bare," I said to him later, a note of glee creeping into my voice, and he nodded, somberly. "Yeah, that was not good." But there was still part of me—and this was both the blessing and the problem—that felt that it was good. In some crucial way, the world really was good.

¶ pika-pika: the sound of my floors and your trainers and our graveyards

I'M CHATTING TO A COUPLE of women I met through an art writing group, one of whom, by total coincidence, spent two years in Fukushima around the time I was first in Japan. Hanging around before the group starts, we're talking about what we've been working on recently, so I explain that I'm trying to work on some essays about Japanese onomatopoeia.

"Oh, like peeka-peeka!" says the Fukushima friend.

"What does that mean?" asks the non-Japan friend.

"It's like sparkling, right?" She glances at me for assurance. "That was what they used to tell me about my trainers at school. I bought these brand-new trainers to wear indoors in school, and they'd all be saying it: 'Peeka peeka!' 'Peeka-peeka!'"

Listening to this description, I can immediately picture the children crowding round the shoe lockers pointing at the sparkling white trainers, as vividly as if it were my own recollection. Although I don't tell my friends this, I also learned the word pika-pika at school, in the context of cleaning. Or at least, I think I did, but this is one of the problems I have with my early time in Japan: my memory. It's as if, with the influx of new sights and sounds to learn and process, and the lack of knowledge about what was real and what wasn't, my mind went into storytelling overdrive, my powers of imagination growing so fertile that I often struggle to differentiate my own recollections from anecdotes people told me around that time, or things I've dreamed up to explain and fill in the gaps. There was definitely a period after lunch when the children routinely cleaned the school, and I believe it was there that I heard it first, the teacher saying, "You need to clean the floor until it sparkles." To look at the kids lethargically pushing flattened old mops around the sludge-green laminate, it was clear that this was if not exactly irony then at least wishful thinking, and yet pika-pika was tied in my head to the surface of that swirled green floor.

Standing beside my Fukushima friend, I hold this sludgy laminate up beside the image of her perfectly unsludgy trainers, and think about the strange specificity of the associations we form when we're learning a foreign language, in a way I can't imagine doing for a newly acquired English word. I might associate a phrase with a particular scene or person, certainly, but it is far rarer for that word to be defined wholly with reference to that association in the manner of the sparkling trainers. At least, that is the case now; thinking on it for a little, it comes to me that my images and associations were far stronger with words I learned as a child. Words were wedded to a particular person or advert or song through which I had discovered them, or shrouded in a certain smell, or gifted with a backing track. I felt more about them as well: their spellings were irritating or weird, their sounds were silly or disgusting. And then the familiarity born of endless repetition comes along to wipe words free of these associations, and what is left us is simply the ability to use them without thinking too much about them. In a way, it is a form of desensitization—in order, I suppose, that we can be sensitized by other, more complex aspects of the linguistic game.

Thinking about these words I wonder, in a way I know to be meaningless, where all of those associations go, and as if in answer, another association leaps to mind, from back on the island. At that time, I would spend all my spare time going for long walks, often by the sea, but one day, with a whole afternoon to spare, I took an inland route instead. I set off walking down the big main road, which cut directly across the center of the island; on a whim I turned off, left by the video shop, and kept going. Suddenly away from the cars and parking lots, I was surrounded by rice paddies, a stone-banked stream threading its way through them. I walked the path traced by the stream, headphones in my ears, gaze fixed on nowhere in particular until I made out some way in the distance a patch of concrete, scattered with tall white objects. Drawing closer, I realized it was a maze of vending machines, facing chaotically in all different directions. In fact, the layout and the whiteness of the slabs put me in mind of a small country graveyard. By the time that I reached it I saw that in some sense, it really was a graveyard; these were disused machines, which had been dumped there, who knows by whom, or why.

Taken by an uncontrollable curiosity, I moved inside the gathering and stood among the machines. Now, with my eyes darting between their multicolored logos and the explosion of items in their display cases, the slab-like impression began to fade, and they started to take on a character of their own, even a faint sense of humanity. Their positioning no longer seemed to indicate randomness but rather volition, group dynamics, like a group of semi-reluctant guests at a cocktail party. Some had their front panels smashed, so you could reach in with your hand and touch the plastic replicas of coke cans and cigarette packets with their tops flipped open, three or four protruding cigarettes arranged at gradated intervals like cabaret dancers.

One day in the future, a few months after this initial discovery, I would wedge my wrist right in through the spiky-fanged crack in the front panel of a cigarette machine and extract two of the plastic packets that had been dislodged from their original places, lying helplessly at the bottom of the blue display case: one branded Hope, the other Peace. The packets were small, and both their shape and their graphic design seemed to call back to a bygone era: they struck me as precious loot, imbued with some kind of talismanic value, and I kept them with me for years.

Before finding the graveyard, it had never occurred to me to think about where old vending machines went; it had never really even struck me that they aged and faded into obsolescence. I didn't know either how the vending machines arrived at this enclave or where they went from here, but something about the idea of a truck driving up to unload or else to load up and carry off these cruddy machines, once so pika-pika but now deemed below par, made me feel quite strange.

¶ jara-jara: the sound of a flash of metal in the blood

A HANDFUL OF SONGS FROM back then. Different, all very, but there is an internal, musical similarity that goes beyond the simple fact that when I put them on now, boom, there are the feelings, as if they've been handed to me on a platter, there the memories of walking down the narrow alleys, the national highway, the constant possibility of walking to your place as the best and most inevitable of all possible options. Inhabiting such a small world, where at any given point you are simultaneously there and not there for me. A proximity, such as I have never experienced, at least not when I wanted to. A sense that you are in some way the symbolic order itself, that it breathes you.

The internal similarity has something to do with the jangle-jangle of those guitars and the way it cuts through me like a fleet of small knives. And yes, I know, that is what music does, that is its stated purpose, but my gosh did it feel different when I was as I was then, absurdly young and infatuated, or whatever you want to call it. Impressionable, dependent, lonely, in need, living with a plethora of unprocessed feelings, over-reliant. But also: actually loving you. Actually loving the way that it felt to be in your flat, the clutch of its safety, the state of being able to reach for your square hands at any point, the way we would wake up on your futon like a dark raft floating on a sea of light coming in through the paper screens, the only landmass in sight your big volcano of books by the wall, how whenever I had a drink or two that was all I could think of, sleeping with you there, and so I would buy more drinks and cram them in my rucksack and walk the hour and a half to your place, high, high, high, and sometimes terrible too, a glorious illustration of why the Japanese government should not pay fresh graduates from overseas decent salaries to move into its rural communities. Picking up and taking home the sprays of fluorescent plastic flowers attached to the lampposts, with which I was so obsessed. Or once, on a glorious summer night when the wishes that local children had written out on multicolored slips of craft paper for the Tanabata Festival had been strung up by the side of the street, I walked to you as a light rain was falling and stole some of the wishslips, drunkenly grasped and tugged a few off, out of some ridiculous curiosity, but also out of the computer-game sentiment that everything was all right, how could it not be, these melodies ringing in my ear through my earphones that said, the world is made for this, jingle jangle, the sound of: what? of everything suffused with romance, and lust, and goodness. Late balmy nights and streetlights and colored paper. Attachment, and attachment, and attachment.

Not long ago I translated a sample of a book, a work of veritable genius which nobody will publish because it's 850 pages long, written largely in dialect and mad as a bag of frogs, and the excerpt I chose as a sample contains a mimetic I found almost impossible to render in English: jara-jara suru. Literally, this means to jingle, to jangle, like the chinking of keys, chains, bangles or tambourines, but in the sample it means metaphorically, to fool around, to get it on, to get jiggy with it. We are in the middle of a summer dance, and the protagonist is preoccupied by the thought of wanting to go off and shake, strike surfaces, chime, ka-ching with the girls, except of course those are all terrible translations, in part because they all sound simultaneously naff and vulgar, but also because here we are in the context of an Obon dance in the late 1800s, the whole village is out, and it is the night of the year when the souls of the dead return to earth and everyone drinks and dances and has sex to placate and welcome them, everything is turned on its head to mark the flipping of the natural order, and you can hear the music for miles off. So the jara-jara is also this, the jingle-jangle that seems to get into your blood and stir it up so that sleep is the last thing on your mind. In the end everything faintly literal I try in English sounds ridiculous, and I settle for something colloquial: "getting it on with the girls." But maybe I should have taken the plunge and gone with jangling with the girls, maybe that is what I will go for if anybody ever publishes this book and asks me to translate it, because the jangling, really, is very important, and it's the same jangling I hear, the crazy metallic throbbing of the guitars from "Modern Romance" by the Yeah Yeah Yeahs as I set off down the road to your place and I have no idea how it will end, or when it will end, but that's the whole point.

¶ koro-koro: the sound your teeny little identity makes as it goes spinning across the floor

SOMETIMES, WHEN I'M TALKING ABOUT what I do for a living with non-translator friends or acquaintances, typically those who speak only one language, I start to build up a picture of the practice of translation as they conceptualize it. Its pale contours coalesce gradually, like a polaroid forming. In this representation of it, translation is akin to an elaborate autocorrect function, and it works like this: I am a good Japanese speaker (this must be true, as I am a translator), and therefore my brain houses the correct English translation for each Japanese word; to move a text between two languages, all I have to do is switch the Japanese words over to their relevant English correlates, and then maybe fiddle about with the order a little, in order to yield the correct translation at the sentence level. Often in these kinds of conversations this exact phrase, "the correct translation," will be used multiple times, and each time I will feel a sort of pang, which I don't quite know how to interpret. At times I wonder if it is a yearning for the days when I could still place trust in the meaning of those words, and use them with no critical awareness, no sense of suspicion towards the assumptions on which they rest. Or maybe it's closer to an imagined nostalgia for the world if it were really as my interlocutor believed: if there really were a singular, correct translation for each word, and translation operated on the word level, and the task of the translator were to reproduce the exact number of words that appeared in the original, and so on. I wouldn't want a world like that, but it would make things a lot more straightforward.

In any case, even when people tell me that the profession I've chosen is "mechanical" or "more a science than an art," I don't resent them; it makes me wonder what preconceptions I'm carrying about jobs I know nothing about. What I find less easy to laugh off is other polyglots, even other Japanese translators, who still have a very firm idea of what "the right translation" is, who go around liberally sowing definite articles as they speak of their craft. These people are not thick on the ground, but they do exist, and I end up praying for them that this is either just an entrenched speech pattern or else a rhetorical front, an act of bravado to protect their egos—in other words, I pray that this is not what they really think. Surely, I reason, they must have had the experience of looking down at two alternative translations of roughly equal merit which respectively draw out different aspects of the source text that seem important, but cannot be incorporated at the same time. What happens to singular correctness in that moment? And what about the tension that exists between the requirements of a sentence in the source language and that in the target one; surely they must have taken on board that the definition of what constitutes translational perfection is always going to vary depending on whom you ask, so that to declare a translation not just good but uniquely correct seems tantamount to legitimizing the demands of one culture over another?

What I find the most extraordinary, though, is reflecting that, as translators and therefore, to some extent, surely, also speakers, these people have most likely had to express themselves in multiple languages, which raises a point that feels even more fundamental: have they not wrestled with the brain-warping activity of having to translate themselves across different languages? Have these people not, as I have, watched their identity contort into rainbow fractals, vanish entirely, and then return as a pink-spotted dragon? I know that it's unreasonable to expect everyone to have gone through existential crises over this—although part of me does really think that if they were sufficiently invested and sufficiently sensitive then they would have experienced at least minor ones—but surely at some point down the line, they must have stared into the face of this difficulty, and watched the possibility of a definite article fizzle up and vanish? And if they have, then what prevents them from connecting this experience with what they do for a profession?

———

I'm aware that this picture of adversity in self-translation does not conform with the received picture of multilingualism. The conventional, monoglot sense of what it means to be bilingual, trilingual, and beyond does not permit of difficulties in self-rendering, let alone existential crises or identity trauma. We prefer to believe unthinkingly that what it means to be yourself across different cultural-linguistic contexts is clear-cut:

you say the same things translated across your various languages. That the reality is often hugely different is something to which the majority of those who speak another language with some fluency will testify: a survey of over a thousand bilinguals found that two-thirds attested to feeling "like a different person" when speaking different languages. To imagine a language means to imagine a life-form; to assume that you would be the same person in different languages, when not only the norms and rules but most likely also your social status and domains of experience and proficiencies within those languages are likely to be at least slightly if not fundamentally different, seems, when examined, plainly bizarre.

I should confess that, growing up monolingual, this flawed picture was mine for a long time. I never waded deep enough into the French and German I studied at school to disabuse myself of the notion that translation was switching one utterance for a roughly parallel one. Speaking a language was knowing what I wanted to say in English, and saying (or trying to say) something that to my mind *meant that* in French. Despite the desires for rebirth that propelled me to Japan, it didn't occur to me that acquiring the language spoken in a culture very different from mine would mean developing a new persona, and the revelation dawned only very gradually.

I suppose that part of the reason that this revelation takes so long to hit is that for a long time, speaking a foreign language feels just that—foreign. Which is to say, new, and transitory, and very hard to link up with thoughts about our identity. Another, I believe, is because when learning a language in another country, the developments we make are so heavily socially rewarded, meaning we process our transformation as sheer success, or at least I did: I'm finally communicating! I'm doing this! I'm being approved! Following the crowd felt like something to be celebrated rather than ashamed of, and I kept it up until one day, I was confronted by the sudden yet now blindingly obvious awareness that this was conformity, pure and simple. For the moment, I was saved from total assimilation by the inaccuracy of my mirroring, which was why I was still able to feel more or less myself. But if I continued to get better, I reasoned, there might come a time where there was no longer room for the me I recognized to exist alongside this increasingly expert mimic. In other words, the extent of my skill in pretending to be like other people was exactly the extent to which I ceased to be myself. Was it really that simple? The whole thing resembled a brain-teaser, and it made me think back to studying identity as an undergraduate. For a while then, it had been fun to muse on the various ways that philosophers had sought to address this issue over time—until it had promptly become tedious. Either way, though, it had been an intellectual exercise that had little point of contact with my real life: ultimately it didn't really matter how you conceptualized it, because in the real world everyone just got on with it and was fine. Now, I felt differently. The conundrums still had that tricksy, puzzle-like quality to them, but now the concern I felt was real. I wanted a branch, either emotional or cerebral, onto which I could grip as I crossed this swamp of doubt, but I could see none.

I had already set down the path of imitation, and society rewarded my progress thereon, so I kept on tramping, and at some point I found myself in the swell of a further wave of identity doubt, where a symmetrical suspicion drifted in

about my original self: maybe this original "me" which figured in my thinking was more nebulous, more tied to English
than I realized. Wasn't a large part of being "me" simply the
fact of having been (very ordinarily) talented at mimicking
the people around whom I'd grown up? Was it fair or valid
to attach any kind of primacy to that form of mimicry just
because I'd practiced it for so long that it had become a thoroughly unconscious competence? And the more I thought
about it, the more it did seem to me that there was nothing
desperately inner or innate about this self; that the relationship I had with it was constructed from the outside, and structured by language.

Even just thinking these thoughts felt intolerably teenage-
angsty to me, and I wanted it over with. Perhaps the important thing was just to plow on through; perhaps, eventually I
would get to the point where I shifted between different selves
among which there was no hierarchy of primacy, and barely
paid their difference any mind. And yet, I couldn't stifle the
doubts that I was doing this all wrong, missing a trick in some
way; that I should just be finding it easier, managing the transition better. This perception was reinforced by the comments
people directed my way. I didn't know if this was par for the
course or not, but each time it happened, it felt like a stab
in the back. "Your voice is so much higher when you speak
Japanese!" "You know you're really different in the two languages? How do you feel about that?" "You're much softer
and cuter in Japanese," "You're serious and scary when you
speak English." These are all things that have been said to
me, by different people, and each time the presentation was
that of simply stating a fact, as if to disown any idea that the

statement could be taken the wrong way. As I felt a twinge of dread in my chest—*see, I am a spineless person after all*—I would wonder to myself why it was exactly that I found it so hurtful. Did I actually believe that it was bad to change, or did I just know that, belying the apparent innocence with which these comments were voiced, changeability carried a negative social value?

————

The Japanese mimetic phrase for "changing all the time," koro-koro kawaru, is a personal favorite. Koro-koro by itself is the sound of a round object rolling, or something round and fat; I picture the trundling of a little red ball as it moves over a hardwood floor, flashing with light. Used alone, koro-koro is a neutral phrase, but when combined with "kawaru" or "kaeru," transitive and intransitive versions of the verb to change, a dose of rebuke creeps in. That's exactly one of the things I like about this phrase: I learned it from a friend, N, who was a very rational person, and demanded a large degree of reliability from people around him. Delays and inconsistencies would always be pointed out, and particularly people who frequently changed their tune would have this phrase directed at them, graded by terms of its severity in intonation. In really serious cases, the emphasis would fall hard on the second ko—koro'KOro—which generated an expressiveness that always made me smile. And it wasn't a mocking smile either—on the contrary, the demand for consistency was very comprehensible to me. It seemed to be woven into the cultural fabric of both the place I'd grown up and this new one I found myself in: a person should be consistent in their behavior unless they want to avoid being immature, self-centered, flighty and irresponsible—all terms taken from the thesaurus in which the phrase "koro koro kawaru" is listed. I loved the feel of it in my mouth also, a feel that can't be reproduced with the English "r" with which this is commonly transliterated—it has to be the Japanese sound, somewhere between an r and l where the tongue stretches up vertically towards the roof of the mouth (the best explanation I've heard is that it's the same as the "tt" sound in most American-English pronunciations of "butter").

Yet as time went on, I started to feel that expecting consistency from people in terms of languages was essentially an unfair and contradictory demand. More specifically, it is a contradiction when this demand for what we could call intrapersonal consistency is amalgamated with another demand we make of people: interpersonal consistency, or fitting in. We expect a person to behave the same across different contexts, and we expect people to behave the same as those they are with, and we are mostly blind to the fact that this is a double bind, because different places often have wildly different codes of conduct. We don't even have to be speaking about multiculturalism for this to be clear: within our daily lives, the different circles and settings through which we move are likely to place different demands on us, and we are expected to respond to these by adapting our performances from situation to situation. We reserve an admiration and fascination for historical characters like Ludwig Wittgenstein who were notoriously unwilling to compromise their principles for the sake of harmony, etiquette, social integration; there is something noble, we think, in this integrity, while in reality we find such people intolerable to be around. Although chameleonship is outwardly derided and disdained, it is implicitly not only accepted but actively demanded. Majority culture in monolingual societies expects people to assimilate—and this is particularly true of those from other cultures, who we expect to assimilate and fit in while simultaneously maintaining the idea that to change makes one slimy, snake-like, untrustworthy. To change, yes, great, very useful, but to be changeable—which is to say, *to be caught in the act of changing*—no thanks. Maybe it comes down to a self-image issue: we would prefer not to think of ourselves as demanding anything from people. Or perhaps it is that we cannot bear to be confronted with what the chameleon makes visible, namely how hard we work to conform. We prefer not to think about the changes people navigate as they move across cultural contexts, and continue to demand the impossible: that people naturally fit in wherever they go, without altering themselves.

This discrepancy between the sort of interlinguistic fidelity we unthinkingly require and the reality was something I'd thought on ever since I first started to sense myself adapting and to have it pointed out to me. It wasn't until a few years ago that I came across something which seemed to bring everything I'd been musing on to a head, and give me a specific frame within which to think about it: an article that came up on my Twitter feed about multiple personalities. The article reported findings from a survey of bilingual Japanese women living in the San Francisco area, asked to complete the same sentences in different languages; in the extract I read, the examples given were all taken from the same speaker:

1. WHEN MY WISHES CONFLICT WITH MY FAMILY . . .
    (Japanese) it is a time of great unhappiness.
    (English) I do what I want.

2. I WILL PROBABLY BECOME . . .
    (Japanese) a housewife.
    (English) a teacher.

3. REAL FRIENDS SHOULD . . .
    (Japanese) help each other.
    (English) be very frank.

I remember the mixture of disbelief and affront that spilled over me as I read these responses. The idea that there would be variation in how people represented themselves across languages was not something that took me by surprise in and of itself; having briefly studied sociolinguistics as part of my MA, as well as living for years in Japan, I was primed to believe that some variation was to be expected—but up to a certain degree. For example, the article reported an earlier study by the same researcher, Ervin-Tripp, which asked French–English bilinguals to complete a Thematic Apperception Test, where subjects were shown a picture and asked to construct a narrative around it. Each participant took the test in both languages, with a six-week interval between, and findings reported significant topical differences between the stories told in the two languages: "English stories more often featured female achievement, physical aggression, verbal aggression toward parents, and attempts to escape blame, while the French stories were more likely to include domination by elders, guilt, and verbal aggression toward peers." This was the kind of result I could deal with, the kind of variation that seemed natural.

This sentence-completion exercise, on the other hand, felt like too much to digest. The degree of changeability shown by this Bay Area woman felt frankly caricatured, and certainly not psychologically healthy. *But these are actual beliefs*, was what I kept thinking. These were not themes in a story but, at least ostensibly, avowals about closely held beliefs, desires, and behavior, about which there could only be one truth. How was it possible for one person to contain two people like that? I understood, even as these thoughts formulated themselves, that the matter was far more complex than that—and that complexity was precisely why this was both so fascinating and disorienting. The truth it so vividly pinpoints is that when we complete a sentence, we are not merely reaching inside ourselves and producing an answer which has formed in there independently of influences, but rather subconsciously echoing that which we have heard said around us. As functioning members of society, our own ideas about what we want to do, our pronouncements about them in assorted contexts within our lives, are subject to external influence—in fact, these conversations are located within linguistic communities. As children, adolescents, adults, we are initiated into the practice of having them, and our extrapolations about what we really want come afterwards; even then, they are conducted with reference to linguistic concepts whose definitions exist for us within a web which encompasses all of our experiences and learned practices and behaviors. As Ervin-Tripp, responsible for both the French and Japanese studies, beautifully puts it: "The internal imitations of external speech constitute a kind of portable society, both the voice of conscience and a categorization system, promoting socialization even of private behavior."

I knew all this, in theory I absolutely knew all this, and still there was the outrage, the tendency to reach straight for moral judgment. The spinelessness, the shamelessness of it! A housewife *and* a teacher! Surely there has to be a truth about what this woman really thought, what she really wanted, outside of her linguistic communities?

Maybe there was one thing this woman wanted to be, which she thought about while alone, or maybe what she experienced was more like a pull between different desires and obligations; we will never know, and more to the point, this is not what matters. In fact, we could articulate the takeaway of this study as the idea that the mistake is to believe that that is what matters, even if it is a mistake we are set up to make. Our languages and the cultures surrounding them are very good at sustaining us in the belief that in standard conversation, what we are expressing are ideas and opinions grown inside ourselves like fetuses, with no exposure to the outside world. It can be that it is not until inconsistency creeps in for the first time—or we first become aware of it doing so—that we begin to question the stability of the attitudes that we express across contexts, across languages, and wonder if we are not all like this Bay Area woman.

Back in Japan, I began to notice myself being spineless and unfaithful on an almost daily basis. I would notice that Japanese concepts made sense while speaking Japanese, only to find myself later talking with friends in English and commenting on how "bizarre" they were. Then it began to happen the other way round too; I would put down the English language, Anglophone culture, Anglophone customs, or at least adopt a distant attitude to them. I felt like a hypocrite, and in most definitions of the word, I was one. As time went on, I would learn ways of ameliorating that feeling of hypocrisy. I would learn to carry with me the awareness that I felt very differently when speaking in a different language, even if I couldn't at that time remember the feeling itself, and that made me both less vehement in my expressed opinions and less bewildered by myself. As I controlled the degree to which I changed, I also grew happier with the idea of changing—more accepting that having multiple identities was neither avoidable nor shameful. Yet the creeping sense of hypocrisy has never entirely gone away, and my guess is that I'm stuck with it, until the day I can fully and deeply accept that social survival across languages requires our koro-koro chameleonship.

¶ bishi-bishi: the sound of being struck sharply and repeatedly by a stick-like object, or (infrequently) of branches breaking

LIKE HOW YOU USED TO hit me. How I'm not even sure that it's fair to say that—*to hit me*—and how I'm not even clear in my memory about what it was that we did that made those bruises, but it was nothing that would blow any enlightened minds, or even any less-enlightened ones. Still, how you were the only person I've ever really done that with, certainly the only person I've really wanted to do that with, and how it's not surprising to me that that's the case. How, for better or worse, you were the only one I've ever trusted in that way. How I'm pretty sure it was me who instigated it, and how I don't know specifically what that looked like, in fact when I look back in my memory it's as if I was never there when it actually happened, but is that absence of memory because I was drunk, or because I was not able to be fully conscious in some more fundamental way? And how the next day you would say, "I feel sin." "When I see your bruises, I feel sin." "Maybe we should stop the bishi-bishi stuff, I don't know if it's good." How you would refer to it like that, bishi-bishi, and how at the time it seemed to me to belittle the whole thing, and why? Because it wasn't my language and I was immediately excluded? Or because the word sounded faintly comical to me, like you were making light of it? Or was it that any verbal representation of it, in any language, would have made me uncomfortable? And how, even as the discomfort formed, I sensed that it had a counterpart in you, and maybe the function of this word was in some way to temper that discomfort, that embarrassment, like maybe all words are there to temper our discomfort and embarrassment, the terrifying thingness of things. That same thingness that I felt one day when I was with a friend on the island, lolling about on her sofa and realized just in time that the bruises were about to show, pulled up my top, and that feeling of thrill that ran through me, together with a fleeting thought that went *I have passed to the other side.* That went, *I am now incontrovertibly a mess.* And the silly satisfaction of that, a new and more incontrovertible way for the outside to match the in. How I secretly liked those bruises, the wisteria spraying out darkly across skin that was so white, I only realized now how luminously white it was, and how whiteness was now a new thing, a color here: desirable, and related to disease, and bleach, and a certain strangeness, and I possessed all of these things, just as I possessed absolutely nothing at all, least of all myself.

¶ mote-mote: the sound of being a small-town movie star

SOMETIMES I FEEL THAT THE anger, irritation, frustration, and the overwhelming desire to punish this new world of mine for failing to conform to my expectations and refusing to comprehend me stand in conflict with the love that I feel for it—that these are two rival states competing for control. At others, I glimpse the larger structure that holds these in place, within which the contradiction between the love and the hate dissolves. The structure is: I am in a pseudo-romantic relationship with Japan, which is jealous, intense and full of burning, flailing ego. Japan adores me, and I adore Japan, and if we don't always see eye to eye, it's because we have so much invested in each other. This is a narrative I never dare bring to my lips, even really to my consciousness, but it exists in my way of seeing the world. The epicenter of all this feeling is the man with whom I am in love, with whom I tell myself that I am in love. It extends also to all of society, in a manner that is unfair, irrational, and anything but adult.

And so. At a staff party, a teacher who has not said a word to me since he arrived new to the school a month ago begins, bolstered by alcohol, to talk to me in Japanese. I'm drinking too, of course, and sometimes when I'm drinking I'm quite good at drawing people out of themselves; the conversation goes well, and the better and longer it goes, the closer he moves in. He isn't smiling exactly, he's not the smiling kind, but his facial muscles relax. I can feel his inhibitions unfurling. I can feel the little tremors of connection in the air between us, and I like this sense of having facilitated this. I relax into it, nodding and smiling and all the rest. His shirtsleeves are rolled up. I can't recall even a glimmer of our conversation now, although I would imagine it was something to do with foreign travel, or foreign countries, or foreigners. Then before I really know what is happening, his arm is around me—not around my shoulder, but around my neck, pulling me in toward him with insistence. I resist writing the word force, because it is not violent, exactly, but there is, in fact, a steady, sinewy force to it.

I suppose what renders me immobile is mostly the shock of it, but maybe it's also my training these past months in not reacting emotionally, and being at all times aware of where I am, as now, surrounded by colleagues, although that doesn't seem to be so much of a worry for him. In any case I do nothing, just let myself be pulled limply by the neck, like a goose. It's down to Y, who is sitting opposite, to rescue me. He breaks off his conversation with the person next to him, leans in and says, "Mr. K, I don't think Polly likes that." Obediently and silently, Mr. K releases me, and our conversation ends, and I don't remember a thing from that point on.

When I wake the following morning, there is a cloud inside me. There are often these clouds inside me, and I am vaguely, peripherally aware that they are made up of some kind of vaporized emotion, but today the cloud is particularly dense. Driving to school, I feel like I am thinking and seeing through a tunnel. The headmaster, who has seen me drunk on numerous occasions, picks that day to ask me with a sardonic eyebrow how my "physical condition" is, in a way that seems calculated to shift the blame for what happened onto me. And then I am in the staffroom, and nobody speaks to me, and everything is back to normal, and they chatter away, and I am again the still, blind eye of the storm. As I sit at my desk, the injustice stings at the back of my eyes. I can barely bring myself to talk to Y, despite the fact that he was the one to save me. He is part of all this, my insides say. He is part of this Japan that has let me down.

Usually by the middle of the day I'm already plotting how I will secure the invite to his place that evening, but that day I don't, and so for once it isn't a collaborative venture. As I leave school at my home time, which is earlier than his, he looks into my eyes with the prompting sort of look that I have learned by now means some sort of worry. "Will you come later?" he says.

And I do go, but even as I show up, and secrete my car in the usual place outside the temple, I feel heavy and detached. So what if we get caught, I think; it'll serve the fuckers right. Although who the fuckers are in this case, I don't quite know. Inside his flat, I am quiet. In what has become unusual between us by this point, I speak only English, as some feeble protest, dressed up as a return to self. I am damned if I'm going to assimilate to this goddamn country. That is how I feel.

"You are upset," he says, taking my cue and also speaking only English. "Because of—" He pauses and then says with a wry smile, "Because of headlock."

Even in my fug of annoyance, I almost smile at this. It hasn't occurred to me before, but I suppose it was a form of headlock that Mr. K performed on me. I haven't fully turned my thoughts on what happened last night, but reflecting on it in that moment, I see that, aside from the obvious way that it was disturbing and indigestible, there is also the fact of how bizarre it was: of all the gestures to represent closeness, to choose that one.

"Yeah," I say.

"It's such a pity," Y says, and his voice suddenly gets very expressive. "You were having such a nice time speaking."

"It's not a pity," I snap back. It irritates me beyond belief that he could even conceptualize that interaction in a way that isn't subsumed by its conclusion—even though of course I'd also felt it was a promising interaction before it had taken the direction it did. And with the force of the anger, I continue speaking, not saying words that mean anything, but just discharging the cloudy feeling.

"It's not even that, you know. I feel just, I dunno, fed up with Japan."

"Fed up?"

"Angry," I say. "Really angry."

"I understand," he says, solemnly. "This is a fucking country."

"He never even spoke to me before, you know?"

"I know. Because he is shy." Then there is a pause, and he says, "I think maybe everyone wants to do."

"To headlock me?"

He smiles. "I think so." Then as if his rational mind requires him to provide a justification, he adds, this time in Japanese, "Polly wa mote-mote dakarana."

Mote-mote: the quality of being intensely popular, fussed over, a man- or a lady-magnet.

At this stage, I've only ever heard Y use this word, and only about me, and always semi-vindictively—I'm sure you'll find plenty of guys to sleep with when you move to Tokyo because you're mote-mote, and so on. It has always felt like a way of holding me responsible for the way that the world—or Japan—sees me. He's never used it like this before, though: factually, and plaintively, but in a way that places us more or less on the same side. It stings as it enters my wounds, and I feel them start to heal. I am not angry with him anymore. The evening goes on and, before I know it, Japan and I have made up.

I wish I could say: All I care about is what he thinks about me, I couldn't give less of a shit how Japan at large sees me, whether or not I'm thought of as attractive—but that would be a lie. Being told, constantly, that I'm kawaii—cute, pretty, adorable—is not enough reason to be here, but these signs of approval aren't something I'm immune to, either; they don't fail to touch me, even if there's little doubt in my mind that I'd be better off not being touched by them. They are part of the ego dance. They are part of the romance that I spin, this narrative of the love affair between me and this country, this childlike certainty that I am in fact the center of the universe.

So let's talk about Japan and narcissism. Though it feels at the time like it's all about me, I now understand with categorical certainty that it's not really. Not every Japan-bound Westerner becomes mote-mote, but my perception is that most who live there for a while experience the phenomenon of league promotion. There are ways one can present—attractive, slim, neat, pale-skinned, possessing the ever-sought-after "small face"—and there are ways that one can act—ingratiating, polite, smiley, curious, kittenish—which will up one's quota of attention, but almost everyone who is visually identifiable as non-Japanese, and who enters a rural setting in Japan will experience, at least at first, the feeling of being a minor celebrity.

I come and go with how I feel on how redemptive this can be: for someone who hasn't had enough of this in the environment in which they were brought up, can it be healing to be made a fuss of in this way? For me, personally, I don't think it was; it stoked an ego-fire, made the world seem more exciting, but I don't think it brought me closer to truly liking myself. What I do feel clear on is how pernicious this kind of objectification can be in the long run. It is pernicious in the same way that celebrity is pernicious: because this sort of attention thrills in the moment and disappears the next and is never enough; and because it places women and men alike in an atmosphere where their criterion for judging themselves is how much people are fawning over them, and where they are positively encouraged to sit back, preen, and self-infantilize. Most people will revel in it for a certain length of time, but only the serious narcissists fail after a while to feel the cracks.

As Japan holds you up, tells you how adorable, glamorous, exotic, unprecedented you are, it is also telling you even as it reaches towards you, even as it headlocks you, that you are unreachable. It needs you to be unreachable. It needs you to be on the outside. It requires your alienation in order to better admire you. The more used to it you get, the more you come to require your own alienation, come to regard it as a condition of being appealing.

There's another event that always comes to mind when I think about all of this, from when my brother, George, came to visit me on the island, and I brought him into school with me, taking him along to my morning classes. He'd just turned seventeen, so for the middle-schoolers he was prime crush territory. Even the boys seemed to want to court him, dancing their bodies in his gaze, eyeing him up in a way that was both more equal and more adoring than the way that they looked at me, and made me feel a stab in my chest. That was an affection that I craved also.

For my brother's visit, the normal lesson plan was abandoned; we played instead self-introduction games, and the kids said his name over and over again: Jōji, Jōji, Jōji. One boy was especially chuffed because his name could also be read as Jōji if one used different readings of his characters, although as it was, it was said Takefumi. I remember even after six months of Japanese this fact was still pretty mystifying to me, certainly as sufficient cause for excitement; for my brother, I imagine, it was another in a scrolling list of phenomena that seemed beyond comprehending with his everyday mind, along with the gift shop boasting a presentation box of nine small cans of tuna labeled Sea Chicken, and the sweets in the convenience shop called Melty Kiss, and the kid who asked him the question "do you like hard gay?" when he didn't know that Hard Gay was in fact the name of a Japanese comedian, and how my friend had taken us to a yakiniku restaurant and upon learning that my brother didn't eat meat, had said blithely, "Don't worry, they have sausage," and opened the laminated menu to a page with pictures of thirty different kinds of sausage.

At lunchtime, we went down to the dining room, and sat with Y and the three girls who were the most academically brilliant third-year students; one in particular seemed very attached to my brother, blushing and laughing behind her hand, saying the odd faltering sentence in English. Before we left, the two of us had our photograph taken with her, and she gave him a small piece of Disney notepaper with her address written on it.

I had no lessons in the afternoon, and so the headmaster gave me permission to go home early with George. My car was undergoing post-crash repairs at the time and I was vehicle-less, so we walked out the front entrance of the school across the large tarmac car park sprawling in front of it, making for the bus stop across the street.

I remember what it was like to step out of the school building with my brother, into the fresh air. We'd only been there for a long morning, but the time had taken on a fairground quality: dizzy and vivid and heightened. I remember that we looked at each other out of the corner of our eyes, and I had for a moment the feeling that we were exhaling together— that our breaths were clearing the same lungs. Everything was so clear, so calm all of a sudden, our feet ringing out on the tarmac, our eyes skimming the bright flowers planted in beds between the cars, and we didn't need to speak. And then we became aware of a sound behind us. At first it was just that, a sound; not voices so much as commotion, but then out of the blur emerged a name, knife-like and unmistakable: Jōji.

I turned around first, I think, and then he did, and being

so used to that school building, I found it hard to take in the change. The windows to the classrooms on all three floors were open, and there were heads sticking out of them—shiny heads glinting black-white in the sun and hands waving from extended arms. As we watched, other windows opened, other heads appeared, boys and girls but mostly girls, clean-shirted arms competing to stretch the farthest. And all of them were shouting: "Jōji, Jōji, bye bye Jōji, I love you Jōji."

We kept on walking, glancing over our shoulders, but at some point we had to stop, turn ourselves around fully, face what it was that was happening. And then, at least in my memory, the ai rabu yū's became more dominant until that was what every mouth was screeching, they were falling towards us from the windows in sheets: "I love you Jōji, I love you Jōji."

Just like we'd understood that we had to stop walking before, so we understood that we had to walk again now, that this was a goodbye ritual that would not end until we were gone, which had to be bathed in while exiting, and so we set off walking again, hands cast diagonally behind us in waves, heads occasionally turning.

Even as I glanced back at it, it seemed like the reception that would be given to an actual rock star in a stadium—except this was more affecting, in a way, because it was taking place apparently wholly spontaneously, and in the far more drab setting of a middle school.

I'd never had the rock star treatment as fully as that, never did have it as fully as that; because of my age, my gender, my situation, maybe. But I'd had the essence of it, and I was glad that my brother had got to experience it, too—not only the adulation, but the weirdness of it also, and the alienation, of which I'd tried to speak to him, in emails, in phone calls, in the previous few days, and mostly failed.

It was only as we were about to step across the threshold of the car park and onto the road that he looked furtively up at me out of the corner of his eye.

"That was bizarre," he said. His voice was impassive, but there was something trembling under it. The tremble said that he didn't know how much he was allowed to take this as his.

"I know," I said. "It really was."

And it flashed through my mind to say to him, teasingly,

"It's because you're so mote-mote," or rather something more English of the kind, but I didn't, because I wanted to let him know without a shadow of a doubt that I was on his side.

¶ kasa-kasa: the sound of the desert heat
in the heart or the desert heart in the heat

THE MORNING I TOOK MY leave from Y, he came to his door to say goodbye, as he always did. In the genkan sat his gladiator sandals: thick leather strips woven into a burned pie lattice, so well-worn that the leather had grown soft and saggy. I loved those sandals. I loved them and I loved the world that contained them. It was a world where every item had a provenance, which I could ask about and which would be related to me with satisfaction, even relish; which would be interesting to me because it mattered to him. He slipped his bare feet into them as he faced me, so he wouldn't be standing on the dirty floor. I was now over the threshold.

"Goodbye," he said in English, then leaned over and kissed me, and stroked my cheek. "Have a nice life."

Of course, he wasn't to know how "have a nice life" sounded—by which I suppose I simply mean, I don't think he did know. I think he wanted the words to say exactly what they seemed to say, but they stabbed me regardless. I might have lingered, talked it through with him, but it was too risky to stand about outside his flat in case the neighbors saw me.

We touched hands, and I moved off, down the steps and onto the road, and he closed the door softly.

————

Outside the day was young and half-fresh, there was still an hour or so until the humidity dump that would make the world unnavigable. Wherever I looked, surfaces were picked out in flashes or blocks of morning sunshine, and beyond the car park, the rice field glowed green. Everything seemed almost oppressively healthy and functional, poised to leap into action. *And there was me, a castaway from the world of functionality and usefulness*—even as the thought formulated itself, I knew how questionable it was. Up until just a few minutes ago, I'd been clinging to the narrative that I had no choice but to go. However large a cog I might have become in Y's reality, I was not an operative part of its mechanism: like an element whose function was purely decorative, I spun free of the other interlocking parts. A luxury, as he'd once called me—and that had stung as well. But now, as the reality of it all began to seep in, I started to catch glimpses of a different way of seeing things. However untenable my current situation was, however reprehensible it would have been regarded by people on the island if they were ever given the chance to regard it, this was the only one I had. If I were really invested in our relationship as I said I was, if I loved this island like I said I did, I would have chosen to stay and see things through, until we were discovered and shamed. Instead I had chosen to leave him to his flat and his sandals and flee into the easy embrace of the big city. At no point down the line had this really felt like a choice, but now I saw incontrovertibly that it was one.

What I wanted more than anything was to run and hide myself away, to turn off my mind and my body. The thought of walking along the main road and potentially encountering someone I knew seemed too much to take, so I swerved off at the first street on the left, passing down semi-familiar backstreets which were mercifully both deserted and shaded. Stumbling along, looking around me for somewhere I could sit and regroup, I eventually came across an old petrol station on a corner of the street.

By now, I'd worked out that the island had the power to absorb things into itself. On my daily walks down the alleys to the beach, I was used to seeing the ways that the salty air and the breeze staked their claim over all kinds of surfaces, and the same happened in inland places like this one too. Nobody could have called this petrol station dirty or ruined, and there were no creeping plants intruding on its plain surfaces, but it was notably lacking the cleanliness and the sharp edges of sites tended by humans. The white dusty stone of its smooth floor and walls seemed far removed from any industrial process, and in their muted colors even the metal signs appeared more like archaeological ruins than the product of modern capitalism. It looked like a place you'd find on the outskirts of a desert, its concrete assuming the texture of blasted bone, replete in its silence. My wish to hide had reached desperate heights, so I snuck in and crouched at the back of the plot, behind a stone block that looked like it used to be the oil-changing station.

Leaving here was too much to be borne. Crouching there on the bone-dry concrete, hot sun beaming down on me, I felt the emotional reality of this truth I'd always rationally known swell to fill my body. I began to stab myself with a question: Why are you walking away if it really means that much to you? I didn't have an answer, and sitting there that morning as the heat amplified around me, none came. I couldn't even feel real sadness. What I felt instead was a scrunched up, dry despair. Kasa-kasa—that was the word that Y would some-times use when he ran his fingers over the dry skin on my shins scriddled with tiny lines. I'd looked it up in my diction-ary to find that it was the rustle of dried-up leaves, the feel of flaky skin and parched land.

If the me today could explain to the girl crouched down on the floor of an abandoned petrol station why she was feel-ing so confused, she'd try and explain how it was that there were two Japans she was experiencing simultaneously. Exter-nally, I would say to the girl, she was utterly replaceable. She had been granted a place in the system but scarcely, as a mere place-marker, and the more that time went on, the more she got the sense that the idea she was marking, the concept of foreigner she was being paid to symbolize, was in fact defined by its unreachability—that she was something like a flagstick on a golf course, marking out a hole. It was expected that she knew nothing about Japan, could say nothing in Japanese, socialized exclusively with other Westerners, or else with Japanese people who spoke English. She was a mascot, and she would be loved to the extent that she could accept that the attention given to her was premised on the fact that she was bigger and clumsier and differently shaped and colored to other people, and the notion that the sweaty person inside was the same as everyone else was of little interest. This was not something that she liked, or something she was able to accept without resentment, and that was why she did not excel at this job.

And then, I would explain to the girl that, in a way that felt qualitatively other and spatially distinct from her mascotry, she felt absolutely involved. There was the intimacy that had grown between her and Y which was something that she'd not experienced before, the friendships formed from bouts of strangely consuming conversations, and the bonds that formed between her and the children, whose intensity seemed almost uncontainable. But while she found these ties to be utterly necessary, found the thought of being here without them untenable, she gradually discovered, like bumping up in chemistry experiments against the sharp edge of a scientific law, that they had to remain on the inside. They were not ratified by any outside structure, and so there was no way of manifesting them. Externally, which is to say visibly, linguistically, publicly, in the dimension which observably mattered, she was still an outsider, and the fact that she had swapped little bits of her life with people was something she had to keep within.

She resented this, and the resentment would rush out at times in a way she recognized to be futile only afterwards; it would manifest itself in speaking in a certain tone of voice about Japan which often sounded like possessiveness or arrogance, or worse, sheer ignorance, but really she just wanted some way of marking socially that bond which she felt, and on which she staked so much importance. She wanted the right to belong on the outside as well as in. Her decision to leave the island was fueled at least in part by an understanding that this was never going to happen, and that such a condition was unsustainable for her, and that was the truth—but when she was dwelling on that truth, she almost necessarily wasn't thinking about the other one, namely how attached she felt herself to be. The truths seemed to live independently of each other, up until the point of her departure, when for the first time, they emerged into sight simultaneously. And that was why she was sitting rendered immobile with an emotion she couldn't properly feel.

———

Whenever I was at Y's flat and he found a new patch of scaly skin on my arms, he would go to the windowsill to fetch the tube of cream. I remember one time hearing him muttering to himself as he rubbed it in: "It's because you don't take care. That's why it gets all kasa-kasa like this."

He spoke in Japanese but used the English word, kea, for care. As I mostly did in those days, I took this to mean exactly what it would have done in English, failing to consider that it might be a faux ami like so many katakana words were; not realizing that here, kea meant specifically skincare, the application of products.

And so, like a petulant child in a bad film, I objected: "I do take care! I do!"

Y looked up at me curiously. "Oh, you do?" he said, his voice placid. "Well, okay then. I didn't think you did."

Now, looking back, I think that however you defined care, Y was right. Certainly I didn't have a good skincare regime, but more generally, I didn't take care of myself properly, because I didn't know how to, and I especially didn't know how to when such wildly different things seemed to be wanted of me, and I myself wanted such wildly contradictory things. I didn't really understand what was going on around me, and if I could see to a certain extent what was happening inside, I had no idea at all what to do with it.

And so it was that I ended up like this, crouching on the dusty floor of a petrol station, cracked, sore, and broken.

¶ bō': the sound of a ship leaving shore

I SAW IT ALL THE time, before it happened, after it happened, an event whose symbolic value far exceeded that of its actual happening: the ferry pulling away from the harbor for the last time with me on it. There would be the whirring of the engines, the smashing of the gong as it moved away, and then once it was onto the open water, the ferry would let out a deep bellow that seemed to emanate from its very bowels. I don't actually know now if the horn was ever sounded, but this was how I saw it in my head and that image surpassed everything else. Bō' is how you say the sound in Japanese. Spoken it is very low, half animal and half mechanical. I'd learned it recently, and was fixated with it, but even that seemed a meager approximation of the sound of the ferry as I heard it in my head. That sound resonated forever.

¶ kira-kira: the sound of a #magiclife, or embracing your shining future

TOKYO: IF I CONCENTRATED ON the word carefully enough, I could feel it giving out tiny vibrations of light. Tokyo, I had convinced myself, would be the place where my life came together, where I learned to shine, where the seeds I'd been scattering would cease to be messy flecks littering the ground, and would leap up in green to become a coherent, unified growth. The desire to change and be changed was upon me again, and now it had an urban flavor. My branches would grow neon baubles, and they would pulsate and twinkle. My life would be charmed, and effortless, and magic.

In retrospect, I think my experience on the island had been genuinely magical. That's obviously a simplification, but it feels like a true-enough one. Things were awful and they were wonderful; they involved endless quantities of panic, alcohol, doubt and joy. They felt, for the first time ever, unmediated and raw. But I was having an affair with a married man with whom I worked, and for bureaucratic reasons I wasn't allowed to stay on the island, would have had instead to relocate to the mainland in order to renew my teaching contract—the situation, I knew, was not a sustainable one. Besides, as wonderful as the island was, it was not a place where things happened. "It's like coming to England and staying on the Isle of Wight the whole time," my mother said to me on the phone at some point. "It's good to try somewhere else, no?" Even Y agreed that "someone with a shining future" was better off in Tokyo.

One of the aspects of being on the island I'd liked most was precisely the fact that I hadn't had to think about my #shiningfuture, but I also knew that I couldn't put it off forever. I had visited Tokyo a couple of times after my orientation week there, and it had seemed to me like a place where one could have wild adventures. On those visits, I had indeed had what passed for wild adventures, the only notable detail of which I remembered was a man calling out in his best English to me and a friend on the street, declaring "I have a big cock." It was such perfect katakana pronunciation—ai habu a bi'gu ko'ku—that I couldn't help but think back to the ko'ku sa'kingu gēmu, and realize that I was now living that reality that had once seemed so far off. I didn't find this man's behavior remotely appealing, but maybe, in the chaotic mess of my mind at the time, it somehow symbolized that Tokyo was the right place for my new adventure. In any case, I applied to one of Tokyo's countless private English schools, and found myself a job.

The Japanese verb for moving to the city, noboru, is related to that for climbing a slope or a mountain, albeit written with different kanji, and this seemed apposite as I made the journey over from the island. I was wedded to this idea of climbing, because emotionally, everything told me that I was sinking, that I had fallen through into nothingness. Back on the island, we had moaned and joked about how much attention we were paid, people stopping us while we were out walking, staring into our shopping baskets and later recounting their contents to us. Now I felt utterly invisible, even as I was universally stared at.

As if in response to a subconscious realization that this new job and this new life of mine were really not right for me, time began almost immediately to pass strangely, woozily. I had trouble sleeping, and adrenaline deluged my system. Returning home to my tiny box flat, I forbade myself from drinking out of the fear that I was going to turn into an alcoholic, and some desire for asceticism. Instead, I would sit out on a cardboard box on my balcony, a large wedge shape almost the same size as the flat itself, smoking cigarettes, reading, skirting around a black hole of loneliness in my chest as the motorbikes roared past on the street below. I was miserable, I felt utterly unsafe, and all I thought about was how much I wanted to be back on the island.

What is alarming to me when I think back to that time now is not how low I was, which makes a lot of sense considering my total isolation and how out of touch I was with my feelings, but the way I struggled to console myself with a sense of how great, how cool, how magic my life was. Being infatuated by the strange newness of my life had come naturally on the island, but now it was an effort, a stiff, unwieldy thing that I clipped onto the front of my unclothed misery, like a paper-doll dress with its fiddly little tags. I had an artist boyfriend who took me to art museums, and to eat vegetarian ramen with field mushrooms in a trendy part of Tokyo. I had a bright orange mobile phone with a toy dangling from

it, half lion half panda, that I'd bought in a vending machine
in one of said art museums. I booked myself in to take a Japanese exam that was far above my capabilities, and began to
study Japanese like a fiend. I lost weight, wore red lipstick
and red shoes. Never mind that this me who was doing all of
this felt so detached from the balcony-lonely me that I find it
hard, now, to position them in the same mental space. If I can
convince myself, I thought, that I am going places, then I will
really go places.

————

In this magical-thinking mindset, where everything takes on
some symbolic value, music played an especially transporta-
tive role. If I felt a song deeply enough, if I knew all its words
and I entered into its spirit, then it could free me and make
me happy. As far as the Japanese music which I had begun to
listen to went, it would also improve my Japanese (in fact, it
wasn't untrue that it facilitated improvement, given how much
I pored over and studied the lyrics) and make me accepted
within Japanese society (again not entirely farfetched, since
this kind of cultural knowledge aided communication, but
this of course was not the miraculous, all-consuming sense
which I envisaged). In particular, there was a song I was
obsessed with while in Tokyo and in fact for some while
after called "Kira-kira," sung by a young singer I thought
extremely pretty. I would listen to it over and over again, and
write out its lyrics in my best Japanese handwriting. I already
knew the word kira-kira, which meant sparkling, dazzling,
shining, because it cropped up in the Japanese translation of

"Twinkle Twinkle Little Star," which I'd sung back at my Saturday morning kids' class, but now it took on a new meaning, namely, to signify the hope that my life would come to have. Kira-kira, to signify my magical life.

The thought of this seems almost unbearable to me now, not just because of how fan-girly it is, but because the singer in question seems a close to perfect exemplification of everything I have come to feel great resistance towards, less musically and more in terms of the type of womanhood she represents: infantile, saccharine-sweet, subservient, a magical pixie dream girl for a society where "small" is the second greatest compliment you can pay a woman after "cute." And then there are the lyrics, segments of which I stuck up on my wall, about a woman waiting for her lover who is away in some unspecified destination: "When you come back, I'll tell you about all the things that have happened to me," she sings. When her lover returns, she promises, she will tell him of how she grew wings and talons, how her silver ring turned black. If the world vanishes before he returns, she pledges to become the wind and wait for him. "That's how I get through the sad days."

I find it uncomfortable to remember now how enamored I was with these lyrics, but it also seems fitting. Of course, they paint a typical picture of the faithful, stay-at-home wife idealized by society, waiting with great endurance for her man out bravely adventuring in the world, but they also offer a startling insight into the kira-kira mentality, where the fantastical magicalness of one's life is offered up as a kind of totemic sacrifice. And what do you earn when you have proved you are magical enough? I'm not sure that I could have articulated the answer to this question, but what I really wanted, or at least what I really needed, was the day when I could stop presenting to others or to myself as magic, stop objectifying myself, and just feel. Feel magic, potentially, but most likely feel very ordinary, and have that be okay.

¶ shobo-shobo: the sound of persistent drizzle on a thirteenth-century Scottish castle

SOMETIMES A STUDENT WILL ASK me what a particular English word means, and I will sit there in the classroom
turning it over in my mind, feeling the way it seems to tug in
different directions depending on the angle at which it's held.
At these times I feel like I'm dealing with a whole personality, a body of sensory associations; the richness of the various contexts where I have heard this word lingers on in me
like an aftertaste, where my entire self is tongue. "Ahhh, it's
tricky," I say, moving my hand to my head. "It's really quite
hard to explain," and lurking somewhere is the feeling that
it is, genuinely, impossible. The meaning of this word is this
feeling, full stop. It starts to seem quite miraculous that as
speaking people, we deal day in day out with these entities
housing such exotic powers inside their innocuous-looking
exteriors. The quality of this feeling is something Wittgenstein (in English translation) repeatedly describes as "queer";
when we understand a word, one of his unnamed interlocu-
tors remarks, it is as if, "in a *queer* way, the use itself is in
some sense present."

   In fact, it is one of Wittgenstein's key tenets in the *Inves-*

tigations that there is no unitary "sense" of a word as such, no ineffable, alchemic essence which appears before us as those conversant with it. What we think of as the soul of a word is really just the conjunction of its uses, in much the same way that a person's identity could be said to be the sum of the myriad ways in which they perform. The "queer" feeling ensues precisely from dangling it outside of its natural context, a goldfish we've plucked gasping from its bowl.

Often the best cure for confused essentialist feelings like these is a good dictionary definition. A solid definition with at least two separate meanings, none of them particularly brief, can mostly untangle the knot in our chests: *Yes, of course: we use it like that AND like this, and that's where that sense of being tugged at by opposing forces comes from, and this sense of richness.*

Another good thing about a meaty definition is that its salutary effect is not restricted to those who know the word it defines. While it dissolves the torment in the speaker's chest and provides clarity around the various associations pulling in assorted directions, the definition can also perform a magic trick for the unacquainted too: by simply enlisting the clutch of meanings a word holds, it can immediately summon its soul into existence. A good dictionary is a talented painter of pictures.

Which is useful, because I would here like to give you my brief spell in Tokyo as a word, shobo-shobo, and this I will now do courtesy of a dictionary of Japanese onomatopoeia.

shobo-shobo:
1. Rain which falls weakly and with a dejected quality.
2. The shabby look when trees or a beard or hair grow sparsely.
3. When the eyes, owing to fatigue, sleepiness, tears, brightness of the light, mental strain, old age or so on, do not open properly and you blink weakly.
4. A pitiable weakness resulting from a lack of physical or mental strength.

———

Where it did not sparkle, Tokyo shobo-shoboed. It drizzled, it sleazed and it shabbed. It was bleary-eyed and seedy. It's hard to know how much objectivity to ascribe to these impressions, now they have been filtered through the lens of everything that came before and after. For instance, the brief spell I spent in Tokyo spanned August through to December, and much of it must have been humid and hot, but in my memories it is almost always raining. A similar confusion applies to the feeling I had of it being sleazy: objectively, I was living on the very border of Tokyo in a neighborhood reputed for its yakuza, so it stood to reason that it wouldn't be the most salubrious of places. Yet, I felt sure that a certain degree of sleaze would have been found in the island, if I'd looked for it. The point was that I never had, and it had never sought me out, and so while the place had occasionally struck me as provincial and run-down it had never once seemed seedy; now I wondered how much of that was simply to do with my personal circumstances, with the structure that held me aloft and in place. In

Tokyo there was no such structure. I felt, almost immediately when I arrived, like I'd fallen through the cracks.

The tiny, nondescript flat into which I fell was in a block home to several other teachers working for the same chain of schools, but there was no attempt to put us in touch. It took a while for my internet to be connected, and so for a good few days I had no way of contacting family or friends outside of Japan. At some point I started worrying that maybe something dreadful had happened to them, a worry which was probably just a front for feeling isolated and abandoned, so one gray afternoon I set off into town in search of an internet café. I assumed I'd find one in the built-up center of town, but I couldn't; even casting my net wider yielded no joy. Feeling by now somewhat frantic, I began to traipse the backstreets, not even sure if I was looking anymore or what I was doing, and then I spotted it: the katakana for internet—netto—on a neon sign. That I don't remember feeling any great rush of joy suggests that even at this stage I was aware that this might not be the best of ideas—that it might in fact prove to be a perfect example of how a little knowledge can be a dangerous thing—but a desperation to check my emails had left me single-minded, and I went clanking up the circular staircase on the outside of the building.

Inside, I found myself in a place for which I had no previous model, but which I gradually figured out was some kind of porn search facility: an internet café, but specifically for pornography. There was not a soul in sight, so I could take a decent look around. The main room contained a reception desk and a bank of four computers. At the side were two booths with chairs and boxes of tissues strategically placed on low tables, faded magenta curtains that could be pulled across their entrances. It was the tissues, I think, which convinced me beyond reasonable doubt of the true nature of this place. And yet, incredibly enough, my reaction was not to walk straight back out, but instead to call out for the owner. Equally stunning to me in retrospect is how, when nobody showed, I sat myself down at the bank of computers and began to use one. I suppose both these responses were testament to the sorts of people I'd encountered on the island, and also to the fact that I still at this stage had a healthy dose of bolshiness in me, which age and Japan would eventually train me out of.

After some time, the owner emerged from what I assumed was a back room behind the reception desk, chain-link curtains jingling. His face, at finding a young foreign woman using one of his computers, was a picture to behold, and he chortled in the way a fairy-tale dragon might when a plump child came stumbling into its lair, but he didn't seem like a creepy or dangerous proposition. When I explained my purpose, he agreed I could continue using the computer.

After tapping away for a while, I sensed someone come in and settle down in a seat beside me. I knew that this was the time to go, but I was midway through an email that I wanted to finish, so I tried my best to shut my neighbor out of my awareness. This worked alright until the owner came over to help him search through the porn and asked him about his preferences, and I overheard him say "Stuff with foreigners in." Immediately, I felt my heart leap into my mouth. Half-doubting my ears, half-wondering if this was just a common statement to make in a porn café, I hurriedly finished off the email I was working on, then stood up to leave. I remember that the owner refused to charge me. Reaching the bottom of the covered staircase, I saw that it had begun to drizzle, and as I was standing under the porch of the ground-floor entrance sorting out my headphones, rooting around in my bag for an umbrella which I'd forgotten to bring, rearranging my thoughts, I sensed a dark presence behind me. I whirled round to see the man who liked porn with foreigners in standing behind me.

"Which country are you from?" he said, and then, "Here, would you like to share my umbrella?" Saying this, he stepped forward and raised one of the see-through umbrellas you found everywhere in Japan over my head. "No, that's okay," I said. Holding on tight to my bag, I set off at a run down the dusk-blue street, strands of rain dribbling down my skin. When I was able to formulate thoughts again, it came to me that he must have taken me for a sex worker. Given where he'd encountered me, I suppose it wasn't an unreasonable assumption to make.

———

It wasn't that I was shaken by this episode, particularly. The man himself I found surprisingly unintimidating and I'd never felt any sense of real danger to my person. Yet it did somehow set the tone of everything that had happened afterwards for me in that neighborhood. It seemed to me like a sign that I was no longer invulnerable, that my divine protection had worn off.

This reversal seemed bizarre: on the island, what I'd been doing had been actually bad, and there were occasionally things Y said and did that made me feel uncomfortable, and I'd crashed my car once and got it stuck in a deep gutter another time, and walked around drunk and at risk, yet I'd mostly felt as though someone had my back. In all honesty, I'd felt for the large part like the world had my back. Now that I was living a pretty upright sort of life, scarcely drinking, without access to vehicles with which to damage myself or other people, and yet with no sense of structure to keep me aloft, I felt that society would sink its teeth into me if it could. For sure, I was working in a private English school, but that was a very different thing to being sponsored by the Japanese government to work in its public school system, as a part of a nationwide program with its own infrastructure. The Tokyo private language schools I visited were grimy, windowless places above supermarkets, full of children who wanted anything but to be there. The other teachers I encountered were often decent but sometimes they were unnerving, and a couple were downright frightening, pestering the Japanese receptionists at the school to go on dates with them. I may, in the barest sense, have been part of something, but it didn't feel like anything I wanted to be part of.

I imagine that many people in my situation would have tried to shut out the signs of danger or create a burrow of safety for themselves, but that was not how I functioned. Instead, having identified some feature of the landscape that felt dangerous, I had to fixate on it. If I looked at it hard enough, I thought, then at least it wouldn't take me by surprise. At least I would be prepared. And so my thoughts bent more and more towards the vein of sleaze that seemed to run through everything around me, in the attempt to come to terms with it. At night, after getting home from work, I sat on my balcony reading a thick red book called *Pink Samurai: The Pursuit and Politics of Sex in Japan*.

Although I wouldn't have characterized it thusly at the time, it was, ultimately, the politics of it all which I was trying to get my head around: the politics, and how they touched me. It wasn't exactly a revelation that society construed me in a certain way, but now with no buffer zone, I felt it more directly. Fending for myself, the points of contact between society and me were greater in number, which meant it was increasingly obvious to me how I was being seen. There were times back on the island when I had felt genderless, more or less: that seemed unthinkable to me in Tokyo. I was not just a foreigner, but a single foreign woman, and that was a rare and marked thing to be. More was assumed of me here, and more was wanted, which fitted into a greater picture of what was assumed and wanted of everyone. I needed to understand when it was happening, and preferably why. I needed somehow to make my peace with it, if I was to have any hope of staying.

One particular form this peace-making process took was a fixation with my local love hotel, which was positioned not so very far from the netto café, beside the station exit closest to my flat. Love hotels had been a source of fascination for me since I'd first heard rumors of them—the kind of juicy rumors that fresh-off-the-boat Westerners loved to trade about the revolving beds and heart-shaped ceiling mirrors and gynecologist's chairs in the rooms. There was something I found endlessly fascinating about their theme-park kitsch aesthetic. At the extreme end this meant Santa Clauses, giant teddy bears and jungle animals hanging from the external walls, but even the less extravagant ones still had a flashy quality to their signage, their lighting, their architecture and so on—a sort of third-rate bling which I couldn't seem to get enough of.

My local rabuho, into which my fascination had been poured since my move, was no less intriguing to me. The Eilean Donan was a ferro-concrete tower, its front a warm orange, its right wall graced with a painting of an orange tree laden with fruit and encircled by a green fence. If anything, it seemed to be aiming for a Mediterranean feel, and it was hard to find any connection between the appearance of the building and the tidal island in the Scottish Highlands from which it drew its name; the only explanation I could conceive of was that the sluggish green-gray river that the hotel was perched beside symbolized in some way the three lochs over which real Eilean Donan castle looked out. From the moment I'd laid eyes on it, there was something that seemed to me exquisitely chaotic about its semiotics.

Of course, the chaos was a matter of my own perception. I was still unused to the aesthetics of the Japanese metropolis, and the overwhelm was also tied up with an unresolved feeling I had about love hotels in general. I'd read a description in *Pink Samurai* about the standard Western reaction to the love hotel: despite believing ourselves above prudery, the author wrote, "centuries of conditioning still taint our sexual outlook with shades of guilt. Thus, if no longer sinful, the love hotel is slightly improper." It is for these reasons that we are unable to see it as "a haven for something perfectly natural and as completely deserving of celebration as its fanciful architecture suggests." And I suppose that was a fairly accurate characterization of how I felt, in one way; it seemed if not quite uncouth then at least unusual to me that the love hotel could announce its presence in such vivid shades. Yet in my case, this improperness was anything but repellent; indeed, in light of my quest to look the sleaze at the heart of society directly in the eye, there was something about the realness of the love hotel which brought me great relief. Here, at least, the cat was out of the bag.

When I came back from work late in the evening, there would be women waiting with umbrellas by the turning to the Eilean Donan, calling out to the men spilling out of the station with me. I knew that the thing to do was not to look at them, to stare at my shoes instead, but I found it almost impossible. So I looked at them, and sometimes I would nod, and at some point we started acknowledging each other. The walks I took on my day off would always include the bright orange beacon, even if all I did was to stand and look at it from a distance.

"Sex is a kind of crucible of humanness," writes Garth Greenwell. I felt this to be true; or rather I felt strongly that it should be true, but it also seemed that when I took my eyes from it for a second, sex would cease to be a real human thing and become some nebulous power pulling the strings of the world around me. I needed to track it, to ensure that it stayed concrete. And so I went back again and again to the Eilean Donan, itself a kind of crucible of all my unsettled feelings, and squinted through the drizzle at its orange walls.

¶ chiku-chiku: the sound of kicking against the pricks, or the ugliness of learning a language as a native English speaker, or the manner of stabbing repeatedly with a sharp-pointed instrument

I'M IN THE LIVING ROOM of the family with whom I've begun to spend time in Tokyo, eating dinner and drinking, as I do about once a week. This arrangement has come about because the matriarch of the family, a woman in her sixties, joined a group lesson I taught at the English school above her local supermarket, and one day after class palmed me a small square of paper with an elaborate hand-drawn map to her house and instructions for me to be there at 4 p.m. the following Saturday. I didn't feel too enthusiastic about the prospect of visiting in the first place, but 4 p.m. seemed especially objectionable as a time to arrive for dinner, and so out of some mixture of conscious and non-conscious resistance, I arrived closer to four-thirty, only to find her standing up the hill from her house on the lookout for me, waving frantically and letting out loud, relieved noises. Oh god, I remember thinking, what have I got myself into?

This sense was promptly heightened when I entered the house and found it was just her and her husband at home, and that the husband didn't speak. I think that of all the surprises my cultural nervous system received in Japan, this was possibly the greatest, or at least, the most visceral: Why was he not speaking? Why didn't he respond to her? "Why don't you speak?" she asked him, voicing my thoughts, and then turned to me and said, "This is Japanese men for you, they're very shy."

"Shy" was one way of characterizing this behavior, I thought; I would have opted for "cold," "dismissive," "misogynist," or any number of other adjectives first. I began to feel quite panicky: for her sake, having to live with this every day, and for mine, at the prospect of having to endure this for the next few hours. But for me, at least, there didn't seem any other option; perhaps that was her conclusion too. In any case, we sat down and began to eat and drink, and at around the point when the husband transitioned between his first and second shōchū screwdriver, a transformation occurred: he began to speak. A great deal. At some point in the evening, their grown son returned home from work and joined the party, and we all stayed up late and had a crazy old time, and I rolled out of their house steaming drunk with a bag of snacks to take home, wondering what on earth had happened.

Since then I've been coming round to their house a lot, even though my feelings about it remain no less conflicted. The general flavor of our interaction runs thus: the husband and his son will speak at a very great pace on topics dictated by a consciousness of my presence, and the wife will occasionally notice that I've said nothing but "mm" for a while and attempt to involve me, usually by asking me how you say a particular word, plucked randomly from the conversation, in English. I will struggle, and be incapable of providing an immediate definition out of context, and will thereafter feel a sense of itchiness at the perception I feel clinging to me: that I am a failure and that I have not understood as much as I am pretending to, even though this is almost without fail actually the case.

The subject at hand right now is America, as it often is. I don't have an American bone in my body, but I sometimes suspect that that fact has gone unnoticed in these discussions, at least by the family patriarch. Ultimately, there is one name for Western nations, and it is America. This is not unintelligible to me as a perception, and nor is the antagonism shown towards this arch-nation. I also know that after the events of the Second World War and the Occupation and its aftermath, the emotional stakes run particularly high between Japan and the United States. Besides this understanding, though, it strikes me that there's something faintly paradoxical at work here: that the very qualities which supposedly form the bone of contention with the United States—its size, power, and supposed crassness—are in fact ratified by singling it out as uniquely visible, as if only such places deserve attention. It puts me in mind of a time back in my first year of junior school, when the playground was ruled by a pair of identical twins. At some point, the twins had an argument, and in no time at all, the entirety of the year was split into two factions, with everyone forced to pick sides. I remember how bizarre it seemed to me, even as a four-year-old, that such a dynamic had evolved between two people who lived in the same house, and whom none of the teachers could tell apart—and although the situation with Japan and America was clearly different in almost every way, there was some of the enmeshed quality which felt of a piece.

Except unlike in the playground, here I am not permitted the luxury of picking sides. I am white and an Anglophone, so I am placed with America.

"The thing about America is that everything there is straight up, superficial. They have no fuzei."

"Mm," I say. Honestly, a lot of my energy is focused on just keeping up with what he is saying.

The wife turns to me. "How do you say fuzei in English?"

I open my mouth to speak—I have recently learned this word, I think—and he's already speaking: "There's no way that there's an English word for that."

I look up blankly.

"Oh no?" the wife says. I am continually impressed by the responses she makes to his dogmatic assertions of this kind, where the dissent lies exactly in the tone and can therefore pass unremarked, keeping the pot of marital tension bubbling but never flowing over. Or perhaps dissent is the wrong word: it's just distance, the sad distance of someone humoring someone else.

"There's no way that English would have a word for a concept that delicate."

"Hmm," I say calmly, although I can feel that my blood is starting to sing, and the urge is rising up within me to argue back. To argue back not in an arch, nuanced, centered way, but an unrefined, meaty, brattish one. The way that I used to argue more frequently when I first started coming here, and about which they still tease me now:

"Remember how R wound you up that time?" the wife

says, frequently. R is the son, and he does do a lot of winding up. She has a word for this: chiku-chiku. I've no idea what it means when she uses it at first, but after a while I work out that it's something like provoking, or being provoked. Now, over a decade on, I can tell you that chiku-chiku is a prickling, tingling, scratching, pins-and-needles sensation, the sound of itchy woolen underwear and scratchy woolen blankets. It is the noise of a "piercing emotional pain," and "the state of using sarcasm and criticism to produce this pain in others."

It is also, I found out just recently via the online dictionary, the state of eyes stinging with unshed tears.

"He was winding you up—chiku-chiku, chiku-chiku— and you got so enraged!" She clenches her fists and pumps her elbows to portray my outrage. In this depiction of myself I am literally a stroppy child. "Oh Polly-chan, you were so worked up!" And she throws her head back and laughs merrily.

————

There's an emotional as well as a lexical element to feeling yourself an infant in a particular language: how powerless you can feel, and how powerless to rid yourself of that powerlessness. How this seems to leave you at the liberty of anybody who wants to take a dig at you, and the sense you have of walking as if mesmerized straight towards their bait. Of course, the option is always open to you to remain quiet when provoked, but in my experience, the feeling you end up with is more or less identical whether you stay silent, or speak up: if you do speak you almost never present your case the way you want to, and if you don't, the other party's opinion goes unchallenged. Either way your eyelids sting with unshed tears because you feel misunderstood, in a particular way that feels as old and inevitable as the hills.

Even if the consequences feel the same for the learner, evidently the choice between these two options is socially weighted: it is always better to be the quiet, embittered adult than the struggling child spouting impassioned, semi-coherent nonsense—at least, in Japan it is. The longer I spend in Japan the more I understand the extent to which this is the case. And so whenever I'm faced by this option, I try to think Japanese things; to remember I am at their house, he is far older than me. To remember also that I'm extremely grateful to these people for providing me with a surrogate family. To remember that if I could express myself calmly and eloquently the situation might be different, and it would be fine to talk, but with my current linguistic level I have the subtlety of a lawnmower.

Even so, there are times when I feel compelled to choose the less graceful of the two failure options. Holy shit do I feel a lot of love for Japanese, and holy shit have I spent what feels like a lot of time buying into this mythology surrounding it, much of which is rooted in linguistic reality: its subtlety, its ambiguity, its profundity, its sometimes outrageous beauty. I would rage at people from the UK, from America who doubted these things about it, forever. Maybe it's just a desire to stick up for the underdog at any given time, or else it's a knowledge of all the beauties of the English language that I've seen nullified or simply slipping under the radar as they make their way into Japanese, that makes me feel like I have to pilot a defense attempt, and I just have to pray that it won't end up getting too heated, and I won't end up exploding.

Which I'm doing now. Except even as I gear up to engage with the challenge, I am thinking, how the hell could you say fuzei in English? and I can't remember.

"I'm sure there *is* a similar word," I say. I key it into my trusty dictionary, and three words come up: *tasteful*, *charm*, *elegance*.

"Maybe something like ambience?" I improvise, praying that nobody at the table will identify this as French in origin, or, more importantly, realize that this isn't an adequate translation of fuzei.

"Hmmmmmm," he says, clearly having no idea what I'm saying.

And this is ultimately, I remember in a rush, why this whole model of conversation is logically doomed to failure, because if I were speaking to someone with an understanding of English that could accommodate nuance, and who could therefore serve as a decent judge of my contribution, we would not be having this conversation to begin with. More specifically, when someone demands a good English translation for a word they've already decided doesn't exist in English, they will be dissatisfied if you tell them an English word that they don't know because they cannot trust it, and dissatisfied if you tell them one that they do, because it's patently inadequate. The latter response, particularly, I understand. It's very hard to see how anybody could love katakana English words after seeing them in comparison to Japanese and Sino-Japanese words, with their history and their resonance within the language. English words float. You can feel their paucity, feel how flimsy and superficial they seem in comparison.

"Can I see?" He reaches out his hand for my electronic dictionary.

And just as I could have predicted, he bungles his way through pronouncing "tasteful" and moves on without comment to "charm," which he knows because of chaamingu, and "elegance," which he knows because of ereganto, both of which are summarily dismissed.

"Chaamu," he says. "Yeah, that's not quite it."

I have heard this phrase so many times—"That's not quite it," or more literally translated, "No, it's a bit different to that," delivered in a tone that says, "Never mind, good try." Let's just say it, for the record: I feel in this moment like I could break something. I feel like I could howl with anger. That I could open my mouth and take him down with a torrent of furious English, my arms pumping by my side like a little cartoon character, or I could yell at the very top of my voice, in Japanese, that's not true! But I also know that by doing so I will be outing myself as an American, this time irreversibly. And so I sit there, and feel the unshed tears of rage pricking at my eyes. They go: chiku-chiku chiku-chiku.

¶ giri-giri: the sound of just about getting by, or being weighed on a moment-by-moment basis

AT SOME POINT, MAYBE AROUND the one-year mark, I reached a stage in Japanese where I could navigate my way through a lot of conversational situations. Obviously, this competency required producing whatever items of linguistic currency I had in my (still very shallow) pockets, but perhaps a more crucial part of it was knowing how to get by with the limited funds I had, understanding how best to arrange and stretch them. An especially key skill, it seemed to me, was that of knowing what not to try.

My Damascene moment with this had come just a few months into life on the island, when I overslept one Saturday morning after being out the night before with friends, and showed up late to the school sports day I'd agreed to attend. Standing there in the playing field as children wearing red and white bandannas mounted one another's shoulders and prepared to wage some kind of battle with a gusto that made me feel on edge, I managed to apologize to the headmaster with something approaching an appropriate degree of politeness, as I'd practiced doing in the car on the way there. Now, I can tell you with unequivocal certainty that given the abysmal state of my Japanese, that was where I should have left matters, but back then I couldn't shake off the feeling that the apology was too terse, not personal enough, and so, through a combination of techniques such as mime and enumerating all the relevant items of vocabulary I had at my disposal, I'd done my best to explain to him that, when I'd seen the time on my clock that morning, I'd almost had a heart attack. Even his expression of total incomprehension wasn't sufficient to convince me to accept defeat, because that evening, at the teachers' after-party, I mounted another attempt, this time with my electronic dictionary at hand. And it was only when I saw the alarm and confusion spreading over his face as he peered down at the screen I'd proudly placed on the table in front of him where the words "heart attack" were displayed in his native language, that the revelation came for me, not dissimilar to a dwarfing sense of humility, and quite possibly my first truly Japanese impression: the intense selfishness of thinking that what mattered in this situation was how I had felt about being late, and taking up this man's time in the convoluted attempt to explain this. Even delivered well, a quip about having a heart attack, though it would be entertaining in British culture, was not appropriate in this context; delivered badly, barely understood, causing only worry and concern, it was far worse. Thus I learned my first major lesson: do not, for the time-being, attempt to directly translate anything even vaguely idiomatic. Also, if you don't feel sure about whether or not something is idiomatic, it probably is.

With these tenets and others under my belt, as well as a faiɩ amount of study, I came to a point where I was just about able to get through a decent proportion of interchanges.

There is a mimetic to express this concept of "just about," giri-giri, which is in such common usage that it's one of the first mimetics most Japanese learners master. So it was with me, and I used it for over a decade without realizing it is, more literally, the sound that something makes when tied very tight, as it grinds and chafes and heaves at its constriction. *Oh my god*, I remember thinking when I made this discovery, *yes!* Here was a phrase I'd always classified as vaguely positive, at least in so far as it was mostly used for events classified as successes, yet I now saw that when you peeled back the surface, the reality revealed was one of enduring stress and huge energy consumption, in a way that struck me as profoundly true, at least with respect to language. "Just about getting by" in a language might sound relatively enviable but it feels like a precarious and profoundly taxing way of going on, and just because you have managed once or numerous times to carry out an interaction correctly doesn't mean that it will go right the next time. You know this, the people around you know this, and these fears and doubts amplify one another.

Living through these days of constant chafing, I thought a lot about Wittgenstein's remarks on the acquisition of skills like reading and writing, and our propensity to apply to them the same sort of binary ontology we apply to objects and beings: we can either read, count, or we can't. As so often, Wittgenstein attempts to erode the certainty of our perceptions through a spate of practical examples, in particular what we might term borderline cases, which serve both to instill doubt about the yes/no nature of a skill like reading, and also draw our attention back to the performative setting in which we learn such skills, their embedding within community practices:

> Consider the following case. Human beings or creatures of some other kind are used by us as reading-machines. They are trained for this purpose. The trainer says of some that they can already read, of others that they cannot yet do so. Take the case of a pupil who has so far not taken part in the training: if he is shewn a written word he will sometimes produce some sort of sound, and here and there it happens "accidentally" to be roughly right. A third person hears this pupil on such an occasion and says: "He is reading." But the teacher says: "No, he isn't reading; that was just an accident."—But let us suppose that this pupil continues to react correctly to further words that are put before him. After a while the teacher says: "Now he can read!"—But what of that first word?

Now, my entire life felt like a borderline case, where the judgment on whether I "really" understood something, whether I was "really" reading something or had just memorized it, was too complex for me to call. What was perhaps more surprising was how quickly I accepted that this didn't matter, at all; I gave myself up to the community's judgment. This wasn't motivated by any philosophical allegiance; it was simply that doing anything else felt like too much. With surprise I noted to myself that my aim in this or that interaction was purely to pass in the eyes of others. I didn't fully understand, or I was too exhausted to give my attention to the interaction, and I focused all my attention on giving the correct responses and behavioral cues, on making sure the other person believed that I was on top of what was going on.

In part, I felt horrified that my true nature had revealed itself to be such a shameless one: that I transpired to be concerned only with how I came across, making interactions run smoothly, treating the whole thing like a game. But another part of me recognized that this shameless part was right, and language was a game, in precisely the way that Wittgenstein famously deemed it to be: a communal, rule-bound activity. And, seeing as it was all a game, this cynical mode of play to which I often gravitated was arguably the wisest strategy for anyone who wished to become proficient. Of course, I could have made my incomprehension known whenever I felt it (on occasion I did, and sometimes it manifested itself regardless of my intentions to the contrary), but then the nature of the interaction would have changed: my interlocutor would have switched to English, or found someone to interpret for them, or brought the conversation to a close. And that was not the way that progress lay, because what we need as language learners is precisely the time to learn, to absorb, and to improve. Gradually it was dawning on me what every child knew instinctively to be true: pretending to understand buys you more time. Eventually the pretending morphs into real understanding.

Yet this morphing is gradual and piecemeal, and it is the spiritual condition of the language learner to feel like they have only *just* managed, and to be in touch with the precariousness of this state. Despite all the problems I believed myself to have with articulacy, until moving to Japan I had never experienced what it was like for someone to turn to me with eyes sharp with the suspicion, sometimes bordering on certainty, that I would be unable to express myself, and see this flash through their eyes again whenever I stumbled; I could never have imagined how much this would derail and strip me down to a nothing. And once I had experienced it, once I had reorganized my social persona to try and ensure this didn't happen, it became radiantly clear to me that a single success, that passing once, even with flying colors, was not sufficient to redeem a person. On the contrary, performing well once, whether by hard work or fluke or some combination of the two, only makes you appreciate the danger that it might not happen the next time. The praise and congratulation heaped on you, either internally or externally, makes it clear that doing less would in fact be a failing of some kind. When you are giri-giri, you can feel that tension creaking in your abdomen, as if your belt is ready to pop open at any time.

———

Thinking about this phrase, I always remember an occasion from the end of my first stint in Japan. I was getting ready to move back to the UK, and a man from Japan Post came round to collect three huge boxes of stuff that I was attempting to send home by sea-mail. He took off his shoes, came into my flat and started to measure the boxes with a tape measure. One of them exceeded the permitted dimensions, but the other two were fine, so he took out his scale from his bag and bent down to lift the first one.

"Yoisho!" he said, which was the noise that accompanied an act of physical exertion, then immediately gave a much more visceral groan. "This is heavy," he said. "I think this going be too heavy."

Perched on the scales, however, the box was just—*just*—within the permissible weight range. He gave a wry smile and wiped his brow with a handkerchief he produced from the pocket of his Japan Post uniform. In this moment, he was the living embodiment of the grinning emoticon with a drip of nervous sweat on its brow.

"Giri-giri daijōbu!" he exclaimed—just about okay!

"Giri-giri!" I repeated, and then he repeated it, again.

"Giri-giri!"

This performance was repeated for box number two, since box number two, as it turned out, was also "giri-giri."

There was a look on his face which seemed to say, *you absolute chancer*, but he was still, just about, on my side—impressed I think, in some way, with my pluck. Having no idea that there even was a weight limit, I'd waded in and got away with it.

"Call me again," he said, "when you've repacked the other box and I'll come back and get it." Then he wheeled my two giri-giri boxes away on his trolley to be loaded onto a ship.

After he'd disappeared I sat in my room, staring at the one large box left behind. Unlike many interactions with officials that I had in Japan, this one had been pleasant. I felt that the man from Japan Post had engaged with me in a respectful and human way. At the same time, I felt oddly encapsulated by what had just happened, as if it wasn't the boxes but me who'd been placed on the scales. In fact, it had been me, for a long time, and once again I had just about made it through.

¶ poka-poka: the sound of stepping into a warm obliviousness that is probably not what a higher self would want or need

WE MET UP IN TOKYO, three days before Christmas and two days before my flight home, and it was my first time to see him since leaving the island. He had planned to visit me once before, but the ferry had been canceled due to bad weather, as it so often was into the autumn, and after that I had told him that I couldn't speak to him anymore. I had to try and convince myself that it was over, that I had a new life. On good days, I could half-convince myself. But then he texted me for the first time in months—"Are you in Japan?"—and I felt like a huge bell had rung out, through my head, through my flat, into the world beyond. I remembered how that felt, to have my head and the world feel as though they were just an extension of the same place.

———

And so he came to my neck of the metropolitan woods and we made the pilgrimage together to the Eilean Donan. It was my first time to step right up to those orange walls and then through them, to enter that totem of untouchability which I had tried to make my friend. I found out soon enough that the inside was not shabby-kitsch like its outside seemed to promise, but just drab and unremarkable. The only visible differences between our room and a regular business-hotel one were the big TV with both a karaoke and a porn selection, and the small dish on the bedside table holding three condoms in cellophane wrappers that read Eilean Donan. Y, also, seemed not exactly a different person than the one I'd been expecting, but at least not quite the one that I longed for in my loneliest balcony moments. Back at the station where we'd arranged to meet, which had far more exits than I'd realized, we'd spent an hour trying to find each other, and in the end I hadn't recognized him as he came walking towards me, a fact which he kept reminding me of and which, to him, I blamed on the nerves that had made my vision swim. Truly, my vision was a mess, but also truly, when he'd approached me I'd seen him for a second as a middle-aged man looking at me with slightly letchy eyes, who didn't necessarily wish me well. This was on me, I knew; nothing about him had changed, and I was culpable for trying to make him something that he had never made himself out to be.

Now, as we sat down to dinner, he started to tell me a story about the pay-per-view porn that he'd watched on his hotel TV the night before. Russian girls—he explained that he'd chosen Russian girls because he'd been looking forward to seeing me. He seemed not just unashamed, but genuinely enthused by this anecdote. They were so pretty, he said; kawaikatta na, the "na" invested with wistful feeling.

Helplessly, I watched as the hazy forms of the Russian girls floated up faceless in front of me like pale kittens, all thin limbs and blonde fairy princess hair, and as I stared into that vision I wondered how I was supposed to process this, this sense of discomfort, now, when I was here with him for maybe the last time ever. A part of me prayed that it was going to emerge that I'd simply got all of this wrong, our so-called romance. That it was just as he'd always said, and I'd just wanted someone to drink with, and now the illusion would be shattered and I would be radiantly free.

I knew that it wasn't as simple as that. Already I could feel the glimmers of certainty that, whatever this was, it was what I needed right now. Already I could feel myself drawing comfort from the specificity of this need, its acuteness, and the way that it seemed to enable so much blurring. The blurring of facts. The blurring of the very concept of truth and the need to pin things down. I was in love, I was not in love, it was real, it was an illusion, I fancied him, I found him sleazy, it was all true, everything was clumped together, and it didn't really matter at all because here we were in the love hotel and if I looked out the window I could glimpse the painting of the orange tree in fruit on the wall outside.

————

There is a story I once heard from an English-teacher friend about a student of his who'd been desperate to get a job at Tokyo Disneyland. She had spent her years at school and university dreaming of it and had prepared assiduously for the interview, but in the end had not been offered the job and had been disconsolate. "What did you do when you found out?" my friend had asked her, to which she'd replied that the only thing that she could think of to make herself feel better was to get on the Disney Resort Line, the monorail that circulated Disneyland and DisneySea. She'd traveled out to Maihama and ridden the monorail round and round on loop, and after a while she'd finally begun to calm down. I remember how incredulous I felt when my friend had told me that story, sure that such behavior could only make a person feel worse. But after a while of imagining her looking down at Disneyland spread out beneath her from the Mickey Mouse–shaped windows, I started to think that I understood the psychology of the choice very well. It was most likely sheer projection, but I imagined the sense of comfort and familiarity flooding her, the security she took in nestling into that, even as she questioned whether she should really be seeking solace from an entity that had just shown it was not going to save her in the way she'd wanted. The more I thought about it, the more it seemed like an animal-like rooting out of warmth, which ran on a separate track to principles, even if in some more stable individual those tracks would converge.

———

We were lying naked on the bed, and I was shivering, and he noticed.

"Let's have a bath," he said. "It'll warm you up."

Poka poka ni naru yo, is what he really said, with poka-poka the word for the toasty warm feeling that springs up from taking a bath. I don't know if I could have defined it as such before he said it, but when he did I knew it instantly. *Why the hell have I not been learning Japanese from you the last six months?* was the thought that ran through my head, and that was a sign that I was now fully on his side. Maybe it was just that the sex was out of the way, that I didn't have to think about it anymore, that we could just be people now, and that was what I'd wanted. In divesting him of his desire, I'd made him safe.

And thus I discovered the third thing that made a love-hotel room different from a regular hotel room of this size: the bath was not the usual square kind, but long and big enough to accommodate two. I got in and he slipped in behind me, wrapped his arms around me, and then it happened. Without warning, the world fell away from me, and I was floating in something like total peace, cut from time, happy for this moment to go on forever and ever, happy to die, happy for all the clichés to rain down on me and for me to swallow them all in an everlasting gulp.

Was this just poka-poka writ large, I wondered. Was this what happened when you were cold and you took a bath with someone you loved, or was there more to it than that: was this feeling here because I'd been cold, not just today, in late December, but for much longer? I didn't like the idea that suffering and saving made what Y and I had better—in fact, didn't like the idea that they were a part of it at all, but I found it hard to deny that they had been an integral piece from the start. He was the only person I'd ever been with who had offered to protect me. It was pathetic, and it was true. I could barely believe that I could just let the Russian girls slip from my mind, that my need was that acute, but there no longer seemed much point in denying that either. I felt, for the moment, warm to the bone, and all the sleaziness dissolved away.

¶ kiri-kiri: the sound of the small sharp dark piercing feeling, or not loving anime as much as you should

THERE IS A WOMAN AT my Zumba class whom I have been admiring for a while. Not only does she know all the routines by heart, but when she dances her limbs fill with a tremendous lightness, and she throws her head back in pleasure, as if she were in her early teens and not her fifties. This week, we get chatting for the first time. We talk about how amazing this class and the teacher are, and then somehow we slip into talking about our daily lives, how it is we are able to attend class on a weekday morning. I'm a freelancer, I say, and she asks me what I do. When I tell her, her face lights up.

"Oh, my son loves Japan!" she says, her voice soaring. "He's been studying Japanese, all by himself, and he went there recently actually for the first time, and he said he just felt immediately at home there, you know really comfortable. I mean with him it's mostly the, the, the—"

My brain silently fills in the next word: anime.

"The animation and so on, you know he's really into technology. I mean he's only seventeen, you know so who knows what is going to happen. But it does seem like, you know, a real thing for him."

"Right," I say, and I nod. "That's great."

Sometimes at times like these, what fills my head is the things that I do not and could not ever say. For example: "You have no idea how many stories I've heard exactly like that one!" Or: "You know, even though I'm generally reluctant to admit the existence of 'types' among people, I'm often shocked by the parallels that exist between the kind of young men who like anime and all things Japanese, to the extent that I sometimes struggle to believe that a group of people with such intensely similar interests are in fact individuals." Certainly I do not say: "And what would you like to bet that he ends up marrying a Japanese woman and becomes an academic teaching the world about Japanese culture while she gives up her job to bring up his children?" But even if these things flicker through my mind, I'm not anywhere near as rageful as any of that makes me sound.

In fact, if anything, what I feel in this particular moment is something like envy, for this son of hers that I've never met. I understand that taking refuge in Japan and being shielded from the demands of full adulthood is a privilege offered to predominantly white, educated, Anglophone men, because they are deemed the most desirable that the world has to offer; that it feeds off power relations that date back to the American occupation and beyond, and which hew closely to the colonial paradigm even if there are important differences (and even if Japan also has a history of colonialism of its own to reckon with); and that even leaving all of this aside, this Peter Pan status is not something I am interested in. And yet I can't help but look at the sort of person who feels "immediately" comfortable in Japan and wish that I had felt like that, not only because it might validate the way I've dedicated a lot of my life to the country, but because the security of that sensation in itself feels like something I would love to experience.

For the record, this is not just a matter of liking or not liking anime, even if that is its most noticeable external manifestation; ultimately it's a lot bigger than that. What I feel towards Japan fluctuates, but even during my most enamored periods the feeling could not have been described in terms of simply "feeling at home" there. The feelings that I've had towards Japan have always been hopelessly ambivalent.

———

These days, it is clear to me that this is no coincidence. After years of therapy, one of the central frameworks I find most useful for understanding aspects of myself and other people is attachment theory, and within such a model, people who relate to others as I do are known as "ambivalent."

A key feature of ambivalent (or anxious) attachment, one of the two insecure attachment styles laid out by John Bowlby when formulating his theory in the sixties, is a tendency towards hypervigilance or "neediness": ambivalent infants perpetually monitor the availability and emotional responsiveness of their caregiver, out of a simmering fear of being abandoned. This forms the polar opposite of the other insecure attachment style, known as avoidant, where infants learn to numb themselves by suppressing emotions of any kind; this tendency develops in childhood and beyond into an aloofness and resolute self-sufficiency, born out of the underlying perception that reliance on people engenders rejection. Both of these "insecure" styles stand in contrast to what is known as "secure" parental attachment, for that blessed group of people (estimated to account for about 55 percent of the population) who grow up feeling comfortable and safe to depend on others, and to be depended on in turn.

I was slightly taken aback when my therapist prescribed me an attachment theory book after our very first online session. Sat in my Osaka flat, hunched over a screen where her severed head hung blurred and spectrally pale, the hour had passed for me with a supernatural rapidity, and I struggled to believe that my therapist could have managed to glean anything about me at all, let alone the nub of my issues. But when I settled down to reading about the traits of the ambivalent personality as it developed throughout the life course, it wasn't long before recognition began to dawn. Here was the person I had tried to suppress in my close relationships from as far back as I could remember—the panicking, manipulative, explosive twin that I did my best to lock in the closet, and who always managed to find her way out. It took me longer to acknowledge to myself the breadth of the repercussions of this; particularly that my "ambivalence" affected not just my behavior in certain situations, but the kinds of people that I was drawn to, and my expectations of what a relationship should deliver. In particular, I remember how scandalized I felt upon discovering that securely attached people tend to find other securely attached people and form secure bonds together, while the two insecure archetypes are drawn magnetically to each other. Now this seems almost predictable enough not to mention, but at the time it seemed radically unfair, like I was looking with open eyes for the first time at a rigged, elitist system, which favored those lucky enough to have grown up in the bosom of safety and stability. And yet, even through my outrage, I could feel the truth of this vision. I'd always known that I'd been attracted to emotionally inarticulate people who lapsed into a kind of distance and coldness that drove me wild; now I came to see that this was not just bad luck, but a kind of inevitability. After all, fear activates the attachment system, and fear and attachment work in synchrony. Through each other, the avoidant and the ambivalent can play out the endless dance of explosion and recoil along the brink of terror.

Thinking on how all of this had affected my life and the choices I'd made, I would find myself drawn back again and again to Japan, and especially to a thought I'd had peripherally in the past but which had always seemed ridiculous—which still seemed ridiculous, in fact, but which now could be formulated clearly. The thought was this: if Japan was a person, it would be male, and it would be avoidant. Japan would be a composed, impassive man, inarticulate and secretive about his feelings. Precisely because they were hidden, those feelings had always seemed to me imbued with a smoldering inner richness. My default assumption, rarely made fully conscious, was that he was waiting for someone to come along and draw out those bright insides, and that I was the person who had been born for that task.

The ridiculousness, of course, lay in the fact that Japan was a nation, which had neither an attachment style nor a gender. Yet it was also undeniable that framing the impression in this way felt helpful for me, and gave certain aspects of my situation a new resonance. Avoidant people have never learned to allow others to depend on them, I heard, and I thought: Japan. Or, at the very least, Japan didn't want *me* as a dependent. It came to me that the rapport Japan and I had could be boiled down to the linear, repetitive dynamic as attachment theory described it: me returning, time and time again, like a wave washing up to shore, for comfort that I was barred from receiving. It felt crazy to admit to myself that I was in some sense extending to a place my general pattern of interpersonal relations, but overriding that sense was one of things falling into place. My instincts had been real, I had been having an imaginary human relationship with this place, and like every other relationship in which I'd found myself up until that point, it was like a constant treading between two poles. The thrill of the attention, and the cold, wracking feeling of having been shut out. Abandonment, redemption, repeat.

———

One of the things I found the most challenging in therapy was being asked to describe specific feelings in a physical way— *what is it like, to feel abandoned?* When I tried to move in closer to the feeling, I couldn't make out its shape at all. It was like a shy plant, its leaflets recoiling from my touch. It was the coldness and the darkness of being untouchable, a feeling that turned in on itself and pushed the feeler away. I knew what real hurt, real rejection, felt like when it came—although I avoided it like the plague, I had always found something strangely comforting about its searing, all-body quality. This was very different to that. This was more like a fear of the fear, which can only be seen from the corner of the vision, never scrutinized directly.

Sitting in front of my therapist, groping around for the right words, I sometimes think about how I wish there was a way of avoiding descriptive language altogether. How I wish I could just pull it out and hold it out in my hands and say, here, look, it's this. I know that this isn't how our words work. Yet for some reason, Japanese occasionally does better at sustaining me in the delusion that this is what I am doing with my language. Used on its own as a one-word sound-sentence, a Japanese mimetic often feels more like a simple, direct naming of a particular feeling than anything I can think of in the English repertoire.

Here it is, then: kiri-kiri. "The state of feeling a sharp, stabbing pain," defines the dictionary. It's not that we don't have the words for this in English—we can say "the stab" or "the cold, piercing feeling" or "the sudden hole inside"— but to me at least, none of them have this sense of being a live feeling that can be cupped in the hands. Anyone who has watched Takashi Miike's *Audition* will likely remember this word from the scene where the protagonist's girlfriend sticks innumerable needles into his body, crooning in a child-lulling voice, "kiri-kiri-kiri-kiri!" and it's hard here too to imagine what a satisfying English translation might be. I look it up to discover that in the subtitles it was rendered "Deeper and deeper."

For a long time, whether I was there or whether I was away and yearning for it, Japan rewrote my past and became the ultimate site of this kiri-kiri. It was the sick certitude of abandonment and alienation, and the dizzy hope of it being different sometime in the future. It was the darkness and the ache and the romance of perpetual longing for something bigger and better. No sooner was it felt than it folded in on itself, transmuting from visceral feeling into solid conviction that I was bad and undesirable, the understanding I would succeed only by transforming myself. Painful as it was, being in touch with that cycle in such a tangible form somehow felt edifying—like I was doing the real thing. Deeper and deeper.

————

Now here I am, flying back from Japan on Christmas Eve, aged twenty-two. The cabin attendants wear Santa hats, and there is barely anyone on the flight, so I have a row of three seats to myself. When the meal has been cleared away and the drinks trolley has made its final round, after the cabin lights have been lowered and everyone else has fallen asleep or fallen to quietly watching seat-back films tucked up in their blankets, I sneak to the back and ask for another mini-bottle of red wine, adding that I can't sleep without it, but in fact I don't sleep. I sit by the window, listening on loop to the same Japanese break-up song whose lyrics I understand with sufficient ambiguity to give them the perfect degree of tragedy, and I cry.

I feel the kiri-kiri like I've never felt it before, like I've always felt it before. I've left the island, and now I am leaving the archipelago; both times the departure has been my choice, and both times I have still managed to feel shut out. I have failed. I have failed to make them adore me. I say to myself that I will go back, I will learn Japanese properly, I will do it better. Next time, I will feel immediately at home.

¶ gara-gara: the rattling sound the inexplicable makes as it becomes manifest

MAYBE EVERYTHING I WANT TO say can be boiled down to a single joy, which is the joy of the unprompted discovery. *Figuring something out for yourself*, I start to write, then realize how wrong this is because what matters is not who does the figuring but how it is done. What matters is the leap you make, into the arms of the speakers who are there to welcome you, and it never feels like something you do by yourself or for yourself. Like when someone in your Japanese office in London uses a word, gara-gara, which you think you know, which you think means for something to rattle or to be empty, an adjective or adverb or a verb or a stand-alone sound effect, but here he is using it in a form that seems to be a noun, talking about "taking a gara-gara along," and you look up at him quizzically, cock your head, say, "Gara-gara?" and he smiles, stands up from his chair and parades the strip of carpet in front of your desk, one hand gripping the air behind him, a pout coming over his face that is pure fashion, and then you remember that he used to be a cabin attendant and is probably very accustomed to wheeling carry-on luggage around in this way, and now he says it again, proudly, "Gara-gara," as if it were self-explanatory, and there, in that moment, it has become self-explanatory, because a wheely suitcase rattles gara-gara gara-gara as it is dragged across the cobbles and the paving stones, and you will remember him and it and this catwalk forever.

¶ shi'kuri: the sound of fitting where you don't fit

AT SOME POINT, I DECIDED I would try to become a translator. Not long after returning from Japan, I'd found a job at a small London-based Japanese publisher, a job whose title wasn't "in-house foreigner" but might as well have been; my task was to handle anything English-related, and it wasn't long before I was asked to add translating to my writing and editing tasks. At this stage, the translation process was painfully slow, as I had to look up what felt like every other word in the dictionary, and extremely risky, because I had such a scant instinctive grasp of what the Japanese meant overall that I was reduced to cramming all the separate elements into the same thought space and trying to deduce logically what the message must be. Whether in spite of or rather fostered by these hindrances, what I felt during those first few dalliances with translation was not only a thrill and a satisfaction, but also a sense of something I want to term "fate."

Certainly, there were practical factors that came into play in deciding that translating was the line of work for me: I sensed it was a good match for my skill set and was something I could develop a talent for, and it also seemed like a crafty way to ensure I got better at Japanese while still making a living. There was a different kind of pull there too, less reasoned and more immediate. I think of a midwife in one of the first books I translated, who describes being a young girl seeing a cow giving birth and knowing immediately that she "wanted to be in the place where that was happening, always. Even if it meant not sleeping, missing meals, not making money, I wanted to be where the births were." That was how I felt too, except the births I wanted to assist were not of cows or people, but texts. I wanted to be the one ushering them into this world. The signs that I'd feel this way had been there all along—had already shown themselves in a strange determination to keep improving my Japanese, which seemed less a conscious choice and more something that consumed me. Now, sure enough, when I tried translating for the first time, something seemed to click into place. Even through the screen of my profound incompetence, I felt that translation connected me with the current of things.

After a fair amount of further language study through expensive textbooks, I took up a place on an MA that covered both theory and practical translation. Of the nine of us on the Japanese–English arm of the course, two identified neither English nor Japanese as their mother tongue: a Korean and an Italian girl, both slightly younger than I was. This fact astounded me. Even as a native speaker of English, I felt like I was drowning. Translating into Japanese, as we were required to do throughout the first term, was my first experience within an academic setting of being set a task where I felt fully incapable of judging how bad my offerings were.

The homework assignments would take me the entirety of the weekend. I couldn't imagine what it would be like to feel any less of a sense of legitimacy than I currently did.

Clearly the Italian girl was struggling. I found her response admirable, because it seemed to come not from the sort of shame and embarrassment I'm sure I would have been riddled with in her shoes—with which I was already riddled, in fact, about how bad my Japanese was—by which I mean, she made no attempt to hide how difficult it was for her, but didn't complain either. She just put in extraordinary amounts of work and worry, and though the teacher on the course took her aside at one point to say that she was concerned about how she was going to manage, it was evident that the teacher liked her a lot.

Things were very different with J, the Korean girl. Both her English and her Japanese were excellent, and she spoke with a confidence that came from years of successful communication with people. I'm sure that without native competency in either language she must have been at a distinct disadvantage, but she never gave the impression of lagging behind. Her only perceptible shortcoming was with literary language—her studies in Japan had been in something practical, I forget now what, and while I believe her Japanese translation of an NHS leaflet had been relatively decent, when we were asked to render a couple of pages of Margaret Atwood into Japanese, the teacher was unimpressed by her attempt.

Indeed it was clear that our teacher was unimpressed by the Korean girl in general. The teacher was Japanese and softly spoken, though you saw flashes of an unbending, metallic core beneath her reserve. J, on the other hand, was forward, and she expressed herself vocally without self-doubt or modesty; within the teaching environment the teacher fostered, based on the Japanese model, this was behavior that stuck out.

I remember we were discussing the choice of Japanese word for rendering a particular English one, which I have a sense was something like "sighted" or "spotted," when J piped up to voice an objection to the translation that the teacher was endorsing.

"Right. And what did you put, J?" the teacher asked. Her voice carried a coldness that already felt like a rebuke—an impression fostered by the way that instead of defending her choice, she'd reached straight for the counterattack. Calmly, J explained the word she'd chosen, which translated to something similar to "witnessed."

"Hmmm," the teacher said with a frown. "But 'witnessed' is very formal and clinical-sounding in Japanese. It's not the sort of word we use in literature." It was rare for the teacher to be this unequivocal, and it led me to understand that she was wound up by J. That she objected in particular to J's radiant confidence, and above all, her belief in an even-footed discussion—which was to say, her noticeable unwillingness to show at least superficial reverence for the teacher's words irrespective of content, which all of the rest of us exhibited to a greater or lesser extent.

But J was unbothered. Either she didn't sense the barbs lurking beneath the teacher's words or she didn't have any mind to respond to them. "Yeah, I don't know," she began. "I did consider the word that you're suggesting, but I don't know, it just . . . it doesn't sit right with me."

Shi'kuri konai, were her actual words, a set phrase made up of shi'kuri, the mimetic state for something fitting well, and konai, meaning "doesn't come."

"Oh, it doesn't sit right with you," echoed the teacher. She was almost, but not quite, holding J up as a figure of fun; her tone, for those of us sensitive enough to pick up on such niceties, earmarked J's statement as something which itself did not "sit right" within the program of how this interaction should proceed. I felt as though if I tried, I could tune into the teacher's thoughts like a radio channel: they were a diatribe on the arrogance of using this expression in this context when her use of "witnessed" as a translation had already demonstrated beyond any doubt to what extent she was not a native speaker, and was thus far from having a native speaker's right to express a view on what sat right with her and what didn't.

At least as I read it, though, the teacher's repetition had another facet to it. There was something so forceful, so right, so natural about the way that the phrase sat in J's mouth that it had driven the teacher to repeat it. However inappropriate it was for J to be saying shi'kuri konai right then—which depended a lot on whose cultural standards you were judging by—the phrase suited her, and she spoke it with total confidence. It suited her so well that it instantly branded itself into my mind, despite having never heard it before; was expressed in a way (and of course in a context) that I was left in no doubt about what it meant.

At that moment, I found the Korean girl enviable, admirable, a million miles from me—and also, paradoxically, I felt that she somehow symbolized my extremely patchy mastery, even as she far surpassed it. Her shi'kuri konai rang as a kind of battle cry: I have the right to have impressions and feelings about language even when I speak it imperfectly and am not a perfect judge, whatever that is, and I have a right to express those impressions and feelings without shame, and without taking on the shame that others tried to thrust on me. For the most part, acting that way didn't feel like something I felt capable of doing for myself, but very occasionally, it popped out when I wasn't expecting it to: a little flash of bravura.

From that day on, I began to use shi'kuri, and when I did, I always thought of J. Mostly, of course, I used it in far less controversial settings, but very occasionally when saying it or other words, I found I could channel her bolshiness, and that felt very good.

¶ hi'sori: the sound of being a masochist, or having an unrealizable dream of which you can't let go, or subconsciously aspiring to a form of life governed by discipline, quietude, and an absence of sticky emotions

I AM NEARING THE END of translating an encyclopedia of extinct animals. In truth, I haven't translated the whole encyclopedia but just a third, which the agency will use as a sample to present to publishers in the hope of rousing their interest, but it's been a long journey nonetheless, and I feel a sense of satisfaction at having got through it. All that remains for me now are the biographies for the various contributors.

The encyclopedia, whose title I've tentatively translated as *Not Good Enough*, is a wry look at the reasons animals have died out, the sort of book that is ostensibly aimed at children but also has half an eye on making their parents laugh. It's well written, often ingeniously so, and it's been one of the most enjoyable projects I've worked on in a long time. Not so the biographies, though. Maybe bios rarely make for scintillating reading material, but when it comes to tedium, Japanese biographies take the biscuit. Beginning with the author's date and place of birth, they progress to list universities, awards and publications, relentlessly, with a notable absence of any variation in sentence structure. Often I sense a kind of comfort taken in this on the writer's part—a joyful abandonment of any need to be interesting. *These are the facts*, the bios seem to be saying. *It would be immoral to dress them up or subjectivize them in any way.*

I've made my way through a list of proper-noun-rich facts for the book's chief editor, googling this and that as I go, finding the whole thing interminably long, feeling the beginning of hunger pangs, when my eyes fall on the final line: "He likes big cats such as cheetahs and leopards that live unassuming, solitary lives and give their young a strict upbringing."

I feel my breath catch in my throat. Immediately, I check to see that I'm not misreading wildly. That can't be what it says, surely. But apparently it can, because it is. I scroll down to the other biographies—of illustrators, writers, editorial supervisors—and sure enough, at the end of their listed accolades, they all state their favorite animal, plus a reason. Still, this man is the only one with anything half as shocking as this. A strict upbringing, I mouth to myself, shaking my head. What a freak. Who on earth revels in the severity shown by big cats towards their children? Also, who is so assured in their sadistic tendencies that they're happy to broadcast them to the world, and in a professional context too?

From inside the hush that has descended across my desk, I can feel my heart beating. The bio has managed to catch me off guard, and there is a certain thrill to that. A thrill, too, in the way that this is not only something I wasn't personally expecting, but not something English speakers would say. We would make it cuddlier or we would wrap it up in irony, because stripped of decoration like this, it reads as bluntly and unnervingly confessional. But it's not just that which is niggling me.

I start to think about this man, his feeling towards the lions for which we don't have a word in English half as good as the Japanese akogare, which stands somewhere between idolizing, yearning, aspiring, and fetishizing, but is maybe closest of all to a crush with the lustful elements removed. The place where wanting-to-be and wanting-to-be-with seamlessly elide.

So this man has a big cat crush, I formulate to myself; he admires them for their discipline, their grace, their savagery. And I mull over how the mimetic he used, hi'sori, which I've provisionally translated as "unassuming," has something painfully beautiful about it, like decades of silence folded in on themselves. I start to think that maybe my sadist accusation was too hasty. Mightn't he long for the lions because he feels a lack of those qualities in himself? Maybe he wishes he'd been brought up by a big cat. Wouldn't that make him more of a masochist?

However I extend my tentacles of thought towards him, I can't frame the problem in a way that makes the mystery disappear. His final line swirls around inside me, creating an uneasiness. I'm done with work for the day, so I get up, change into shorts and trainers, and head out for a run. On my way to the park, I open up the dictionary app on my phone and look up the mimetic word from the sentence: hi'sori.

Hi'sori, a word common enough that I hadn't needed to look it up while translating. Or at least, I hadn't felt I'd needed to at the time, but with it still churning over in my mind, I want to check I haven't missed anything that might help me in some way. Applied to a place, the Japanese-to-English dictionary informs me now, the word hi'sori means "hushed" or "deserted," while when referring to a person, it yields a different set of English words: "inconspicuously," "modestly," "quietly." Hi'sori, a relative of the adjective hisoka, meaning secretly, or without catching attention. Taking in these definitions, letting them expand and resonate through my mind, I find a picture emerges for me, richer and fuller than the standard sphere of associations I make with big cats. A life of stealth and elegance, unburdened by a need of company for its own sake; an existence moderated by prudence and discipline; and like a vein running beneath it all, a transcendent understanding of what is truly indispensable.

———

I reach the park gates and I set out running. My course takes me up over a hill, then round and down. I'm tired and I'm marginally hungover and the uphill section is a struggle, but as I near the top something kicks in, and by the time I hit the downhill stretch I'm feeling free, buoyant, and in that newly opened-up window of mental space it comes to me like a bolt: this man is me. Or maybe it's better to say, this man was me. I used to be this man, and I can still feel his traces inside me.

Immediately, the shock and discomfort his biography gave me make a bit more sense. As my feet hit the tarmac one after another, I can remember the buzz of it under my skin: aspiring toward a life form that you will never in a million years attain. The nursing of an unfulfillable dream—except my choice of hi'sori-dwelling entities to idolize wasn't as imaginative as cheetahs or leopards. My big cat was, and maybe will always be, Japan.

¶ beta': the sound of very sticky fingers

I MET D WHILE I was living in Edinburgh, through an online forum for people seeking language-exchange partners. The forum was home to posts from an assortment of peculiar characters, some offering great comic value and others genuinely terrifying, but back in those days, before video chat became ubiquitous, there was still a good number of people who relied on real-life language exchanges for boosting or maintaining their language skills. For a while, I met up every week with a PhD candidate in Scottish literature; I proofread her chapters about fairies in Sir Walter Scott's fiction, and in return, she helped me make the transition from reading passages to reading essays, eventually giving me the courage to tackle my first novel. At some point, though, I realized that I was still lacking for casual conversation, which was how I came to meet up with D one day in the cinema café.

D was thin with a moon-shaped face and shoulder-length hair, and I remember that the day we met she wore a beige trench coat. Her resting expression was one of inscrutable blankness, and her physical gestures, her way of walking, also had a pared-down quality to them. When we greeted each other by the entrance, I sensed a distance from her, which read to me as wariness. Still, we sat down and began to talk, and as we did it came to me that, distance or no distance, we were navigating each other quite well. By the time she looked at her watch and said that she was going to have to go, that two hours had passed, I realized that this was someone with whom it would be possible for me to spend time talking not just for the sake of talking, but because I was interested in what she had to say.

For some time we met weekly at the cinema café and spent an hour speaking each language, but after a while we started to migrate to pubs, and occasionally each other's flats. One day, we met early in the morning and traveled to a seaside town a little way away. We walked along the beach, then sat and had tea and cake in a café. On the train back, she asked me if I wanted to come and have dinner in her flat. After we'd spent the day together, this invitation felt like the ultimate compliment, and represented an understanding that she actually liked me.

Somewhere I perceived D as the shy, graceful, slightly sickly looking girl that as a child and a teenager I had always wanted to be and be friends with at the same time, and never really managed. Now I was managing, and to my delight, the reality was as exciting as the idea of it. It wasn't that we were desperately similar and immediately hit it off: our connection developed in a different, calmer way. The draw wasn't a romantic one, but nonetheless there was a physicality to the way that we were with each other; we spoke of various abstract topics, yet that somehow felt secondary to knowing what the other liked or didn't, was good at and wasn't. This was similar to the kind of con-

nection I'd had with Y, but it was not something I'd experienced with anybody else I could think of, certainly from
the UK; there was a careful yet unembarrassed corporality
which felt decidedly un-British to me. It felt somehow of a
piece with Barthes's description of arranging a rendezvous
in Japan without a shared language in which to execute
the transaction:

> To make a date (by gestures, drawings on paper, proper
> names) may take an hour, but during that hour, for a
> message which would be abolished in an instant if it were
> to be spoken (simultaneously quite essential and quite
> insignificant), it is the other's entire body which has been
> known, savoured, received, and which has displayed (to
> no real purpose) its own narrative, its own text.

Of course, my friendship with D was different to that.
Having two common languages at our disposal rather than
none, we were able to get to the bottom of each other's meaning pretty well. Yet I want to say that there was something
about training our eyes as we did on language that allowed
this physicality between us to grow. Maybe it was simply
that all the repetitions and clarifications, all the consciousness and clunkiness which came with the process of trying to
deepen our knowledge did away with the demand and even
the hope for everything to run smoothly, or for our language
and the selves it stood between to be invisible. The nature of
our connection made it ever so easy for me to memorize her
turns of phrase—although "memorize" is perhaps a misleading choice of word, because her words lodged in my head

without any effort on my part. I liked to flick through the stash I kept in there, remembering and emulating her intonation and gestures.

————

Eventually, D and I moved to London independently of each other and became housemates, and one day, were having a conversation about sweets and their names in our respective languages. Giant gobstoppers, I remember talking about; how I'd pleaded with my mum to let me get one, but found when I had it that it wasn't much good, because you couldn't get it in your mouth, so you just had to suck away at the side, never making much of an indentation.

"We had lollies that seemed to last forever too, that you'd suck and suck and suck and not get anywhere."

"Like push pops?" I said. "I remember those."

"Yeah, they had a little pushy bit at the bottom," she said. "And when you were sucking on them all the juice would seep downwards and your fingers and wrists would be like—" And with this, D pulled a face that rightfully belonged in a horror film, her eyes suddenly enormous, her irises swimming in white, and her mouth just as huge as she pronounced, "BETAAAA." She dragged her right hand down her left wrist, then repeated the gesture with the opposite hands to show the unstoppable tide of sugary gunk leaking down towards her elbows.

I had not heard this word before, at least not in that exact formulation. I knew the reduplicated form "beta-beta"— the state of stickiness, but also the state of two people being all over each other, used a lot in both meanings—and so I could guess what this meant. I could also figure out that this singular—or linguistically put, non-reduplicated—form suggested something less continuous than beta-beta, an isolated instance of the utmost stickiness. Remembering this now, I think of the repulsion on D's face, and also what borders on delight—or is it just my delight?—in the untold overwhelm of that one-off physical moment: being covered in mud or drenched in rain, or having the stickiest hands in the world.

This usage fitted in so perfectly with everything that I knew about D: her sensitivity to her body, her awareness of its boundaries, how careful she was not to touch a single surface on public transport ("Have you seen how many people just *openly* pick their noses?"), how she would wash and gargle the moment she got in the door, how it seemed beyond her ever to be sticky in her relationships with anybody, but how she attempted from behind all that space to share the experience of that body and the ecstasy of that moment when it does, in fact, get communicated, despite it all; and how, although I knew such thoughts were not permitted, this put me in mind of early-period Wittgenstein, and all the mystery and mysticism and difficulty around communicating anything with meaning: "What we cannot speak about we must pass over in silence." Except it wasn't true that we couldn't speak about it, because we had bodies and we had faces and we had onomatopoeic language, and that was more than enough.

¶ pera-pera: the sound of spouting forth, or a bullish market

"ARE YOU FLUENT IN JAPANESE, THEN?" I cannot say how many times I've been asked this question, but certainly enough that I should know the answer. And in a way I do—I know what the answer should be. I should hold my head high and answer in the affirmative, not only because I am a translator and there is an understanding that translators must be fluent in the languages they translate, but also because, when described verbally, I do most of the things that fluent people do. To wit: I speak, on occasion, at length, without pause, to certain people, in Japanese. In some not-too-renegade sense of the word, I am fluent. Yet there are also contexts where I can barely articulate even simple sentences, or miss basic utterances spoken at natural speed; there are cases where people switch to English to talk to me, or look at me with a disdain that seems to quash any prospect of ever labeling myself fluent. With all this in my head, I find that more and more, when I go to reach for a standard definition of fluency, it slips globbily through my fingers, impossible to hold on to.

Nor can my difficulties be resolved simply by adopting a more personal, inward-facing definition of fluency oriented around how it feels for me, because how it feels is equally unstable. There are times when my Japanese seems to rush out from deep inside me, if not perfect in its construction (almost never perfect in its construction), then at least moving through my muscles in a way that feels nuanced and warmly, uniquely mine; times, too, when I don't notice that I'm speaking "another language." And there are others when my Japanese possesses not a grain of interiority, and seems instead like a set of vocabulary, clauses, and collocations which I've tried my utmost to affix to myself so that they won't fall off, as part of a project that seems tinged with both vanity and quixotic absurdity. I picture these words like senjafuta, the pilgrimage stickers with names of the worshippers which one finds plastered at dissecting angles across the insides of the grand gates at temples and shrines, an unexpected burst of punky calligraphic chaos in what is otherwise such an austere and orderly environment. Whenever I'm standing at one of these gates, looking up at the spill of senjafuda, I try to imagine the pilgrims who pasted them there, using some mysterious implement of a great length, both devoted and somehow vainglorious in their attempt to stake a claim, albeit a very tiny one, upon something so enormous and unassailable.

Perhaps it is the fate of language-learners to seesaw between these two states: between thinking that learning is not only something doable but something we are actually doing, and thinking we will never ever get there, with which side we fall on depending on really nothing more than how high our stakes of confidence are running. We are like stock markets, surging up so joyfully when there is enough optimism to be had, only to come spiking back down again when the belief runs out. I think of the time back in school when I first learned about stock markets, in the context of the Wall Street Crash, and how I found it unbelievable that the variable determining the output of our financial system was publicly acknowledged to be something as psychological, as interior as confidence. These days, I understand better that the same is true of almost everything. I know better, too, than to conceive of confidence as a purely internal state, and this is definitely true in how it applies to learning a foreign tongue. To learn a language to the level of fluency, to enter into the innermost echelons of a new cultural context and assimilate its ways is a gargantuan task, and how we fare has as much to do with the levels of support and encouragement we receive from the various communities in which we participate as with our "baseline" levels of self-esteem (which in themselves could be viewed to a certain degree as internalized communities of a historical nature: the degree of support and the type of responses we have been given in the past, filtered through the lens of our development, perceptions and body of memories).

In other words, some people are set up better to learn than others, and I often find myself wondering whether a key factor in determining linguistic success is the ability to rise to the demands of the occasion, in a similar way to the athlete or the actor. Ultimately, speaking a language is not only a performance, but a performance where a single mistake can herald the end of you if you don't have the technique or the mental resilience that day to find your way around it. You need a word, you look inside yourself and don't find it, and the game is over: it's not there and there's nothing to be done about it. In this realm of showmanship, no consultation of dictionaries is permitted. Whether you detect a glimpse of distrust in the other person's eyes or whether the condemnation comes entirely from yourself, you are nonetheless ousted as a result from the community of rightful speakers. There is now a demonstrable difference between you and the competent, natural ones. The question is just whether or not you can bounce back.

———

This dog-eat-dog reality behind fluency, where you can be proven guilty at any given moment with a single word, was not what I imagined in my fantasies before I had set off down the path towards it. Back then, I would say, my concept of fluency was all the more comfortingly firm for being utterly unexamined. I didn't know exactly what it would feel like, I don't know now if I imagined it as a permanent sense of elation, or just a liberation from having to think about being inarticulate all the time, but I certainly believed it would be stable and safe. Slowly it dawned on me that this way of thinking about things was thoroughly misguided, and now even the words seemed to reiterate my misunderstandings to me.

For instance, the vernacular word for "fluent" in Japanese is pera-pera. It was a word I learned early because every cautious attempt I made in Japanese would be greeted by the kids at school with "Ooo, nihongo pera-pera!" (Ooh, you're fluent in Japanese!). This they would invariably say in the specific accent used to imitate gaijin—an accent that most Western people working with kids in Japan will have encountered whether or not they realize it, regardless of the strength of their native twang or what that twang sounds like. To me, though, the way the children said this particular phrase, pera-pera, in their pseudo-Western accent made it sound like Italian, a language that I have tried and failed to speak on multiple occasions. Failed because I felt that forming its words and rhythms demanded more emphasis, more conviction than my hesitant language-learning persona was capable of. And pathetic as I knew it was, those kids speaking in that pseudo-Italian drawl while ostensibly imitating me gave me the fear. *This is how you will seem to us when you are fluent in Japanese*, they seemed to be saying—*an overconfident, smarmy foreigner.* At the same time, the association with Italian was also signaling to me: *This is something that you cannot do.*

As I came to know more about Japanese, I found out that pera-pera wasn't just the state of being fluent in another language, as I'd supposed; it was also the mimetic word for speaking at full speed. You might naturally use it in sentences that would translate as "He was spouting all kinds of nonsense," or "She was talking at full pelt." Once again, I felt a burst of disproportionate dismay, because what this intimated to me was that I would never be a truly pera-pera person because I am not one in English. Because I find speaking difficult and painful, a lot of the time; because I am not a confident talker.

―――――

Nonetheless it would be a misrepresentation to present myself as a sad squeaky mouse by whose side confidence has never sat: there were times when I could speak, and times when I would clam up, and the gulf between these two states felt extreme. It was extreme in comparison to people around me, and it was extreme just as a thing to live with. At first I imagined that which side I fell on was close to random. It was only once I began to tune in to the contexts in which I felt okay speaking and those in which I didn't that I started to understand more about located confidence. I think here about Wittgenstein, and the suburbs of our language of which he spoke:

> Our language may be seen as an ancient city: a maze of little streets and squares, of old and new houses, and of houses with additions from various periods; and this surrounded by a multitude of new boroughs with straight regular streets and uniform houses.

As linguistic newcomers, we are likely to be familiar only with one or two regions of the city and the most intuitive way to define these geographical regions would be in terms of topics. Typically, if a language learner has come to the language through trips abroad, for instance, they might be able to navigate adeptly restaurant and hotel speak, but be slightly lost outside these contexts. A child might be at home conducting a conversation about a picture-book or a farm, for instance, but not speaking about politics or cooking a meal. English conversation schools in Japan advertise "business English" classes, wielding the term with an assurance that bothers me, as if it were an independently defined suburb—as if people within the business sphere only speak of contracts, photocopies, and inventories. And yet, there are indeed jargons, conversation types, vocabularies, and models for transactions that are specific to business contexts.

I started to wonder whether we shouldn't also try to offer

a more emotionally driven definition for those "regions" of language to which speakers are accustomed. To acknowledge, for example, that linguistic competence buds from a place of being listened to, facilitated, made comfortable, rooted for, and that this applies to the child but to the language learner too. That it comes from wide-reaching communities but far smaller ones too, where a community can at its smallest comprise a single other person.

Ultimately, my inquiries into what made me fluent and what caused me to clam up led me to people: those who exude an atmosphere of judgment, and those who create an atmosphere where one feels listened to. I think of how I owe so much of my development to a few people from this latter class of backers, without whom I would never have got to a stage where I can sometimes, if need be, assert myself for a short time even when faced with someone who thinks very little of my capabilities. These are the people who are not overly attached to the shiny facade of the performance, who don't require a flawlessly smooth interface, and who are not scared off by awkwardness or discernible effort and struggle. It feels to me that often the presence or absence of these people is the factor that determines on which side I fall on the fluency question—of whether I can temporarily join the ranks of the pera-pera.

¶ uwaa: the sound of the feeling that cannot be spoken

THE HANDFUL OF TIMES I'VE seen an English-language article referencing Japanese onomatopoeia, it's almost always in relation to the sound for silence: shin, or shiiiiin. I'm struck each time by the apparent reverence and romanticism extended to this by Anglophone journalists as an alien and somehow bewildering concept, since conceptually I don't think it's so far removed from words like "hush" or "schtum." That said, I will readily admit that "shin" is far more prevalent as a straight-up sound effect, particularly in contexts like manga, where the long midbar of an enormous しーん is often found traversing the awkward space between two characters, or spreading through an entire room to indicate the voluminousness of the silence. In fact, the manga SFX dictionary I consult doesn't even list "hush" as an option for translating shin, showing instead *stare*, *silence*, and *frozen*. In that they are less likely to be confused for imperatives, I suppose these are better options but they still read to me as a little forced. One could argue that this very awkwardness points towards a kind of untranslatability that serves as proof that shin is special, but I don't think this holds, because in fact a proximate level of awkwardness seems to cling onto so many of the SFX translations: *cozy*, *menace*, *flustered*, *throw up*, etc. The truth is, such awkwardness is kind of inevitable, because there are lots of situations where Japanese mimetics are used in which we simply wouldn't use a sound effect in English.

I'm not going to talk anymore about shin, but I do want to talk about the linked phenomenon of words that give sound to non-sound, words which touch upon the difficulties of sound. Specifically, I want to talk about finding a man who had killed himself.

This isn't an easy story to tell, and I have debated many times about whether I should be telling it, either to people I know or here on paper; I have wondered repeatedly whether it is mine to impart. It's been years now since it happened, and I would like to say with assurance that in that time, I have thought a lot about the damaging power of silence in perpetuating shame, isolation, and disconnection, and come to believe that passing on your subjective version of events is in many ways the most respectful and responsible way of being in the world. Yet it is also true that when I think back to that day and everything that happened afterwards, I feel a veil of silence drawing over me, a silence with an organic, all-enveloping quality to it like a forest, and I am tempted to think that I'm bound by it, that it's that which is demanded of me. Paradoxically, it's the darkness of that draw to silence which has impelled me to try and speak of it.

After many years of being away, I was back in Japan, teaching English in a small, semi-rural city somewhere between Tokyo and Osaka, famed for its beef. Like most of the famous Japanese beefs, Matsusaka-gyū was extravagantly

fatty, a mottled white meat known by the name shimofuri—
"a dusting of frost." This picturesque-sounding phenomenon
was achieved by putting the cows on an intensely high-calorie
diet, which allegedly involved feeding them beer to stimulate
their appetite and massaging them with shōchū to make their
flesh softer. Despite living in the region for a year, I saw one
of these beer-fed cows only once, right at the very end of my
time in the region, when a student of mine gave me a tour
of her village. We pulled up outside a slightly ramshackle
shed, inside which stood a short, fat black cow, hunkered
down among the straw in the dim of the back of the shed.
When it saw us it backed farther into the darkness, its white
eyes gleaming with trepidation. For some reason it had never
occurred to me that the cows would be kept alone, and while
I could recognize that to some the sight might have betokened
great care and attention, it seemed to me too unspeakably sad
to properly face. With the simple nondescript shed, the whole
scene seemed timeless, and I could imagine it rendered by a
seventeenth-century Dutch master.

Matsusaka had paddy fields and ramshackle houses and
endless bridges painted in pale blues or bright reds or oranges,
and a river running through it over which rows of billowing
cloth carp with gaping mouths were strung out in time for
Children's Day on May 5. I found it lovely, especially in the
beginning, but it was not a tremendously exciting prospect
for a visitor unless your visitor enjoyed aimless wandering for
hours on end. So when D, the Japanese friend I had met in
Edinburgh and who had since moved back to Tokyo, came
to visit me for the weekend, we decided to take the train to
Toba, a port town in the same prefecture known for its fish-

ing and its beautiful views. In Toba Bay was Mikimoto Pearl Island, where women dressed head to toe in white dived for pearls that were fashioned into jewelry to be worn by rich ladies. There was an aquarium, whose website promised dugongs and rare giant isopods as well as the usual sea lions and dolphins, and which we were due to visit later that day. But we had decided—I think in fact it had been my suggestion—to begin by climbing a mountain that I'd read about in the guidebook.

The mountain was densely wooded and had various paths up it, but as a British person to whom the word "mountain" still connoted a daylong expedition, the fact that it took only twenty minutes to climb meant it was hard to conceive of as anything other than a hill. We followed the main path up and emerged into a small clearing that gave on to the sea. There was barely anybody around, but another couple who seemed like fellow tourists came up at an opportune moment and we asked them to take a photograph of us. It wasn't exactly anticlimactic, because neither of us had had very high expectations, but there was something that felt small-scale about it, the peace and comfort that comes from visiting a remote village and giving yourself up to its limited delights, of scalping all that there is and getting the most of it, which was such a different mentality to visiting Kyoto or Tokyo, whose attractions felt boundless and overwhelming. We turned back, deciding to head into Toba and see the port we'd just looked out across, and as we were making our way down, we ran across a wooden signpost that pointed to an Observation Deck. How was that different to the place from which we'd just come? Neither of us knew, but since we had time and energy, we decided to go and see that too, circling round and round up the hill, and as I came out at the top, I saw the figure of someone hanging from a tree. I saw him from the back: the black ball of a head, white expanse of shirt, a length of yellow-and-black striped rope.

When I think about people unable to respond to emergencies unfolding in front of them, I imagine them immobilized by the rapidity of the situation, but this was the opposite. The scene was a flat, stock image suspended in front of me, dislocated from the temporal and spatial context in which I'd come upon it. It was so stationary that I found it impossible to counter its stillness with action. I stopped, and looked, and then I turned back and looked at D. Her response was immediate, and she broke the spell.

"Yadayadayadayadayadayada," she began, like a chant, *no, no, no, no, no, no*, shaking her head, doing everything she could to magic away what had appeared in front of her. This reaction of hers, the intensity that I sensed from it, hit me more than what I was seeing. With its colors so crisp in the morning sun, I could only see the scene as some kind of museum exhibit, a film set. I opened my mouth and said, in my slowly dawning panic: "It's not a joke, is it?"

This strikes me now, possibly struck me as soon as I'd said it, as a bizarre and alarmingly childlike thing to say, but at the time, it felt like the only means I had at hand of crossing over from the pool of sensations in which I was immersed to a shared linguistic world that included D.

"No, it's not a joke," my friend said, and she returned to her chanting, turned away from the scene.

A few minutes later she was on the phone to the police. I

was aware that it should have been me who was speaking to
the police, that she wasn't really in a state to do it, but this was
Japan, where a Japanese person was always the right person
to do everything. In a sense, this was probably judicious right
now: I'd never phoned the emergency services before, and I
didn't even know what was the right, polite, official way to
say that someone hanged themselves.

And so I stood there, listening, and just as she was beginning to sound calmer, I heard her let out a cry.

"No!" she said down the phone, almost hyperventilating,
"No, we can't take him down, we can't take him down."

Take him down, take him down—the Japanese word,
in her mouth, orosenai, orosenai, had something nightmar-
ish about it. It stormed through into my daze and planted
in there a single thought: What if he was still alive? I still
hadn't seen the man's face, so it seemed like a distinct possibility. What if I was about to let this man die out of cow-
ardice and squeamishness? For the first time it occurred
to me that however still this scene might seem, it might
actually call for immediate action. He might be breathing
his last as I let the time run over me like water, and so
while D stayed on the phone I stepped onto the flat surface at the top of the mountain and walked over to where
the body was hanging, my heart a percussion instrument
in my chest. The peak of the mountain was shaped like a
thin cone, the path encircling it all the way up in a way you
might imagine the top of all mountains to be if you'd never
encountered one outside of fairy stories, and the rope had
been tied deftly to a tree branch that was jutting out over
the side. The weight of the body had pulled the rope taut

as a rod. Without a knife, I realized, it would be literally impossible to release him.

Just then I heard D's voice behind me, hysteria weaving through it like a shiny thread. I turned back.

"I wanted to check," I told her. "That we couldn't get him down."

"No," she shook her head, shook it like she was trying to shake the reality away, and I knew with confidence that "orosenai" on the phone had not meant physically, but something else. She had meant: taking him down is not within the realms of my possibility at the moment. I still wonder, pointlessly, what I would have done if I could, actually, have got him down. Whether I'd have had the guts. Whether I'd have felt in that moment that it was right to do so.

In order to wait for the emergency services, we moved a little down the path and leaned against a big tree positioned to its side. After not too long a time, we heard sirens, and then stirrings from deep in the bellows of the mountain. Descending a bit farther, we could see flashes of figures in dark boiler suits with reflective strips around their chests carrying a huge stretcher. We started calling out to them, eventually moving halfway down so as to lead them all the way back up. At some point when we were nearly there I looked up, trying to gauge how far we had to go until the top, and there he was, right in front of me, and I saw his face for the first time, gray-beige in color.

I had never seen a dead person before. I suspect that even if I had, seeing him there it would have felt as if I hadn't. At the top of the hill I had seen his back and thought him an exhibit, a piece of artifice, a sudden incursion of the human world into this natural space, but from this angle he seemed not-of-this-world in a different way, the still gray of him strangely of a piece with the muted greens and browns of the mountains, as if nature were already claiming him as one of her own. Yet his expression, his slumped head, were all taken straight out of a scary film. Slowly, slowly, and then fast, it dawned on my struggling, panic-weary brain that this was exactly the sort of reality that scary films were based on.

Perhaps the standard instinctual response at a moment of crisis like this would have been to cry out, at least register in some way what I'd seen, but my instinct was to remain silent. All my mental blood flow was directed to digesting this internally—I was back to being the wordless child who'd been stung by a wasp at a friend's house and was too bewildered and embarrassed to say anything to anyone. And if I was back to childhood, it didn't escape me either that D was playing my parent, here, wavering on the verge of an outburst of some terrible emotion; the last thing that I wanted to do was alert her to the face of the dead person, to plunge her into hysteria that I would then have to deal with.

The men whose jackets announced they were from the fire department set to work, instructing us to wait around; as the ones who had discovered the body we would have to make statements to the police when they got here. Once again we walked farther down the hill, stood with our backs to the large tree trunk that marked a turning in the path. Now I told D: I'd seen his face, and it was alright. It wasn't clear to me what "alright" meant in this context, but I knew what I was doing with this sentence. I was making an offering to calm. There is nothing more that is ghastly, I was telling the two of us—an entity that had taken a more solid form than I remembered it having before.

After a while, a man came down the mountain, a policeman this time, who must have joined the firefighters at some point. The man was dead, he told us. From the onset of stiffening in his body, they could tell that he had hanged himself early this morning. After seeing his face, I'd known he was dead; now a part of me felt something like relief at the knowledge that even if I had by some miracle managed to get him down, I couldn't have saved him. I didn't have to feel responsibility. The other part latched onto the word for early morning: sōchō. Now that word had a new definition for me, knocking the other, more standard one, to a lower position. Sōchō: the time at which he had killed himself. Even months, years later, people would say to me, "I got up early in the morning to go running," and I would think of him, the man whose name we never came to know, and feel a lump in my throat. I would imagine his trip up there. Would the sun have been up or not quite yet? The rope in his pocket? He had no bag.

Beautiful places like these, the policeman said, places with a view—that was where people wanted to do it. He seemed utterly unaffected, as I suppose you would be, or would have to be, after so long in this job. A short, stocky, friendly man, with an animated way of speaking. Everyone knew how high the suicide rates were in Japan, the widespread problem of people jumping in front of commuter trains, the "Blue Monday" phenomenon where suicide rates would surge when people returned to work after the weekend. When I was first back from Japan, I had tried to write a novel centering around a suicide; now I could see how little it was that I knew about anything. It wasn't shame I felt exactly, but a sudden sense of wide-open humility.

Would we like to see him? the policeman asked. We looked at each other, said nothing and so he went on: We recommend it, people find it helps. And to my surprise D nodded, said she would, and so we went up to the so-called Observation Deck, which wasn't a deck at all, but just a spread of earth. Now, laid out on the ground, the rope cut away from his neck, he looked different from when I'd looked up at him—he looked like a man. He looked like a person who you saw on the train, who had a job, who didn't smile, who meant no harm, who didn't find it easy to talk about his feelings. A meter away sat the machine they'd brought with them with which they'd have tried to resuscitate him if that had been possible.

The policeman took us to the side and began to interview us. Maybe ten minutes previously, D had said to me by the trunk of the tree, "I think I'm going to be quite traumatized by this," and my response had been, "Really?" Such was the degree to which I was numb, but also feeling an almost absolute divide between what was going on in the inside world and the outside one where language happened. After standing over him laid out on the earth, after seeing him become a person within history, the numbness was starting to unthaw. I tried to stay calm as I was speaking, but describing in Japanese what had taken place an hour previously felt a Herculean task. I spoke, but my voice was cracking, and it was no longer clear to me which details were important and which weren't. Eventually I got to the end of what felt like my account, and the policeman smiled at me.

"Okay," he said, pencil poised on his paper, "so you were

coming up the hill, going round and round in a circle, and then you looked up and went, 'Uwaa!'"

It seemed to me I could feel my insides turning white. I knew that this man was, either consciously or not, attempting to make my experience manageable for me. He could sense, I am sure, the mist of fear that was hanging over me and D, and was being friendly, and kind, in the manner of a hospital worker, a nursery school teacher, guiding us steadily back into a world which was not laced with traumatic discoveries. He was providing us with a normality within which to couch our experiences—experiences that he dealt with, I imagined, on an almost daily basis.

Yet rarely in my life have I felt a greater discomfort at being paraphrased. Barely, only just barely had I managed to eke out what it was that had happened, and it had been immediately recast, into what I felt was the anime adaptation, the manga version of my story. Uwaa: the sound that you make when something shocking happens. I enter it now into an online Japanese/English dictionary, and elicit the following list of translations:

> *aaaagh*
> *yikes*
> *oops*
> *eep*
> *wow!*
> *ew*
> *oh my God*
> *whoof*
> *wow-ees*

ew

man

whoah

gee

gosh

goodness

zowie

I said nothing. I did not say yes and I did not say no, I stared at the policeman, again silent in the face of this thing that was happening inside, which I had no way of carrying into a world shared by him.

Again and again as I learned Japanese I had been struck by its expressive possibilities; now, more viscerally than ever before, I felt its banality, its normalizing abilities, and how oppressive those things were. No longer was this about the delight of dressing up my thoughts and feelings in new guises: now there was a feeling which it seemed very important that I hung on to, and I didn't want it stolen away from me by language that smoothed, made communal, made palatable and comprehensible. I felt something I'd experienced before only in English: the sense that if the possibilities for expression were going to misrepresent me so radically, to cartoonify me, then I wanted nothing to do with them.

Now years on, older and wiser and a more proficient speaker, no longer in the grips of shock and a more underlying sense of linguistic insufficiency, I know better that this is just how language works in this context. The policeman was not attempting to describe what it was that I felt, the feelings that moved in me and the associations I made, but rather to storyboard the situation. He was doing this not to supersede my version, but so he had what he needed for his report. And it is a simple fact that a storyboard, in Japanese, is far more likely to contain sound effects.

Yet I still can't bear to think of my feeling at that moment through the lens of that uwaa. To represent the complexity of what I was going through in a single word, and for the word to be that one, felt not only that I was betraying myself, but also betraying the person who'd made me feel that way, and the world that had brought it all about. If it came to that, I would have chosen silence every time.

¶ ba'sari: the sound of nevermore, and how
it comes when you least expect it

THE STORY OF THE MAN on the mountain should have no
epilogue, and yet for me, the episode had a second part. Its
content is of a very different kind, and yet the two lie insepa-
rably beside each other, twins grown together in the womb of
the same memory.

As it happened, D's prophecy of trauma came to loom
larger over us than I imagined, although now I suspect that
lack of imagination on my part was just the effect of some
kind of shock. By the time the police were done with us it
was almost afternoon, and neither of us had a clue what to
do next. We could either carry on with our day of sightseeing
as planned, or return home with nothing to do. Both options
seemed equally awful, but after conferring—as I recall, our
deliberations took place in a deserted bus station—we agreed
that it was better to have some kind of distraction, and so we
decided to stay in Toba. When we arrived at the aquarium
we'd been planning to visit, though, and stood looking up at
the huge poster of a sea lion plastered outside, listening to the
high-pitched strains of the woman doing the dolphin show
carried over to us on the sea breeze, it came to us that entering was impossible. I don't know if either of us could have said

exactly why; entering felt to me cruel and superficial, and the entire place dystopian, but I couldn't have defended any of those impressions. In the end it was D who voiced it: she just couldn't, she said. I felt relief at her certainty, because I would probably have swallowed my distaste and traipsed inside if she'd wanted to, but also a form of panic, and irritation: what would we do instead? We'd decided to stay on here; was she now going to veto every course of action? In the end, though, we found something to do: we got on a bus and visited the Meoto-iwa—the Married Couple Rocks, as they were known in English—a pair of large boulders stationed out to sea and tied together by sacred rope, where people went to pray for luck in love and familial safety. It felt surreal and ridiculous to be there, but at least we were out in the open and not around any animals in tanks and cages.

By the time we returned to Matsusaka it was evening, and D was clear: she didn't want to go back to my flat, she wanted to be out somewhere, so we slipped under the navy noren curtains and inside one of the chain izakaya that dotted the road leading to and from the station. It was only as we slid ourselves along the wipe-down faux-leather banquette in the booth to which we were shown, only as we sat across from each other and looked at each other and let time pool around us that I understood for the first time the reality of what had happened, let that reality assume a coherent form inside my body. That such a thing could happen, I suppose, was a sign that I felt, in some way, protected. I had been dubious about D's plan to stay out, had found the thought of nesting at home more appealing, but now I could understand it better: there was something immensely comforting about the two of us being held there, semi-privately and in near darkness by some larger structure, some abstract body of people. From the speakers emanated an endless looping shamisen melody, sliding up and down and never seeming to go anywhere.

As we began to speak of what had happened, I can remember feeling as though I were talking for the first time ever, and I was genuinely unsure that the words I was voicing would succeed. Perhaps they would describe a reality, in the way that the policeman's summarization of my account had described a reality, but I doubted that I could put words together in a way that would correlate with my version of events. Maybe the problem was that I didn't know what my version of events was, that it was wallowing somewhere in the murky mire of dissociation.

And yet, somehow, we did manage to talk. We didn't touch or lock eyes or move to sit alongside each other as the tears ran down our faces. Still, the feeling of something passing between us was unmistakable, and it grew out of a knowledge that we were the only two people in the world who could possibly be having this conversation—that somebody listening in would have understood the words that we said, but the conversation would have seemed no more than a limp balloon passing between us.

I'd spent a lot of time before this thinking about cultural variations in how to signal that you were listening, taking in, sharing a wavelength with someone. In English, I had been raised to understand, you mostly stayed silent and nodded, waiting for your turn to speak, whereupon you would profess enthusiastically that you understood, or felt the same. In Japanese things were different; more weight was placed on the behavioral cues and interjections known as aizuchi, a term taken from blacksmithing, where the apprentice unleashes strokes in time with those made by his master. As this etymology suggests, there was a focus on continuity, and matching the other; often aizuchi reached a level of vocality that would be perceived in an English context as an interruption or a sign of impatience, and I would occasionally feel affronted by them, find they made me lose my flow. The reverse also happened: when I didn't keep up a constant enough flow of aizuchi in Japanese I would perceive my conversational partner starting to falter. All of these musings made me wonder how much of feeling "listened to" was a matter of social convention; it was around this time that, on my more preoccupied days, I began to catch myself, on the phone to people back home, giving a perfect and empathetic-sounding response to what they were saying while having not absorbed a single word and thinking: I'm too proficient at this for my own good. I can do the wavelength without the wave.

What happened now between D and me felt different to any trade-off of behavioral cues; we were not reacting expressively to each other's thoughts, or encouraging the other to go on, and rather the encouragement seemed to come naturally from the other person voicing more or less what you had felt, of the experience feeling both new and shared. What we mostly talked about was how bonded we felt to the man, though we knew we had no real right to be feeling such when we'd never even found out his name or anything else about him. We talked about getting in contact with the police, asking if it was possible to attend his funeral. And as we talked and wept we both felt it: we were changed. We would never be flippant about death or suicide again, but it was more than that—we felt, even in our terror, bound to life. We wanted to take that moment, and do something with it, although we didn't yet know what. Afterwards it would be difficult to say these things to people without them sounding cheesy and ridiculous, but in that moment in the black-leather booth nothing we could say to each other was trite, because there was only us, and we both felt the same.

After a while, D stood up. "I need to go to the toilet," she said, hovering at the edge of the table, "but I don't think I can go alone."

And so I went with her. Not begrudgingly, either; the request felt reasonable to me, even if I knew it was unusual, and as I was waiting outside the cubicle for her, it occurred to me for the first time how deep we were in this together, and how that was maybe not exactly a good thing, in and of itself, but it was at least a comforting one. It seemed like this: we had both experienced a moment of total loneliness and we had decided that we should band together, with the world, but first with each other.

And thus began our two days of an intimacy for which I really can't think of a parallel. I have had various relationships that were extreme in ways which, looking back, feel ill-advised, but it's hard for me to think of any period of time with anybody that felt more quietly intense than that I spent with D in Matsusaka, even if there was nothing sexual or romantic about it. We drank a lot, accompanied each other to the toilet, slept in the same room. At first D was convinced that she wouldn't sleep, and sat on the sofa as I curled up on the floor, but eventually she did, waking up late the following morning, when we repeated the whole procedure, this time traveling to Ise Shrine. In the evening we went out, came home, and drank and talked until the early hours.

Many times since, in the light of what happened later, I've wondered if I should have handled the situation differently, specifically whether I should have been more boundaried. I wonder this even while knowing that really it would have been impossible for me back then to do so: I felt I had to take care of her, and I also defined my mental state in terms of hers. Possibly I drew solace from being the solid one, but more than that I drew solace from sharing the experience, from nothing being off limits, and in truth it felt good to cry, and talk, because I knew that there was nobody else that would understand. Both of us were aware, I thought, that we wouldn't be able to do this anymore after she went home, and so we should make the most of having each other. But it now seems possible that we conceptualized in different ways what that return to normality would have to entail.

The morning D went home, I walked her to the train station and we said goodbye, hugging long and hard in a way I wouldn't necessarily have expected her to be comfortable with in public, at least Japanese public. The last thing she said to me before she strode off, limbs bladelike, towards the ticket gates was: "I know it was awful, but I feel like the fact that it happened to you and me had some kind of meaning."

I walked home with this statement echoing around my chest—*some kind of meaning.* What kind of meaning, though? I didn't know what she meant by it, and I didn't know if she knew what she meant by it. I didn't know how much significance I was supposed to attach to it.

I half-suspected that D would go away and I'd discover myself amazingly fine, but what I found instead was a world of fear far greater than I'd anticipated. Mostly, if I was around people at work then I held it together, but in solitude it all came out. Everywhere I went I saw bodies hanging from lampposts. I had visions of his face burned into my mind as I tried to sleep, as I woke up. We had discovered him in broad daylight and yet it felt that it had happened at night, so evocative was the darkness. For as far back as I could remember, taking long walks alone had been the best way of shaking myself free of obsessive thoughts, or at least generating space around them, but now I found that coping mechanism outlawed, because walking alone was terrible. Still, life went on, and gradually it did get a bit better. My boyfriend, G, came out to Japan to join me, and I talked to him about the day in Toba, and that helped a lot, although there was still a sense in which talking to him about it was not like talking to D.

Except that sense of what talking to D was like was gradually ebbing away. She and I exchanged emails: she was back with her family, her mother and her sister, they were taking care of her, everything was good—and then it wasn't good, she was thinking about it a lot, she said, but her emails grew more distant and sporadic. We planned to Skype, but she was busy at work and put it off. In one email, I remember, she wrote to me that she'd been researching PTSD; although it hadn't seemed like that to us at the time, she said, what we'd found on top of that mountain had in fact been a scene of violence, and that was why we'd suffered so much. I could understand what she meant, and yet, if I was going through the wringer a bit, I was pretty sure I wasn't suffering from PTSD.

In honesty, I don't know if it was D who taught me the word ba'sari or not. I can see an image in my mind of her saying it, possibly in terms of a haircut, but I don't know if that's a real scene or one I've dreamed up. My early memories of people speaking are sharp, but past the point of a certain familiarity with Japanese they begin to round off and fade, outside of truly dramatic moments. I'd spent enough time with D and knew her well enough that I can put almost any phrase in her mouth and have it work in my head, so probably I will never know for sure who taught me this mimetic for cutting something forcefully, in a single movement or all at once. To have your long flowing locks ba'sarily cut off. To ba'sarily cut off a relationship with people: "used in particular in cases where no reserve or hesitation is shown," says the dictionary. It's also used for killing people, or "mercilessly making them redundant."

D didn't want to be friends with me anymore, she wrote. Our reactions to this incident proved that I was more mentally stable than she was. She didn't quite say "it's alright for you," but that was essentially the message. Speaking to me made her recall the event, and she didn't want to do that. It wasn't up for debate, and there was no apology.

Predictably enough I felt various things: I was hurt, and angry, outraged, and let down. I was alone, in a new part of Japan without any community to rely on, whereas she lived with her mother and sister in her hometown of Tokyo surrounded by old friends. Okay, I wasn't crumbling, but I was up and down, and it seemed rich for her to be making pronouncements on how I was without having even spoken to me. But the most powerful reaction of all, whose strength only deepened the more I reflected on everything that had happened and what she'd said to me at the station, was a sense of astonishment. It stunned me to have bonded with someone like that, and to have bonded so intimately in a way that I didn't want to ascribe to either one of us but seemed more at her instigation, only to have the security of that whipped away from under me. Without that bond, I found that the things we'd dreamed about on the black faux-leather banquette, the cheesy ideas we'd had about making sure that this didn't slip back into silence and that something good came of it, promptly disappeared. Much as I resented the fact, I felt I couldn't do that on my own.

It wasn't that the sudden cut-off was a tactic that seemed totally unthinkable from D. Back when we'd lived together in London, D had once confronted me in tears about how I insisted on always speaking to her in Japanese, even when she began conversations in English. The outburst took me totally by surprise, and we talked it through until we located the source of the misunderstanding: my mistaken analysis of her comfort levels, partly born out of a comment she'd made about how intimidating I was when I spoke English. I was surprised because my behavior as she was describing it to me was undoubtedly shitty, and I could see how upsetting it would have been; not for the first or the last time in my life, I had a visceral sense of how different two experiences of what was objectively the same reality could be. But what shocked me the most was her admission that she'd been on the verge of saying nothing to me and simply moving out. Even to hear her say it gave me a kind of thrill—*how fucked up, how intense, how much like something out of a Japanese novel!*—but I also shuddered to think how I would have reacted if that was really the course of action she'd taken.

Except to dress up the shut-out in foreign garb is not fair, because I understood its mechanism, and understood why it prevailed in cultures where discussion of feelings was not encouraged—a category in which I included Britain. You repressed and you repressed and you repressed, told yourself you were not feeling a certain way, and then the feelings got too much and there was no holding them back and no reversing them: it was cut-off or nothing.

The thing was, this time I didn't feel that was what was happening. If I'd sensed that D was looking for a reason to ditch me, or if the event had been caused or exacerbated by me, even if I'd been the one asking her to accompany me to the toilet, then I could have understood her reaction. In reality, I would never have asked her to accompany me to the toilet, even if I'd wanted her to, precisely out of a fear that it would make me too much, and therefore liable for ditching. Instead, I got the sense that her connection with me had been severed to facilitate a total erasure of the event from her memory. I was an inessential organ snipped out in order to access the malignant one, tossed into the trash without a second thought.

Looking back through my inbox, I find that I emailed her a year or so on from the ba'sari email—to check, I suppose, that the decision hadn't been rescinded. "I had a dream about you last night," I wrote, "and I think about you a lot. Are you okay?"

D had replied, to say she was fine, not thinking about the event. "Normal life with everything," she writes. "But I still feel fatigue to that direction so I don't feel like talking." So ran the last ever lines exchanged between us. Casting an eye over her words, I still feel like an ice cube has been dropped down my back.

¶ nuru-nuru: the slippery sound of knowing the lingo

I AM TEACHING AN INTERMEDIATE lesson at the language school called "Describing Things," whose aim is to build up the students' stock of English adjectives. The students and I go through a number of photo-flashcards supposedly depicting certain attributes—a cactus, some green gunge, a shag pile carpet—and finish off with a game where one person describes something in the room for the other to guess, hopefully using vocab they've just learned. I'm fond of this lesson, and teach it whenever the syllabus allows, because I feel like this is the kind of English which is actually helpful in real-world conversations. More selfishly, I like hearing what adjectives my students choose to describe certain objects. This tactile, visceral area of language, where English is full of adjectives ending in y—spiky, glossy, shiny, and so on—is a realm of Japanese festooned with mimetic language; students often enunciate mimetics when they latch on to the meaning of an English word as a way of establishing a correspondence, or scribble them down in their notebook as a translation of a particular English word. Those two don't correlate exactly, I frequently want to warn on those occasions, but mostly I don't say anything.

Today's lesson is a one-to-one session with a woman in her late forties, intelligent and reserved but not without warmth. By this point, all my students know that I speak Japanese, and though we're officially supposed to conduct our lessons exclusively in English there are times when, as a last resort or when it seems more expedient to do so, I'll leap in with an explanation in Japanese. I feel less guilty about this knowing that the owner of the English school conducts his own lessons 70 percent in Japanese. We've done "rough" via a picture of sandpaper; we've gone through "silky," "smooth," "itchy," and now I'm trying to do "slimy," for which we don't have a picture.

I try first of all to explain this in English, but the student doesn't get it, so I say, "Like nattō," which is a popular breakfast food here of fermented soybeans, the stringiest, stickiest, slimiest food substance known to man. And then, thinking that I've broken the Japanese dam anyway, and I may as well, I add confidently, "Nuru-nuru shiteiru."

My student turns to look at me suddenly, and for the quickest moment her eyes cut blade-like into me. And then she shakes her head, and corrects me. "Neba-neba." Sticky, I believe this means, but I don't see where the vehemence is coming from.

"You don't say nuru-nuru?"

The student shakes her head again very fast, putting me in mind of an ornamental chicken, and then she sighs in a way that makes it clear she wishes she didn't have to say what she's about to say. "That's mostly for—for sexual things," she says in English.

Instantly the blood rushes to my face, and as it does my mind starts racing: I am sure I've read nuru-nuru in books used about things that have nothing to do with sex. Have I? Haven't I? But however I scrabble around in the vestiges of memory, I can't be sure. Because the truth is, I did learn this phrase in relation to "sexual things," and that's the only time I can remember hearing anyone actually say it.

It's hard to express how much of an idiot I feel like at this point, and I feel it all the more because by now I think of myself as being above making terrible faux pas like these. The Japanese that I speak might not be brilliant, but is at least sensitive, I tell myself; I am above the stage of parroting indiscriminately.

Now, though, I have inadvertently exposed myself in the worst possible way. I have come out with what is tantamount to an unsolicited confession of having sex with a Japanese person, and done so in a lesson I am teaching. If I were a Western man blithely alluding to his dealings with Japanese women, I would have found myself beyond terrible, the scum of the earth, although I suspect that probably from my student's perspective, doing the same as a woman is, if anything, more shocking. In any case I feel at that moment, maybe in the purest way I have ever felt it, dirty. I imagine seeing myself through her eyes: a girl of ill repute who has learned her Japanese in the bowels of society. Helplessly, I picture my colleague at this very English school, a fresh-off-the-boater from the United States who douses herself in awful perfume and speaks awful Japanese and throws herself at awful Japanese men and is at this very moment having a not-so-secret secret affair with one of our students; I am just like her. I feel tears of shame sting at the back of my eyes.

Back in the staffroom, I look up the word in question and

discover my mistake. In fact, nuru-nuru is very much *not* only used for "sexual things"—it's used for snakes, eels, moss, and fish, but not for nattō. I don't understand exactly why the student had come down on me so hard for saying slimy, when a Google image search yields a very mixed array of mushrooms, gums, and sea creatures—even to this day, I don't really understand, and part of me wonders over and over if I've embellished this scene in my memory, or dreamed it up entirely. The way that it has lingered with me suggests not. Even understanding that my mistake had not really been such a terrible one didn't make the fear and the shame go away. I was the girl who had learned my Japanese in the bedroom: the shame stuck because to a certain extent this was true. I don't think I've ever used nuru-nuru since.

¶ uda-uda: the sound of the wild bore

"IT REALLY BUGS ME," A friend from New York says, "when you hear these hip, beautiful, super-functional people talking about how they're such geeks. It's like, I know real geeks, and that's seriously debilitating."

"Right," I say. "It's like they want to have their cake and eat it."

Even as these words are coming out of my mouth, I feel saddened. Saddened not only by how trite they are, but also by the awareness that I'm not really contributing anything of substance to this conversation. I am drawing out my friend in the way I often do when I want to avoid exposing myself, hoping that the episode will pass without me having to make some unambiguous pronouncement.

On this occasion at least, it's not that I don't want to participate in the conversation in a more articulate and meaningful way. I find the idea of laying down some form of social ineptitude as a defining condition for geekdom interesting, and I'd like to thrash the issues out more, but as frequently happens to me in conversation, my head feels like a morass of different possible responses and associations and I struggle to just take one and run with it. That's not the only reason why I don't make a proper reply, either. The other problem is that, as so often happens, a lot of what's in there relates heavily to Japan, and I'm terrified of being a bore.

Now, for example, I'm thinking about a beloved Japanese phrase you might use to describe people who play up their geeky credentials when amongst geeks and play them down in contexts where they're less well regarded: happō bijin. This is written "in eight directions a beauty," with eight standing for "all," and represents the desire to appear beautiful on each of the eight main winds of the compass, i.e., to present an appealing face to whomever one is with. I am thinking, too, about various discussions I've heard about otaku—people with consuming interests, especially in anime and manga. In particular, I think about the way that the word otaku has shifted over the years from meaning something tantamount to chronic reclusiveness, something close to a mental illness, to being something far more socially acceptable, as elements of otaku culture have been commodified and commandeered by mainstream materialist capitalism. And finally I am thinking back to my own experience of feeling like a geek, quite unexpectedly, and very precisely in the sense of being debilitated.

At the time in question, I was visiting London from Japan, an extended visit of six weeks between moving from semi-rural Matsusaka to a freelance life in Osaka, Japan's second-largest city. In retrospect, it was a bad idea to stay in Britain for that long, but I was in a bad place, confused and messed up enough to believe that if I was to return out of the blue there would be a place for me, and people would give me the welcome I was desperately craving. I guess I hoped that I'd slot right back in even if it was just for a little while.

Back when I'd returned to the UK after my first stint

in Japan, I had, mostly, slotted back in. In fact, I had been kind of amazed by how little people would ask about my time abroad. To my closer friends, I spoke about some of my experiences there, but even then it was predominantly the anecdote-worthy events, and for the most part I acted like nothing had happened. It didn't feel like that on the inside—I missed it like hell, and I spent most of my time either working in an office that was essentially Japan but located in London, or writing a silly novel about the Japanese experiences of someone called Alice who was really me. For the most part, I kept this part of me separate from the part who socialized with my non-Japan friends.

As time had gone on, though, and ever more of my choices and my stories involved Japan, this partition between Japan and the rest of my life had become harder to maintain. Eventually I began to translate full-time, and the more I was surrounded by other Japanese translators, the more talking socially about Japan grew normalized—and then I moved back to Japan.

And so it had come to pass that by this point I had, as I promptly discovered, essentially lost the ability to converse about anything that didn't relate to Japan. I knew that people around me didn't have any particular interest in what for them was just one far-away country of many, and I didn't want my contribution to the conversation always to be seen as either a wacky aside or a moralistic reminder of what a big place the world was. I could hear in my head how ridiculous my voice sounded as it began every sentence "In Japan." But if I didn't come out with those kinds of sentences, I was stuck with silence. It wasn't simply that I didn't have facts or anecdotes to contribute, either; I felt that somewhere along the way I'd lost my right to have an opinion because I was now so badly informed about things back home. In Japan, it had driven me insane how so many of the conversations I was invited to participate in as a foreigner were just comparisons—*in Japan we do X, where as in the UK you do Y, right? Oh, you do Z? Oh wow, we don't do that here!*—and now here I was, orchestrating the same kinds of conversations.

———

At the very end of my six weeks in London, I went on holiday to the Kentish seaside with my mother, my brother, and his partner. The holiday had been intended to be the three of them, but I was invited along at the last minute. After my brother and I had lived together for a few weeks, with me in a fragile state, things had grown toxic between us, and the holiday pushed us as close to the abyss as we've ever stood. On the last night, we ate out at a nice restaurant. In the car on the way there, I already felt hated and hateful; sitting at the table, I felt unable to contribute to the conversation, felt hopelessly ostracized. Eventually at some point I said a sentence, quite possibly not the first, that really did begin, "In Japan."

"God," said my brother in a whiny, sarcastic voice, "all you ever talk about is Japan."

It was him being tipsy and making a joke. A little barbed, maybe, but essentially not malicious—the kind of joke that we were used to making with each other. But at that moment I was not in a place for sarcasm; my ego couldn't tolerate it.

"Well, you talk about music all the time," I snapped back

at my musician brother, and we glared at each other across the table.

The truth was, I just couldn't bear to be the bore. Since the first time I'd lived in Japan, I had been what a friend called a "maniakku" about language—a geek, when those geeky tendencies didn't necessarily lie within the narrow scope of traditional otaku interests such as video games, technology, anime, figurines, and so on. I had studied Japanese like a maniac, and it had given me incredible amounts of pleasure privately, as well as being rewarded interpersonally. Far from being socially debilitating, it had enabled me to communicate better with people in the Japanese contexts in which I moved. In other words, at least according to my New York friend's definition, I wasn't a real geek.

Now, I was coming to terms with the fact that not only was this allegiance to Japan not productive in the UK, but it served as an actual hindrance. I felt, all of a sudden, like I had nothing to offer; like the only things in which I took pleasure were actually very boring to everybody else, starting with my family. There were subjects that I wanted to speak about because they had meaning for me, but I suspected that to their eyes it seemed I was being either pretentious, or else had ceased in some way to be myself. The person who could offer anything other than culturally relativist comparisons was gone, and in her place was a strange, uncanny presence who would mumble at you in Japanese when you tried to wake her up from where she'd fallen asleep on the sofa. I felt that now I understood what it was like to be between cultures; not the happy versatile figure who could switch at will, but the person who felt fundamentally other wherever they were. I wasn't the bridge between cultures of which everyone blithely spoke; I was someone bobbing helplessly on the sea.

Although I'm back now in the UK and adjusting to life here, there are still times when I worry that my conversation is like a radio stuck on a single channel; that not only am I a one-trick pony of a person, but my trick is an obscure one which confounds rather than delights. These days this is a concern, rather than a sick sense of certainty such as it used to be; I genuinely don't know whether I am a bore or not, or how acceptable it is to speak about Japan to most people of my acquaintance: how much it reads as boasting, and to what extent it alienates others. And so for the most part I don't really tell people, until they ask, and this is a solution that works, except it makes me less talkative than some other version of me would be. There is a real relief in meeting people who've spent time in Japan, not particularly because I want to speak to them about it, but just because I can turn off while I'm with them my fear of being a one-dimensional loser.

———

In the early stages of writing this book, as I'm thinking about which sounds I want to include, I'm leafing through one of my onomatopoeia dictionaries when I alight on the word uda-uda. I've heard this one before, but I can't remember where; it means to drone on, to talk about pointless subjects. And lo and behold, the example sentence reads: "Children who go on and on in a boring way will turn into wild boars (old proverb)." Droning on and on, I think, like a wild boar, a wild bore, and the coincidence brings a big grin to my face.

There's a particular scene in a book I translated where a young woman named Satomi is recalling how badly bullied she was at school. One day, she remembers, she returned from the school toilets to find the words GROSS OTAKU SCUM scrawled across the notebook where she sketched her beloved anime characters, and the first thought that popped into her head was, "Oh, I'm scarcely worthy of being called an otaku"—because in her mind, otaku is a high accolade. Something about this struck her as funny, and she sniggered, and it's at this point she realized she was being watched, because she heard someone say, "Whoa, she's so creepy."

As I guffaw out loud at this trans-linguistic serendipity with the wild bore, I also think to myself: I've become her. Of course I haven't been bullied for being maniakku about Japanese, and I don't want for a moment to suggest that my pain rivals Satomi's. But still, there's something about her experience which seems illuminative; maybe, if we do define being a geek in terms of finding yourself socially impaired in some way, then we should also stipulate that the payoff is the richness of that inner world, and that the same can maybe be said for standing in between cultures.

So maybe in some way I am a geek, albeit an accidental one. I am a geek because I can make these silly jokes to myself and laugh at them in a way that other people would find incomprehensible, and I'm a geek because I pay some form of social toll. But probably especially I'm a geek because I feel that even if it alienates me in the circles in which I move, that seems like a fair price to pay for what I've gained in return.

¶ don: the sound of the sexy lovely violent
hand slamming the wall

THEY SLIP IT INTO CONVERSATION, my friends who like
manga a lot. The exact circumstances are hazy in my memory, but I remember sending on a group chat thread with the
two of them a photo I'd taken of a poster, because the caption was either ridiculous or referenced some in-joke we had. I
didn't pay much attention to the poster's image: to my mind it
looked like a nondescript cartoon of a man and a woman, the
man resting his hand on the wall above the woman in a way
that suggested some romantic vector between them.

My friends comment on the caption, but the discussion
swiftly moves on to the image, and immediately what they
say becomes totally opaque to me. Living in Japan, I've grown
used to this happening in all corners of life, but right now it
catches me off guard. Here is something that is supposed to
transcend language—pictures are universal, right? Except of
course, they aren't. It's as if the wall of our conversation has
split apart, revealing the entrance to a secret passage of whose
existence I was unaware, and I feel a phantom-limb, almost
metaphysical confusion: I don't understand what it is that I
don't understand.

I think about how, in the past, I have interacted over text

with people I made uncomfortable with my use of emoticons—
people who were unable to understand the way I used images
and were puzzled by any emoji use that wasn't straight down
the line, and how I found this a turn-off. Indeed, one of the
joys of interacting with these two is that they are pictorially
literate: we can tell one another jokes and write one another
stories with emoticons. Before this interaction I might have
said, "They are pictorially literate, like me," but now I see a
huge chunk missing from my so-called literacy. They are the
children of manga, they have been raised on the stuff, which
means they have a whole other vocabulary utterly unknown
to me. So they talk about how bad the picture is, how it clum-
sily combines a hodgepodge of different elements I don't
understand, and then casually they reference the pose: the
kabe-don.

I'm at my desk in my flat when I get this message, and I sit
there staring at this strange hybrid word, 壁ドン: the dense 16-
stroke kanji for "kabe" (wall), and then the two blocky characters making up the katakana "don." I stare and I stare, and
still it doesn't make sense to me. So I put it into Google, and in
a fraction of a second a new world has splayed itself out before
me. A list of dictionary definitions, crowned by an extensive
Wikipedia page. Pressing through to the images tab, I find an
endless array of images from manga, anime, and TV shows,
all showing two figures arranged in a variation on the basic
pose from the poster: one person standing with their hand
flat to the wall above the head of another. Almost always the
hand-owner is a man, and the other party a woman.

In this way, I find out that the kabe-don—literally "the
wall thump"—is an act that takes place in communal housing:

a smack to the wall to admonish one's neighbors for making too much noise. But it has a second meaning too, a move which one finds above all in manga, whereby a man drives a woman back to a wall (alternatively a window-frame or column) and then sticks out a hand—don! thump!—against the surface behind her. From this pose, he can look down at her imperiously, and she can gaze up at him a-tremble: a microcosm of the power dynamic that gets every romance-manga-reader fired up. The first recorded usage for this latter sense of the term was from a voice actress, who called it a "moeru shichuēshon"; a situation that sets the heart in bloom. Widespread application was sparked by the 2014 film version of a particular shōjo manga, L♥DK: it was that same year that the term made it into the Top Ten List produced by the New and Trending Words Awards.

Honestly I love this feeling, the opening up of a previously unthought world courtesy of a single word, the sense of everything falling into a new place. But often when it happens, I spare a thought for how things were back at the beginning of my learning career, when I didn't have the knowledge or the tools to decipher this unfolding, and I would never make it through to the feeling of satisfaction. When, not understanding Japanese, I frequently had to rely on cabalistic English translations that did little to assuage my confusion, translations of the kind I now find when I click through to the English version of the Wikipedia page for kabe-don: "The term Kabe-don first appeared in 2008 when voice actor Ryōko Shintani described it as 'lovely situation.'"

I'd be lying if I said I didn't miss being in regular contact with these kinds of translations; they always seemed to me to have a poetic fertility to them, the potential to spark off new lexical connections, and I used to be somewhat obsessed with them, but I certainly don't miss having to rely on them for guides to meaning. In fact, as time has gone on, I've come to see the phenomenon of the "endearingly mystifying translation" as posing more problems than simply that of bringing us no closer to a real understanding—I think it also plays into a wider pattern of exoticizing and Orientalizing that goes on constantly. If our reaction on encountering a dubious translation was to accept that the information provided was insufficient for our purposes, and perhaps to ask if there was anything we could do to bring us closer to understanding, then all would be well; yet my sense is that there's a tendency on discovering an opaque phrase to leap to the assumption that we won't ever get there, because the concept in question is on some level beyond our understanding—too hazy, strange, mystical. In other words, it's not really about the translation, but rather about some quality in the source language, source culture. It is, after all, very alien.

I'm sure that part of this impulse stems from a sense that if the thing in question weren't something deeply mystifying in the original language, it wouldn't be possible to produce such a plausible-sounding yet deeply opaque section of English. Certainly this is what I would have thought back at the beginning with "lovely situation": it's just two words, for heaven's sake, and one of them, "shichuēshon," is derived from English. How hard can it be to get it right? It's only since I began translating, both professionally and as part of everyday life, that I've come to realize that this is a deeply flawed way of looking at things, because the "right" presupposes that there

is, in fact, a way of expressing this concept in English, which
is often simply not the case. Really, you are not just translating "two words," but also a broader cultural heritage leading
back decades or centuries which those two words conjure up,
and about which the average Anglophone reader or listener
knows nothing. In order to truly understand—in order to
sense things slotting into place or "falling to your internals"
as they say in Japanese—you need more. You need decent
descriptions, of the kinds that you rarely find on English Wikipedia for less prominent Japanese concepts; if you're a translator, and you want your reader to really and truly understand
a context for which no analogous version exists in their own
culture, you need asides, or footnotes.

In this particular case, then, my footnote would state how
in manga and anime circles, kabe-don has become the paradigm of the ultimate romantic gesture to make girls weak
at the knees, and to induce that other kanji-mimetic com-
pound, the "mune-kyun," or tightening in the chest, i.e., the
heart flutter. It would say that the original phrase, "moeru
shichuēshon," references this context, because "moeru" and
"moe" are concepts heavily embedded within the world
of anime (and which merit another footnote of their own).
It would also explain that like almost any coercive gesture
whose power derives from the vocabulary of superior physical
force conceived of as masculine (greater height, a powerful
move of the arm, the sense of making the first move, the physical pursuit), it has a problematic transition out of the fictional
world—particularly the world of shōjo (young girl) manga,
used within the Japanese language as a metaphor for romantic fantasies not compatible with the life of the adult—and

into the real one. In the Japanese reality TV show *Terrace House*, a contestant who shows early and consistent signs of being a sexual predator and whose actions subsequently provoke an arguably overdue *Japan Times* article entitled "It's Time to Talk About 'Terrace House' and Consent," responds to the appearance of a new contestant he finds very attractive and has previously deemed A5-rank, a grade given to the finest quality of wagyū beef, by saying that maybe he'll kabe-don her tomorrow: "If the moment to do a kabe-don presents itself," read the English subtitles, "I'll take it." You'll mean you'll kabe-don her and ask her where she wants to go on a date? asks one of the other male contestants. "If you're going to kabe-don, you can't go *asking*," the sexual predator replies: "You've just got to do it. You go, 'You'll go with me,' and then, *DON*." He reaches out his hand to an imaginary wall to demonstrate. Sitting on my bed watching this on my laptop, I find that I'm making a prolonged retching noise.

The kabe-don is the set-up to the confession of love, or the date invitation, or the first kiss, and it gains its power from having been yearned for, or at the very least, coming from someone towards whom you feel not unfavorably. When performed by someone from whom sexual attention is unwanted, someone who's misread the signals, doesn't care about the signals in the first place, is a sex pest or worse, then it is, to state things mildly, harassment.

These, anyway, are all involved in making up the heady mix at play in the concept of kabe-don which I read about in brief that first day, and as often happens in these situations where I've learned about some new linguistic phenomenon via the internet, I feel like I want to speak about it with real people. It's not that I don't believe it's real, exactly, but in order to fully integrate it into myself I need to pass it through my oral channels. The problem is that I feel embarrassed at my limited knowledge, and sure that the way I bring it up in conversation will be either childlike or geriatric. Obviously the pair from the poster chat are my go-to choice to practice with, and the next time we're out drinking, I raise it with trepidation. But I needn't fear with these two; it's clear from the get-go that this is absolutely their favorite thing to speak about, and the more geeky my questions the more welcome. "Oh yeah," one friend says, "it's sexy alright," and the other tells me, "If there's someone you like, the kabe-don is the stuff of dreams." There are screams of laughter and there is fanning of hands in front of faces to cool the flames of heat that rise up just thinking about it. And so the magic is done: it's there, in my vocabulary. Not just the old dust-covered recesses, like so many words I've looked up in a dictionary, even written out in notebooks or stuck up on post-it notes but never actually said and which register now only as a faint sense of familiarity when someone uses them. No, this is an actual, real, live word, that I can use with relative impunity. It's a gift they've given me.

As always, now that I know it, I start seeing it everywhere. Images of it, that is, and references—I have to this day not seen a real life kabe-don. In particular, I notice it more in my manga friends' conversation, and I don't know if they've introduced it because they know I know it now, or if it was always there and I conveniently skipped over it. Kabe-don sareta-aaaiiii, my friend one day exclaims of some terrible beefcake: *Man, I would looooooovve to be kabe-donned by him.*

¶ dōn: the sound of big drums, bombs, and the good-bad dream

FUCK, IS THE FEELING WHEN you wake up, NOT AGAIN, or sometimes it's slower than that, sometimes it's the awareness of the peace and the happiness that comes first, the warmth held in your body, and you start to query it, ask why? Why do I feel I am made of a different substance from usual, a substance that is not wrought through with anxiety, a soft, endless warmth like cream? And then it sifts back to you, the dream, that you had, of him, again. Nothing major really happens in these dreams. One time he's wearing leather gloves, that's the kinkiest that it gets. A few times he is living in an elaborate cave system on the outskirts of town which you try to infiltrate, sometimes there are hotels or meeting rooms, but either way you end up alone in a room, there is some illicit situation, and you touch. Just that! Just touching, with hands, with clothed torsos, his face looming close to yours, but it's how direct it feels, in the way that no other human contact you can think of ever is, has been, will be. Your body is played like a timpano, an ōdaiko, and DŌN is the sound it makes, the ō stretched, written with an elongating dash, ドーン or どーん, to signify reverberation in time, a more extended sonic event than the slamming hand on the wall. DŌN: the boom of an explosion, a bomb, the striking of a drum. DŌN: the thunder-rumble of waking up like this, and how this is the only time you ever feel this feeling. DŌN: how you can smell his breath. DŌN: how sometimes it happens when you're sleeping next to somebody else, sometimes when you've been single for a long time, but either way it's been a literal decade since you were together, and you know that you couldn't be with him now, that a relationship with that kind of power balance doesn't interest you, and yet somewhere in your body-mind he is held there, motionless, the emotional truth of what he was for you then cryogenically frozen, coming back just occasionally to remind you what it feels like, which is to say, remind you how and why it cannot be reduced to "just" anything, and why nothing else comes close, why however mature you believe yourself to be this can still shake you like nothing else: DŌN.

¶ uka-uka: the sound of always being slightly wrong

A ONE-STEP GUIDE TO BEING wrong in Japan: go there.

Go there and discover that you are wrong constantly. You are wrong in the small, predictable ways, because you have not grown up using chopsticks or taking your shoes off at the door, or because you have holes in your clothes or fluff on your jacket and do not think immediately to rectify these slippages. You are wrong because you do not know the things to say in all the situations, by which I do not simply mean you do not know the word for this or how to say that, but rather, you don't know that at a certain point there is one set phrase that you have to say, which could be something that your textbook translates as *I beg you to treat me well*, or could be *thank you very much for your continued assistance*, or could be *you are working very hard*, or, *you worked very hard*, and that you have to say these phrases in the right register so that you are neither rude nor excessively groveling. Neither do you understand—it takes you so long to understand—that variation around certain greetings, utterances, is not something to be aspired to; that it is better to be conventional than steer towards playfulness or originality, because the whole point is the ritual, which demonstrates respect and generates comfort.

Also you are too large, and your voice is too loud, and you knock things over. Even if you are not considerably larger than the majority of Japanese people, you will feel large and ungainly, and you will bump and crash your body into surfaces in a way that you're sure you didn't do back home. You will look at the way that people slip past one another in stations, and while you are looking you will come close to colliding with at least two different people, and they will swerve to avoid you, putting an arm out to shield themselves, and a faint flicker of irritation will pass over their faces but they most likely won't look at you, even if you can find the wherewithal to apologize, in Japanese, before they've disappeared off into the crowd.

This is, of course, the lot of the newcomer, and it is to be expected, even if the mysteriously tear-jerking property of the feeling exceeds anticipation, and arguably plays out quite differently in Japan than in other popular holiday destinations for Westerners. Maybe the best you can hope for is that you don't realize how wrong you are, and as a tourist the chances of that are extremely high. A less predictable phenomenon takes place when you live in Japan for a long time and your Japanese is of a relatively high standard. The phenomenon is: you still feel constantly wrong. In fact, there are occasions when you think that time makes you more wrong, just as you sometimes feel that your Japanese is worse than it was when you spoke none. A more rational self informs you that this sense is illusory, that you are not worse or more wrong. Rather, in the same way as your perception of what constitutes "being good" at a language shifts with your progress, so your criteria for being wrong are constantly updated.

The list of the things you have to be aware of is perpetually added to.

Once, working in a Japanese office in London, I'm making breakfast in the staff kitchen when a colleague comes downstairs for a cup of tea. This particular colleague has always made me nervous for reasons I find it hard to put into words, and being alone in a small kitchen with him is not an ideal situation for me, but I do my best to keep a handle on my jitteriness. Not so well, though: in the midst of my flummox and our conversation about what I am eating for breakfast (instant porridge), I reach for the bowl through the steam of the kettle. It's a stupid mistake for sure, but I'd say if I'm honest, it's in the class of stupid mistakes that I make relatively frequently. As I'm rubbing my scalded arm in pain, he scrunches up his face in distaste and says,

"Pff, you're not a child."

Only an infant, the implication seems to be, would do something so impossibly clumsy.

What stuns me is neither the scorn in his tone nor his lack of empathy, but rather the way I sense that I am being assessed by Japanese standards. I am not being given the sort of get-out-of-censure-free card held out to me time and time again as a white person. The fact that I look different—and, in my whiteness, different in a way marketed as the most attractive way of looking different—means I have benefited endlessly from the "cute" dispensation, had my incompetence seen as endearing or excusable, been met with inexhaustible patience time and time again. Yet I've also felt the othering force of this patience—felt in no uncertain terms that I'm being placed in a separate category not just of ethnicity but of adulthood. "You can use chopsticks better than my three-year-old!" multiple people have exclaimed to me in surprise, without a hint of irony, after I've been using chopsticks for ten years, and it's their total conviction that this is a compliment which allows me to see, in a very sober fashion, that what it means to be let off in this way is to have one's capacities estimated as less than those of a toddler.

When this man slaps me with the full force of his scorn, it registers even through the sting as a kind of compliment. It also makes me think about my clumsiness: my propensity for making not just cultural blunders but other mistakes with relative regularity. Growing up in the UK dyspraxic and generally terrible with most practical tasks, I was teased and told off, and yet I have managed to get through like this—I am now permitted to be a passable adult, albeit a badly coordinated one. Now, in the face of this little outburst of vitriol from a near-stranger, which I am sure is just the tip of an iceberg of scorn that exists underneath, I wonder what it would have been like if I'd grown up in his country. Especially as a woman, for whom those kinds of practical competences are crucial: making tea, etc. Would it, and could it, have been drilled out of me, ameliorated, with the right training? How painful would that have been?

I remember something that a friend who has lived in both London and Tokyo said to me once about those in Japan having a perpetual awareness of what temperature things are; specifically, of the division between cold and hot, and maintaining it—the sort of constant peripheral awareness that would, presumably, make it not just stupid but effectively impossible for someone my age to reach their hand through a jet of kettle steam. There are other categorizations constantly attended to, she said, a central one being dirty versus clean. My immediate impulse on hearing this, I remember, was to dismiss it out of hand: it sounded like the type of romanticized nonsense I'd heard people coming out with about Japan far too frequently, even if my friend was not the sort to spout such things, and besides, I'd heard enough British people warning their children that things were dirty or hot to know that this distinction existed there too. The longer I kept her point alive in my mind, the more I saw it at work in the actions, the speech of those around me. The dirty–clean dichotomy was wrought into the Japanese way of life—bathing practices, cleaning practices, the very structure of Japanese residences—and reaffirmed by constant verbal iterations. When I started listening for them, I heard more warnings in Japanese about hot things, too: in restaurants, in people's kitchens.

With time, I increasingly came to conceptualize the toll taken by Japanese society for inclusion as a form of awareness. Maybe this is true of every culture; linguistic practice tends to systemically channel our awareness towards or away from certain features of reality. This struck me frequently when noticing the way that English grammar forces us to be aware of the gender and the singularity/plurality of things in contexts where this wouldn't naturally be made explicit in Japanese. The longer I stayed in Japan, though, the more I felt this was not just an issue of vector—what your awareness was directed at—but of scope as well. *Be aware*: so often that felt like the injunction. *Be aware of yourself, and how you are fitting into the whole, but mostly just be aware, all the time.*

Arguably the most significant of the awarenesses is showing concern for other people. In Japanese, kizukai—literally, the usage of one's spirit or energy. It was tiring, people will regularly say upon returning from a work party or event supposed to be fun; I was kizukaing all the time. The expenditure is framed in the manner of a physical equation, in a way that seems quite wise to me: if you give too much of yourself, you will be drained. Except to frame kizukai as giving of oneself is perhaps misleading, because in a crucial sense you are not giving of yourself, but rather the opposite: you are giving exactly what is demanded.

On several occasions in the past, I have struggled to keep my cool during lectures from Japanese people about kizukai. Typically, the more people want to lecture me about kizukai, the less I want to accept what they have to say. The problem is that I have grown up being distractingly aware of people's feelings, hyperaware to the extent that what I was feeling myself was frequently obscure to me, and the last thing that I need is to be lectured about consideration for others as if it were a uniquely Japanese phenomenon. So when I'm told, "Do you know that in Japan we check, before squeezing lemon over a shared plate of fried chicken that everyone assembled likes lemon, because we care about other people's feelings?" and the unspoken clause is *unlike you individualist Westerners who only ever think of yourselves*, it makes me feel sad and irritated.

Yet with time and calm, I start to see how I am wrong: it starts to dawn on me that there are elements of kizukai that do make it unique as a concept, at least compared to anything that plays out in the West. Unique in its articulation, in terms of how it is explicitly formulated and constantly name-checked as the oil that makes the smooth running of society possible, but also unique, or at least extreme, in its various demands, which I feel can be summarized by something I'm told as a follow-up in the fried chicken situation: "But the thing is, in Japan everyone has to say that they're okay with lemon even if they don't like it, because they don't want to disrupt the social harmony."

Wait a minute, I'm ready to object when I'm initially told this. Doesn't this secret pact to suppress all needs, and to suppress them more the lower down you are in the social hierarchy, not mean the entire game is no longer about preventing actual inconvenience to others, and rather a purely ritualized piece of theater? But before this makes it to my lips, I remind myself that, yes, of course it's ritualized—and what code of etiquette isn't? The deferential door-holding back in Britain, for example: the way that in the absence of heavy bags, nobody experiences any practical benefit from having the door held for them, and the "After you!" "No, after you!" nonsense really only uses up time and energy, and yet when you're inside the mindset, the endless negotiations and smiles and laughs and thank-yous make great sense as a grooming ritual. This also is how things are with lemon-squeezing and all the hundreds of other forms of kizukai (some of which, I should state for the sake of accuracy, *are* about genuine concern for people's feelings). The kizukai mindset is like a helmet I gradually become better and better at putting on, and with it on, I can see why people might want to lecture me. From within this space, I can see how those outside of it look, unburdened by this expectation to show care at all times for others.

————

One way to describe a state of being careless, of not paying enough attention, is uka-uka, which has the same stem as the verb uku: to float, to be happy, for your heart to be sunny. Uku also means to stick out, to stand out, to be different. It is hard not to see this tangle of meanings as brutally indicative: the price you pay for being carefree is to be a social outcast. Or conversely, the price that you pay for assimilating is to have your consciousness occupied by other people's feelings. I try to steer clear of clichés about Japan as I feel there are too many of them around as it is, but there is a handful of things people say that are, I believe, actually and importantly true, and one of them is this: a key part of being in Japan is that gradually, without realizing, *the state of being unlike others* comes to seem more and more repellent to you on a subcutaneous level. That this happens even if consciously you totally reject this principle, and even if on a purely physical level you have no hope of doing anything but standing out. Without realizing, you learn to recoil from it.

As friends have told me has happened to them also, I would realize how far my recoil mechanism had developed only with the arrival of overseas visitors. I looked forward to these visits, and then they happened and parts of them turned out to be frankly unbearable, and I wondered in earnest when it was that I had become such a misery. An example: I take a couple visiting from abroad to a gyōza restaurant and they pick restlessly at the remains of the meal, bite up toothpicks into little pieces and use them to prod at the remains of the food in a way that I find so unbearably impolite that I feel like I'm going to scream, a reaction that I'm sure I would not have had with such vehemence outside of Japan.

Another one: my mother comes to stay for a week, and one day in the convenience store across the road from me, while she's waiting for me to pay, she starts singing to herself and plucking at one of the cardboard displays.

"Mum—" I start, and then I can't even finish the sentence. *You don't do that here, you just can't act like that*—but of course the problem is there is no way of unpacking the "like that" to someone who hasn't learned to carry themselves "here." And as I'm watching my mother with a growing sense of powerlessness, the feeling that steals over me is resentment. Resentment and envy at how free and untroubled she looks. What an easy life, I think, just being able to hum and sing whenever you like—and then I catch myself and think, who have you become?

This convenience store incident is one of the moments when it hits me how much I have assimilated, to what extent I am not being careless and uka-ukaing in the way I used to. Also how much this assimilation costs me psychically, how it is not making me happy, and I wonder reflexively if it's worth torturing myself this much. Wouldn't I be better making my peace with not assimilating?

For the record, it's not the first time I've thought about this question. In fact, I think about it all the time. I wonder, is it more dignified to assimilate or not to assimilate, and in short, I don't know the answer. But what I do sense is that it isn't a choice that people really make, in any meaningful sense of the word: the choice makes itself, and it's largely tied up with awareness. By which I mean, to be giant and loud and clumsy and careless and know that you are all of these, and then to decide not to try to change yourself, is not a feat that many manage. It appears to me that predominantly, there are two schools: those who notice that they are "floating" and decide to assimilate, all the while feeling that they haven't assimilated enough; and those who notice neither that they are floating nor to what extent they have failed to assimilate. But if we're being wholly accurate, maybe we should add a third: those who notice, and can't bring themselves to assimilate, and choose rather to float away entirely.

¶ boro-boro: the important sound of things falling apart

I'M SITTING WITH Y IN an Italian restaurant, a dark basement with burgundy walls and no windows, being waited on by one of our ex-students. This isn't a dream, I have to keep reminding myself, although I have dreamed of so many shady, convoluted situations like this one, and could definitely have dreamed up a more imaginative poster selection than the ones gracing the walls, all Tricolores and vintage racing cars. When we emailed to arrange my visit, our first meeting in years, Y pledged to surprise me. Now it transpires that the surprise he had in mind was being greeted at the restaurant door by a former member of the baseball team, looking not dissimilar to how he did at fourteen, when we taught him English. In his white apron, the student shows us over to our table, gives us the menu, chats awhile with Y, and then moves back over to the bar.

Trying to imagine beforehand what the "surprise" might be, I had actually entertained this scenario, only to dismiss it as too obviously a bad idea. So I am surprised, but not in the way I'm meant to be. I'm surprised that Y would do something like this, which reads to the untrained eye like a deliberate attempt to court suspicion about our relationship, now a decade in the past. At first I can only assume the worst: that he is aiming for some illicit thrill, some rush of power that comes from hiding in plain sight. When I tentatively start to quiz him about it, in tones as hushed as they can be without sounding like whispers, this interpretation doesn't seem to fit. He appears genuinely oblivious to the idea that this situation could be risky now, so long after the fact, and so I look for another explanation. Maybe the danger isn't real for him, was never real for him, because I never have been? I suspect there are elements of truth to this, but it doesn't feel quite spot on either.

Then it starts to come to me, less a hypothesis than a remembered sensation: the way he has always gravitated to small-world setups like this one, the comfort he seems to draw from the centrality of his role in them. How he used to bemoan his various duties, the relentless socializing expected of him, all the late nights and needlessly long meetings and hangovers and parents and students who wouldn't leave him alone, and how I always sensed lurking behind his complaints a desire perhaps not to be explicitly in demand, but at least to be seen, held in place, incorporated into the system. *Yeah, yeah, you love it*, I'd say, and he'd vehemently object. Now, I think I was wrong: he didn't love it, but he was sustained by it. Unconnected as I was, I felt like I could practically reach out and touch the gluey spider-thread which embedded him in this world of his, of schools and parents and small communities. I knew it was wrong to resent him for this, and yet I also understood intuitively that it was precisely this sticky in-the-worldness, which he had and I lacked, that was my greatest rival for his affection and that would ensure in the end that I was always a peripheral presence. I would and could never have the realness which all that assumed for him.

And how real was he to me? In a way, that is the exact question I've come here to try and answer. Excessively, seems like a tenable response. It didn't take a perceptive genius to see that I'd made a legend of him, a one-man nation. I'd fashioned him into a Japan that was mine, and that wanted me just as I wanted it. In a sense, that didn't seem like the worst of crimes; it was largely that instinct which I had to thank for my progress in Japanese, and if what I had done had hurt anybody, it was mostly myself. Besides, wasn't that just what you did when you were young and you fell in love in a foreign country—you conflated person, language and land, and threw yourself at them immoderately? With time, maturity and healing, that bond eventually dissolved and was replaced by a more holistic form of social integration, and you moved on.

Yet time has passed, and I haven't moved on, at least not completely. For sure, I think of Y less than I once used to, and our volleys of telegrammatic yet weirdly weighty emails have grown less frequent. For the past year, I've been in a serious relationship that I had high hopes for, although it's in the process of disintegrating. I have my own Japan now, my own nuanced and difficult relationship with this place, and, in theory, my own reasons for being here. Yet I can't shake the sense that really, they aren't what keep me here. That the real reason is inextricably bound up with this far older man about whom I have thought every day for ten years and not seen for six, and the feeling that comes from thinking of him: the tug of rope around my waist, a piercing hollowness and a belonging, a home and a homesickness.

And that is why I have a sick suspicion that another answer to the question of how real he was to me is: not very. I've never had any problems articulating brutally honest things about his fallibilities and my feelings for him, both to myself and to other people, but I wonder whether I can do that precisely because I know that what lies underneath is something unshakeable, the ossified aftermath of a need so pure and primal that it can't be disrupted, even by the reality of him as person.

Now, though, I want to disrupt it. For a long time, I believe I took a perverse pride in how powerful my feelings towards Y were, but that's shifted. Now, its heft is a dead weight around my neck, and I disgust and bore myself by thinking about it, by feeling that time is only taking me further away from ever understanding what it was that we had. As the new relationship I thought might be the one sinks into the dust, it dawns on me: whatever of me and Y remains, I have to try to see it for what it is. I want to see him outside of the dance of need. At least, that is the optimistic version of events. Another version is this: I have come back to see him because I feel like I am possessed, and I don't know what else to do, so I've taken the long-distance coach over to the part of the country where he currently lives.

————

And now here we are, burgundy walls and spaghetti choices. Y orders a bottle of red wine from the student. The minutes seem to pool and stagnate, my head grows thick and heavy. I sense I am not being entertaining company. Y checks his phone to see if he has a message from another ex-student, who will be joining us later, and I feel a pressing sensation behind my eyes as though time is both running out and has vanished entirely.

It occurs to me to wonder: does he really even see me, sitting there in front of him? It's been years since we last met but he doesn't tell me that my Japanese has improved, and nor do I feel, in this moment, that it has. I remember how fast he speaks, how he mumbles, how hard it is to communicate.

All of a sudden I'm saying things, words are streaming up from my stomach, which not only had I not planned to say to him but which I didn't know were down there: *I really liked you, you know, I wasn't pretending, for a long time I felt that you'd ruined me, that I couldn't ever marry anybody but you.* To hear these things come out of my mouth is strange, to say the least. I've never been in a position where marriage was on the cards, I don't even believe in it as an institution, but then, I suppose, the part of me that is spewing this out is not talking about marriage in any worldly sense. I'm talking instead about marriage of the heart, which I almost certainly don't believe in either. Or else, I do. Still spewing out words in intervals, I start to cry. With our ex-student throwing us furtive glances from the bar, I lose control and sob right there in my seat, like only a foreigner ever would.

There's a phrase in Japanese for crying inconsolably which gets stuck in my head sometimes: boro-boro naku, or, "to cry in a boro-boro way." I think maybe it stuck because I'd never been able to put it together with the meaning of boro-boro with which I was familiar, namely to fall to pieces or be in a state of disrepair. My clothes were often boro-boro, at least by Japanese standards, and I'd learned to preempt and defuse any potential criticism of this fact by joking about "my boro-boro bag," and so on. Boro-boro was equated in my mind with words like tatty, scruffy, and shabby, and I found it hard to put it together with weeping. But now, as I watched Y watching me crying, I felt the two meanings slip quietly together. It seemed to me as though I'd never cried in anything like such a public manner before, and the sensation of it was that of the plaster facade of an old building plummeting down in vast white sheets, beyond repair or retraction. I was coming apart, and that had expressed itself in my tears, even if I hadn't ever consciously intended it to.

On the wall of the loo in the suburban London house where I grew up hung a framed poster for the DEVO album *Q: Are We Not Men? A: We Are Devo!* Underneath a picture of a man in a sunhat, and the letters D E V O in red, green, yellow and blue, were written the words: "The Important Sound of Things Falling Apart." The poster, and particularly that slogan, had always seemed to me to embody something both frightening and impossibly adult, although like most of the soupy thoughts that filled my head in childhood, I could never have put that impression into words back then. Any kind of devastation, I felt it was saying, let alone the important kind, was a distant privilege you had to earn. A few not-so-distant things had fallen apart while I was growing up: my parents' marriage had disintegrated, and life at home had sometimes felt like it was on the brink of going the same way, but throughout it all, I carried the sense that it was my job to make sure that things didn't fall apart entirely. Even if I did nothing to make things better in any practical, measurable sense, I felt that at the very least, I had to hold the weight of it. I had to not crumble. Ultimately, I suppose, I didn't feel safe enough to crumble, because what would happen then? If the facade came down, I suspected, the whole building would be promptly written off.

There in that restaurant, as the crumbling took place, I didn't know what it was that I was doing, I didn't yet realize that it was a need to do exactly this which had brought me here. But some part of me must have known, because what also broke, along with every semblance of comportment and glamour I was holding on to, was the spell. Waking up alone the next morning in my hotel room, I was still no wiser as to where I'd obtained the recipe for this exorcism, how something so blundering and clumsy had managed to hit its target, but there was no doubting the change. Y had vanished from the place that was too deep down to really feel, and what was left was a huge, lonely, open space. It had begun. For the first time ever, I began to fall apart for real.

¶ sara-sara: the sound of a very smooth fluid taking you by surprise (and being the most acceptable part of you)

YEARS PASS. I'M SINGLE, AND my life is small and solitary, and I cry a lot, even if I laugh a lot as well. At some point it dawns on me that I've ceased to be attractive as a woman. Throughout my time in Japan I've heard it said over and over again that foreign women are frightening to Japanese men, but I've never struggled much before. I was attracted to Japanese men, and women, and they were attracted to me, and that was just how it went. Now, I have the feeling that I've slipped off the plate. I am not going anywhere—for maybe the first time in my life, I sense this with a calm certainty. This isn't an adrenaline-powered whirl of doom like it was back in Tokyo when I was twenty-two. Life is a snail-like crawl towards wherever I sense safety might lie, but the crawl takes me no closer to it. Most days I feel that I simply don't have the energy to be this different from other people around me, to be treated with so much caution, fascination, surprise, horror. I don't have the energy to be always slightly wrong, to be flinched from in corridors. Of course I'm aware that if I could just relax and stop being so self-conscious everything would be better, but in these days my cells feel like they are made up of uncontaminated self-consciousness. I've always been plagued by it, but now it is a vice-like physical grip.

I could talk here about all the myriad ways in which I feel disgusting, but I'll limit myself to one very specific way— although if I allow my eyes to soften on it for too long then it blurs into every other form of disgustingness I feel to be mine—and that is: how it feels as though all I really want to do is talk about my feelings all the time, and how that puts me fundamentally at odds with almost every member of Japanese society I encounter. Really, it isn't that I want to talk about my feelings constantly, but that I need to know it's okay to talk about them, because only then am I able to relax and not have them constantly tugging at my consciousness all the time like a pack of needy children.

Even this need for empathy isn't something I experience simply, but rather as a convoluted complex in perpetual dialogue with itself. Approximately a third of me thinks I should be able to talk about my feelings all the time to whomever, and people shouldn't be threatened by that. I have a friendly face and I'm frightened of hurting people, and I've endured a lifetime's worth of strangers coming up to me in the street to emotionally offload on me, not to mention those people I do know; now, now, it is payback time. Thus spake my entitled portion. A second third recognizes that a space where you can talk about feelings with someone is something that you build up over time; that I would be freaked out if someone I'd just met launched into a conversation about how much they disliked themselves, and considering that Japanese people are disconcerted by talking to me in general, it is hardly a surprise that they don't open up that space for me. My third third just longs to be different. It wants to have the emotional palette of the people around me, the restraint and the decorum and the talent for repression. It wants to not have to be this guy, this woman, this clammy foreign person whose everything is too gloopy and too much.

––––––––

At some point during this extended fallow period, I take on a private adult student, S. Later, we will end up ill-advisedly dating, but for the time being we are not together. Before it turns wintry and she starts coming to my flat for her lessons, we meet in parks and sit on benches for hours, getting eaten alive by mosquitoes and reading children's books, and occasionally straying off topic and talking about all sorts of weird stuff.

This situation has come to pass because S came to one of the classes I am giving in a café. A few weeks later I bump into her in the street, and we have an interaction that feels highly charged, though I can't exactly say with what. There is something instantly and obviously different about her. Everything she says, each movement she makes is like some minor act of bravery, a brutal stroke through a lake of softness. She is tiny, her hair is short, she moves like a boy, her face is so delicate it could have been cast in porcelain. You can feel the conflict breathing in her, and you can feel how she turns from it. In retrospect, I would say, you can feel the unprocessed trauma, although I don't put it to myself like that at the time—suppose I can't, because that would mean not proceeding down the road we're traveling, not trying to see her as she wants to be seen.

Before she ever told me a thing about herself, I could picture S as a kid: the tomboy who'd not have shown the slightest fraction of interest in me, who ran around daubed with mud and could do anything with her body that the situation demanded. These days she is immaculately clean, but she maintains a morbid fascination with bodily functions and anything commonly described as gross. Cuts, diseases, snot, scars, shit, drool, puke—it seems like she saves up her greatest enthusiasm for anything which it isn't polite to describe in great detail, and when we start reading Dahl's *The Witches* together, I can feel the way the words we read out seem to slot into her worldview.

I learn early on that she struggles when our conversations veer into territory that could be described as emotional. When I make the attempt to go down this path, she looks at me like a stunned rabbit then follows up with a barrage of factual questions. I am with her when I find out my mother has just been hospitalized, and before I know what's what, I am being bombarded by inquiries about the medical system in my country, how it is that healthcare can be offered for free, what the problems are with the NHS, feeling, even as I answer dumbly in Japanese, a numb sort of confusion, until finally my brain clocks out and I stare at her mutely. And yet, so long as we are talking within her comfort zone, particularly on topics for which she has enthusiasm, there is a quality to her attention that feels extraordinary. Maybe it only feels that way because I am so starved of it. But in any case, with all that going on, we sometimes get tied up in strange conversations, more revealing because of what we don't say. At these times I have the impression we are heading down a narrow alley, knowing that it won't take us where we want to go but still ineluctably drawn further and further on, because all that matters for the moment is this forward motion, together.

Now, sitting at my desk in my one-room flat, facing the window that gives on to Osaka Castle, we are talking about childhood memories. Surprise surprise, both of us were weird kids, although differently so. I am describing one of my earliest memories to her, which even now I find hard to explain. I was sitting at my desk in reception class when I felt a tingling sensation in the back of my nose, like it was about to run. The next thing I recall, there was a great puddle of water on my desk, larger than my hand. I remember looking down at it, feeling totally bemused as to how that quantity of fluid had come out of my nose, and not having a clue what to do about it. In fact I don't know what I did do about it in the end; it probably doesn't bear thinking about. In any case, my memory ends with that scene, staring down at the puddle in astonishment.

As I sensed she might be, S is delighted by this conversational offering of mine.

"Woah! Your nose ran *that much*?" she asks, her voice soaring. "You mean all that sara-sara water came out of your nose?"

I know sara-sara as a word, but I never really know it until she says it now. The emphasis—saraSA'ra—seems to express in a way that now feels close to totally intuitive both how runny this water is and how excited she feels about its runniness.

Years later, I will translate a short story with a narrator who hears an anecdote stating that the first time Japanese people in a certain region saw Westerners drinking red wine, they believed it was blood. The narrator doubts the credibility of this because, as she puts it, "as if blood would ever be that sara-sara." I deliberated long and hard on how to render "sara-sara" before finally opting for "runny"; now I think that "watery" would have been the better translation. But either way, it's hard to imagine a native Anglophone focusing on that aspect of the wine, just as it's hard to imagine an English speaker who had been told my nose-running anecdote focusing on the texture of the water, at least in that way. We might say, "Wait, a whole puddle of water came out of your nose?" But to pinpoint the smoothness, the textural quality of the water seems improbable, if not impossible as something to do in English, not exactly because we don't have the muscles for it, but maybe because our muscles for giving expression to the sensate properties of things are less well developed than the muscles of the average Japanese speaker. We sound less good when we flex them.

In this particular moment, this precise tactility of the Japanese language dovetails so perfectly with S's personality that it appears to me like a natural extension of it, and I feel a powerful hankering for this ability to root oneself in the specific, physical sensation. Never mind that S's emotional life is clearly opaque to her, that she doesn't really understand herself—in this moment, I wish I could be like her. I wish I could be smooth and watery, and not constantly attempting to serve up my viscous emotional stew at any possible opportunity. I wish I was different, and that this conversation we are having was the real world, for me as well as for her. Or, at the very least, that this was the only kind of communication that I needed. So we keep on talking, relating our various gross childhood anecdotes and trying to believe that our words are all that is the case.

¶ ho': the sound of the xenophobe returning home, or being restored to magical normality by your friends, or tolerating yourself in photographs

SCATTERED THROUGHOUT THE DOOM I trod were little pockets of breathable air, whose existence I owed entirely to my friends.

I know that when I'd first learned, right at the beginning of my Japanese education, that to say "I found a friend" you said tomodachi ga dekita, which translated literally into English as something like *I was able to make a friend*, I'd found it an amusing and endearingly childish turn of phase. Nowadays I thought nothing of it, but when students rendered it literally in English, as they often did, asking me "Could you find a friend?" or declaring proudly, "I was able to make a friend," it still tickled me because of the way it seemed to imply talent, or effort, or a sense of achievement, none of which I associated with the act of making friends. I believed that finding people with whom to be friends was out of your control, not an art form or something for which you could claim any responsibility.

But then I met T, and before very long I wanted to shout

it from the rooftops: *I WAS ABLE TO MAKE A FRIEND!* The friendship felt no more like something I'd accomplished personally through effort or talent than any in the past, but the sheer importance of what it represented to me generated a sense of achievement. Maybe my change in perception was as simple as this: never had I needed a real friend as much as I did then. But even if need greased the wheels for me and T, our bond never felt like one of convenience. Instead, there were elements of our friendship that I'd not experienced before with anyone. Specifically, I'd never before had this feeling of being safe to talk with someone about anything—to be as ugly and uncool as the occasion demanded, to speak about myself with unlimited seriousness in the knowledge that I'd be heard—and because we'd gone to those places, there was a trust that suffused all of our conversations, so that even when we talked about crass and superficial and extremely silly subjects, as often we did, it rarely felt like there was much pretense or artifice between us. We were both of us good at pretending, and had spent a lot of our lives burdened by a feeling of doing exactly that, as we discussed in great detail, so it wasn't entirely clear to us how we had managed to create a space of honesty, only that we had. And this space announced itself physically—either immediately that I saw T or after a few minutes' conversation, I would feel the relief pass through me, the tension of being inside my body lifting. It was like the videos of drain unblocking fluid you saw in adverts, where a pipe's worth of gunge would be converted to a peaceful stream of clear blue in a sheer instant.

We talked about this feeling that we both had in the other's company, and yet it was oddly hard to find the vocabulary for. Part of that, I think, was that it seemed slightly illicit to describe feelings that grew up between a woman and a man who weren't in a romantic relationship. Maybe that was good; instead of falling back on banalities, we had to actually think about what it was that we felt. We had to speak of drain unblockers. Or: someone who recharged your batteries—that was T's phrase, which sounded a lot better in Japanese than it did in English. We had more improvisational creative alternatives, too, and more emotional ones that came out after a drink or two, but the most standard phrase we used, and which became our go-to choice, was ho'to suru. Ho, with a sokuon after, was the sound of exhalation, and ho'to suru meant breathing a deep sigh of relief, the reassurance of having your concerns and worries taken away.

Up until that point, ho'to suru was not a phrase with which I had particularly good associations. It was common enough that I'd heard it in a variety of contexts, but the strongest connotation was with a certain section of students I'd taught over time who would tell me how relieved and comforted they were to return from a trip abroad and see clean streets and Japanese faces again, smell the scent of dashi billowing out from the restaurants, and speak their own language, because, "When it comes down to it, Japan is the best." Another set phrase that these same people would come out with frequently was "I like traveling but I prefer Japan," and when I asked why, the answer would be formed of some variation on the three big concepts: it's safe, the food is delicious, and I can speak Japanese. And then they might say it again: In Japan, I feel ho'to. Or they'd ask me how to say it in English. From mouth after mouth, across different age groups and in different parts of the country, I had watched these sentiments emerge, dazzling in their uniformity, and when I was irritable I would think reflexively: fuck you. No really, fuck your stable national identity, your crimeless safe haven, your rich and unique culinary tradition. It felt like the smugness attached not just to the qualities of Japan, but also to the meta-activity of leaning back into and parroting the received narrative. And thus, over time, I'd come to associate the phrase ho'to with lazy patriots, uncritical, boring, scared people who lived oblivious to their own privilege, the kind of people who had never even considered what it meant, for example, for their country to accept so few asylum seekers, or why that could be seen as problematic for the third largest economy in the world.

Speaking honestly, I can't promise that if I were back in Japan teaching right now, I wouldn't feel this exact same rage all over again; even in my calmest moments, I believe this phenomenon merits genuine concern. I see something inherently problematic about the patriotic messaging that pervades Japanese society, and however benign and apolitical its expressions might appear in the context of an English class, I feel it shares an ecosystem with phenomena which are anything but. I could go further and say that I think that when "Japan is number one!" can pass as a simple expression of preference without calling for any unpacking, then that society is bound to have problems, and some of the shapes that those problems will take are nationalism and xenophobia.

And yet I would also say this: like most vehement fuck-you reactions, there was a backstory to this one too, a reason why I was taking the affront so personally. I also think that it was in part through being friends with T that my grievances began to heal. It was through experiencing a feeling of unbounded security for the first time in what seemed like forever—and not as a sudden burst of euphoria, but something drawn out across months, years—that I was able to accept (gradually, unwillingly, problematically) that it was okay to want safety. And then, in time, to see that in some way that was all I'd ever wanted, and had therefore immunized myself against ever wanting—scorned others for wanting, and resented when they actually got those desires fulfilled, and recognized it, and expressed it: ho'to. That ho'to was a reasonable thing to want and hope for and enjoy, although that didn't mean you'd always get it.

When I think about feeling comfortable in this way, there's one specific episode I remember; like the thermal imaging cameras you see at the airport that turn your body heat into lurid yellows, pinks and greens, it seems to cast in visible form something I'd never thought I'd be able to visually perceive.

It was summer, and more or less the worst that I'd been feeling. Great waves of self-loathing would wash over me when I was walking down the street or getting out of the shower or standing on the train, and it would take me all my energy not to double over, to physically flinch, from the horrendous spectacle that was myself as it flashed before my mind in the form of images that weighed a ton. Sometimes I didn't manage it. Even when the invitation came to go on a day-trip with T and his boyfriend, N, to Awaji Island, I didn't feel enthused. It was important, my therapist would tell me, that I battled through the waves and met with people, and though I found it nearly impossible to imagine how anything good could come of something which felt so awful, I did as she said. For a start, I said yes to T and N. When the morning of our trip came around, it was blistering hot, and as I stepped into their car, I felt only foreboding for what the day had in store.

Somewhere on the journey there, though, I began to realize that I didn't feel too ill at ease. By the time we stepped into the cool underground recesses of the Tadao Andō temple, which from surface level looked just like a lily pond, I was having twinges of a different feeling: not perfect enjoyment, for sure, but held in place, as if I were part of a family. Was I being perfectly authentic in that moment? I probably wasn't—as usually happened when it was the three of us, we all fooled around a bit, and the conversations we were having were hardly serious. But somewhere, somehow, I felt deeply comfortable. I could feel my lungs, breathing.

The following day, N created a shared folder for our photos of the outing; he had a proper camera and had taken a decent number of pictures. I opened up the folder full of the usual dread I felt at the prospect of encountering photos of myself, my eyes involuntarily narrowing to reduce the impact of the visual blow I was about to receive, but for once no blow came.

To this day, I don't really know what the difference consisted in between these photos and all the others that had been taken of me. Probably there were superficial factors at play: I was wearing clothes in which I felt comfortable, and I wasn't eating or drinking much so I was thinner than usual, but I can say with certainty it wasn't just that. I'm unsure whether it was my comfort that came across in the way I held myself in the photos, or if it was more my memories of that day which affected my perception of myself, but either way, I remember as I looked at them formulating the thought: I guess this is what normal people feel like when they look at pictures of themselves. I wouldn't have gone as far as to say that I looked nice, but I looked how I looked, and for the moment that was okay.

¶ gu'tari: the sound of your words having more power than you thought, or unexpectedly saying what you mean

MORE AND MORE AND MORE, I felt that I was failing at Japan. There was no doubt that I was in a dark place and wouldn't have been happy wherever I was, and I was mightily wary of straying into the expat affliction of blaming all my ills on the country where I had actively chosen to be, generalizing wildly so that everyone who glared at me at the convenience store became not just a mean person at the convenience store but an exemplification of some problematic aspect of Japanese culture and how little it respected me, and so on. This was a tendency I'd observed and criticized in people around me, while knowing I was not immune; now I found myself doing it more often, bitterly regretting it afterwards.

Increasingly, though, I started to suspect that there was more going on than simply scapegoating. As my panic and anxiety gradually lessened, as communicating with people ceased to feel so dreadful and walking down the street less awful, it started to strike me that I would feel even less self-hating and self-conscious if I wasn't surrounded by people who treated me like I was radically other. I knew that acceptance had to come from the inside, but I felt it might be easier in a situation where it was more forthcoming on the outside also.

When this thought first started to formulate itself, it struck me as straight-out wimpishness, and I dismissed it. I homed in on the reasons why I was held at arm's length: was it simply because I was foreign, or rather because I wasn't fully understanding yet of people's nuances? In other words, could I be sure that the failing wasn't mine; could I not assimilate better? It was only after a while that it started to sink in: it didn't matter where the fault lay. It didn't matter if it wasn't Japan per se but my specific situation that was at fault; it didn't matter if there were tweaks that would hypothetically make me feel better. I didn't have to have explored the possibilities exhaustively. I didn't have to play this as an endurance test. I just had to find what was right for me, and do it.

And more and more, it felt like going back to the UK might be right, although that thought also carried the distinct ring of wimpishness. Since first being on the island—which was to say for most of my adult life so far—I'd been adamant that Britain was no home to me. Not only had I always felt incapable of representing or speaking for British people, as I'd been constantly asked to do, but I'd go as far as telling people straight out that I didn't feel British. I'd prided myself on never having felt homesick, and would act marginally affronted when people assumed that I would be returning home soon. It was through therapy that I started to unpick what it meant not only instinctively to pursue the path of greatest resistance, but also to use that as a way of defiantly turning away from feelings of not being accepted: *you won't abandon me because I'll abandon you first.* When I started to entertain

the idea that I would go back—that regardless of the politi-
cal shitshow playing out there, the UK might feel welcoming
in the way that I wanted it to right now—a different kind of
guilt popped up: the incredible, predictable privilege of it all.
Who was I to be lapsing back into the joy of returning home,
when some people didn't have a place they could go to and
feel accepted? When other people in situations unthinkably
worse than this had no choice but to brave them out? And yet,
the gnawing sense grew, more and more unavoidable: acceptance was what I wanted. It didn't need to be total—in fact I
didn't see how it could be. I just wanted to be in a place where
people would talk to me as one of them. I wanted people to
smile at me, and not to remind me constantly of the country
where I was from. I sat with this thought for some time, and
gradually softened to it. I started to make peace with the idea
that feeling this in a sustained way might suggest not a defi-
ciency in me, but rather some unfulfilled need.

Around this time I bought a new backpack, which I first
saw sported by a schoolgirl in the park outside my house, then
tracked down in a Tokyu Hands department store. The bag
was a bright emerald green, made of canvas with a snap at the
top. The fabric tag sewn into its belly region read "Relate"
in red letters against a white background. Underneath, in a
smaller font, were written the words: "Hope many people
are connected by this bag." It was one of those rare times out
shopping when, despite the surprisingly eye-watering price
tag, I felt no hesitation whatsoever, and as I strode over with it
in hand to the cash register, I was reminded of my early days in
Japan when I would gravitate towards items that bore oracular
English slogans, sensing in them some sort of mystical solace

as though they were tidings of hope from the universe. Back on the island, I'd bought a hardback diary for the year with cartoon elephants scattered throughout, whose cover sported the slogan IN LOVE THERE IS NO LACK; *yes*, I remember thinking when I saw it; *yes, that's exactly how it is*, spectacularly failing to recognize that my close flirtation with "lack" lay at the structural core of everything I was experiencing—failing to acknowledge consciously that I was drawn to it precisely because it represented the opposite of my current situation, and somewhere I believed that if I could only swallow it whole, I would become it. Now *Relate* was just the same. All I wanted to do was to relate to people, and with Japan as a whole, and it seemed like everything that I couldn't do.

By this point I had a girlfriend, and I couldn't relate to her either. The saga of us finally getting together had almost finished me off, far overshooting any touchingly awkward marker and landing square in territory that seemed a million miles from the way that two people who cared for each other behaved. This should have been sufficient to sound loud warning alarms about how things were going to go; indeed it did sound warning alarms, but I elected to ignore them. And lo, there were a few moments of affection and goodwill scattered throughout our time together that came when we were in silence or talking about insignificant subjects, but mostly, overwhelmingly, we disagreed about everything, and our conversations were all the more crazy-making for the linguistic difficulties that we faced.

As our relationship disintegrated, I began to be visited by a strange apparition: clarity. Specifically, a certain kind of clarity about who I was and what I wanted. In the heat of my ridiculous arguments with S, where it felt like all my most basic tenets about life and the universe were challenged, my world would spin and I would grow nauseated. Yet increasingly, as I came away, I felt relatively single-minded. It began to dawn on me that I was, in fact, sure about some things after all, and that a lot of these things were the values that she called Western individualism. I balked at that term, of course. Not only had I been set on proving to myself and everyone else that I was as Japanese as the rest of them, I also felt a great distaste for so much of the Western world, particularly as viewed through the eyes of Japan, and most particularly when it was the type of Westernness that was proud of itself, drinking down its sunny liberal values and never thinking to question them. And yet the values to which S referred now—being open with one's feelings, talking problems through, showing warmth, connecting with other people through honest communication, prioritizing one's personal development over unquestioningly going along with what other people wanted from you—were ones to which I subscribed. I didn't see them as Western, particularly because the majority of Western people around whom I'd spent time were light years away from embodying such values, but whatever they were, I believed in them relatively unreservedly.

Except even calling it "belief" felt wrong: these were just the things I wanted, for myself and for the people with whom I surrounded myself. The feeling of letting myself want something just because wanting it felt right was tapping into a force that felt in some way primal, a blast of sunlight through the veins. It felt transparent to me that this was not adopting an identity I'd dreamed up for myself, but returning to what I had always and never had. The longer I sat with it, the more the realizations rained down on me: I didn't have to be a chameleon, at least to quite the extent that I felt it necessary to be one right now; I didn't have to hold in my head at all times the validity of other ways of being. I could understand and empathize with other people while still upholding my values. I wanted to be around people who could say what it was that they were actually feeling; I wanted to be around people who had some insight into their own mental workings. I could arrange my life so that I wasn't met with shock and fear and embarrassment each time I talked about how I felt. I could arrange my life so I wasn't shamed for feeling angry, and saying so.

———

The final straw with S, when it came, was stupid. After a week of exhausting arguments, she sent me a photo she'd taken on her way past a temple, an elegant handwritten sign that read THE HEART OF THE BUDDHA IS NOT GREEDY AND DOES NOT GET ANGRY, appended with the caption "I thought this might be helpful for you," together with a smirking face. Here was the kind of beautiful calligraphy which had seemed to me so fathomlessly romantic at the age of fifteen and for many years after, and now here I was, almost two decades later and capable of reading it, and it was biting me in the ass. A well-deserved bite, probably; payback for all the years of exoticization. Still, S's message was straight-out bitchy, and it cut me as I imagine it was supposed to. Cut me sufficiently that I can remember where I was when I got it, standing in the aisle of the foreign section of a bookshop in central Osaka. I remember too forwarding it to T, with whom I'd been talking through the ins and outs of my relationship for a while, and I remember his reply: *That's enough, no? I don't see why you have to put up with this shit.*

Like so often, I felt like he'd spoken my mind for me, said what I was afraid to fully formulate to myself.

"I don't think this is working, is it?" S said, days later at my flat when she'd come over to talk things through.

"No," I said, and paused. Many times she had told me that she wished I was calmer; now, I found myself serene with detachment. "It's totally all-consuming. I've barely been able to work this week."

"Maybe we should call it quits," she said, scanning me with big searchlight eyes. "If it's having an effect on your work."

"Yeah, maybe we should," I said, sensing as I did that this was not my line. I was supposed to respond with aggression or upset, with my characteristic drama. We were supposed to wrestle our way out of this, have a fight and then have make-up sex all night, face the next morning together sleepless and wide-eyed and in love again. But I didn't feel like I had it in me. I tuned in to what my body was saying, and it was saying something quite simple, so I said it out loud: "I'm exhausted."

Gu'tari: the dictionary on my computer translates it as "completely [absolutely, utterly] exhausted," and "dead tired"; also "limp," and "drooping." A quick Google image search yields a zoo's worth of slumped animals: dogs, polar bears, foxes, cats, raccoons. It was a word that I had only really added into my spoken vocabulary recently, after hearing T use it about a day spent walking around in the sun, but I'd known it peripherally for a long time, and I felt like I understood well enough what it was saying. Certainly, I didn't feel like it contained hidden depths.

Now, though, as I saw the shock pass across S's face, I wondered suddenly if I'd underestimated its impact. I thought of how she'd described her mother's response to learning of my existence: "Her reaction was normal," she'd said, "but her eyes were not." In the same way, it was S's eyes that told me how weighty what I'd said had been: the way they seemed to swell as she breathed the word in. Had I been unintentionally hurtful? Was I being one of those Japanese speakers I was always trying not to be, who wreaked unknown violence with their language? Was using gu'tari in this way tantamount to saying that I was sick and tired of her? Did I have the right to use a phrase like this, or was this another instance of my Western dramatism?

Even if I hadn't known what I was saying as I said it, and even if it was blunt and mean, it felt also like I'd unintentionally spoken the truth: I was really, really tired. I was tired of having to fight tooth and nail to be seen as a person. I was tired of making do, of glamorizing this emotional distance and pretending that it was something mystical and sexy, that one day it would yield me the validation and the love and the affection that I wanted. I was tired of feeling like a freak for wanting those things, and ensuring that I was always in a situation where it felt that way.

I was very sure that change was not going to be easy. I'd become so good at assimilating, at adjusting to the other's terms even as I lamented them, that the idea of it was far less affronting to me than the prospect of trying to build what it was I really wanted. Certainly, the building wasn't going to be as simple as just putting myself in a different physical place.

One thing I now felt sure of, though, was that the solution was not to continue depriving myself of what I wanted and then complaining about it. I was not going to thrive while asking myself every second if I had the right to speak a certain way. In that sense, my gu'tari had been correct. Something inside me was done, and it had made itself heard.

¶ atsu-atsu: the sound of being hot to a degree
that stands just on the verge of acceptability

NOT LONG BEFORE I LEAVE Japan for good, an anthro-
pology professor gives me a tour of the National Museum
of Ethnology.

This was not initially the plan. I'd come to the museum earlier that morning to attend the opening ceremony of a temporary
exhibition for which, thanks to some strange administrative
machinations, I was on the planning committee. Located in the
center of the Expo Park on the outskirts of Osaka, the museum
takes an inordinate amount of time to get to from the city center, but I somehow managed to forget that fact each time, and
that day, as always, I was late. After asking about four different people in the museum to direct me, striding in a panic from
floor to floor, I finally nudged my way into an open space where
a crowd of people stood in silence. Threading through the gaps
between people until I had a view, I saw four grave-faced, black-
suited men standing in a row in front of a red-and-white ribbon
hung across the entrance to the exhibition space and pinned
with voluptuous silk rosettes that I imagined my nan would
like. Each of the men held a large pair of scissors.

A fifth man, this one with a microphone in hand, stood to
the side of the four scissor men, delivering a commentary. If I

switched my brain on I could understand almost all the words that he was saying, but if I didn't make a conscious effort—if I allowed my concentration to lapse as it so wanted to after the surge of I'm-going-to-be-late adrenaline—then I could easily hear it as a wash of sound, the kind of wash I remember being staggered by when I first came to Japan. Something about the uniformity of the intonation, the absence of notable sentence-breaks, called to mind the burble of a river, the outpouring of something inanimate—or at least, something with a superior capacity for incessancy and a lesser need for expressive fluctuation than the people I'd grown up knowing.

Now, the microphone man was announcing, we shall perform the ceremony of the tēpu katto, the "tape cut." The utter banality of how this noun sounded to me, imported from English and then engineered to suit the Japanese tongue, formed a surreal contrast with the exaggerated formality of the setting, the ornateness of the rest of his language. By this point, I was supposed to be accustomed to the usage of these Japanese takes on English words in forms or contexts where they would not be used in the West, and the nounification of everything. Yet there were still examples, particularly ones that cropped up in solemn contexts, which would catch me out, call forth in me a schoolgirlish desire to laugh. There was something about cut, in particular, which seemed to get me—I also had a weak spot for paipu katto (vasectomy).

———

Now, the four men square up to the stretch of ribbon. At the microphone man's cue, their four pairs of scissors cut the tape in unison, and snippets of red and white satin rain down to the floor. Watching them, I spot out of the corner of my eye a professor I know—someone unrelated to the exhibition, whom I hadn't anticipated being there.

Of all the people I've encountered in Japan, this professor is one of those I like the most. His soul seems broad, like an open dish ready to accommodate others, but he also has sufficient reserve and robust enough boundaries to make the occasional bursts of humor surprising and all the more joyful.

When the ribbon-cutting ceremony is over, he approaches and says hello. On our last meeting, when we went out for dinner, we spoke entirely in Japanese, but this time he addresses me in English, and we carry on like that. It's the first time I've spoken English outside of teaching for a while, and I remember how freeing it is—not only because of my discrepancy in ability, but also because I don't have to worry about making cultural faux pas all the time, and because I feel less pressure to show respect to him as my elder. Perhaps he would disagree, but it seems to me less that I now have the upper hand, and more that I cease to have the lower hand—a lower hand that doesn't stem solely from not being Japanese, but from being his junior, in age and position, and a woman. In fact, I've met many Japanese people who've spoken of calling on the power of English to do this in certain situations—to level out, to place all speakers on the same platform.

It's not time for lunch yet, and so the professor takes me on a tour of the museum, which I have seen before. It's arranged by region of the world, and he shows me the sections to which he has contributed research. I see a photograph of him during his time living as a Buddhist monk in Thailand, documenting the lives of Buddhist monks in Thailand. He looks youthful, and dignified, and somehow fundamentally the same.

We come to the end of the world, and there is a section designed as a type of play-zone around the theme of language. Suddenly a memory surfaces: this is the one permanent section of the museum for which I've done translations, back when I was just starting out—the English panels must be my work. I tell him this, and I think that's how we end up stepping inside and wandering around.

The section feels like it's built out of so much that I love—there are retellings of the classic Momotarō fable in different dialects from around Japan, experiments with braille, games with voice recognition software, and so on—so much so that I start to wonder if it wasn't in fact designed with language geeks in mind, and not children as I'd initially assumed. But being mostly set up for two people, these are also the kinds of exhibits that I would feel sheepish about enjoying on my own, and I am really glad to have his company in exploring them. His English is good, my Japanese is good, there is pure, nerdy joy for us in this, sharing the wonder of different languages.

There's an attendant standing in the corner of the section, hands neatly clasped behind her back, and we ask her a question about something to do with a pronunciation machine that we don't understand. Presumably she recognizes the professor, because she then adopts the role of a tour-guide, leading us to the next exhibit over: a mimetic-sound generator. Positioned around the circumference of a circular glass window, like a huge porthole laid on its side, are a crowd of little stamps with katakana syllables on them. The attendant demonstrates how, when you drop two syllables on the glass, the machine identifies them and the explanation of the relevant mimetic word pops up, with an illustration.

While I'm still planning my move, the professor leaps in. He lays on the glass an "a" and a "tsu": hot. Oh, I think and before I know it, the explanation has risen up with a picture of a young boy and girl embracing, surrounded by a cloud of tiny hearts.

Atsu-atsu, it reads, *the state of being fervently in love.*

There the three of us are, staring down at it, like a prophecy that has surfaced there on the water—an answer to the unvoiced question posed by a middle-aged professor escorting me, a young foreign woman, around the museum.

"Oh," says the professor. "That's not what I was thinking, I was thinking about hot food." And of course, atsu-atsu is also used in a more literal sense, to mean hot, steaming, boiling; on the verge of inedibility. "That surprised me."

The professor falls into silence, and I try out a couple. Riffing off his attempt, I put down "me" and "ra," angling for mera-mera and sure enough there's a picture of a house fire: *the state of flames licking an object.* But even as we walk away to the next exhibit, the professor's expression now has a disconsolate cast, floating above its stone base of calm. I imagine it is the embarrassment of this situation: here we are, he as a museum professor showing this foreign woman around a section intended for children, and he picks the saucy word. It's either as if he were deliberately trying to create a bit of a stir, or else, that his choice had inadvertently given us a glimpse into the kinds of tracks his mind moves down. I imagine also, or maybe I read on his face, that coupled with that feeling is a sense of disconcertment at being tricked by his own language.

He had gone for a safe one, an easy one, and it had backfired on him—become something that, had we been schoolkids, we would have laughed at him for. Neither exactly to me, nor to himself, he says it again: "That surprised me."

And quite unexpectedly, I feel in that moment a rush of something that I haven't felt for a while, and which can only really be described as love. Love for this person who is so derailed by this experience in a way that I would most likely also be; love for the language that can do these deceptive looping-backs on itself; love for the total, ridiculous specificity of this situation, just one of an infinite number of possible ridiculously specific situations.

For a long time, and particularly of late, it has worried me that I don't love Japan in the way other people around me do; that all I really like is the language. Now it comes to me that the language has never been anything other than a collection of people, real and fictional, whom I've felt assorted affections for. If I've loved Japanese, I've done so because I've loved the glimpses of people I've caught through it. Which is why, I suppose, my feeling for Japan and its language has always been hot, and embodied, and inappropriate; it has been atsu-atsu. In this moment, at least, I can stand behind it and say not just this is how it has been, but that is probably how it will always be.

¶ uho-uho: the sound of the jubilant gorilla
and the foolish builder done good

IT'S COMING UP TO CHRISTMAS. I've arrived at my
mother's house in London a few days before festivities begin,
and none of the other guests are here yet, so I take over a desk
in a room that used to be my brother's, attempting to put the
finishing touches to a book I'm translating.

At one point in the story, the narrator finds a job writing audio adverts for buses, and a few of the advert scripts
are included in the book, sprinkled with realistically cheesy
jokes. Until just a couple of years ago, I used to translate a
lot of computer games, where these kinds of groan-inducing
puns were a ten-a-penny, and mostly the approach there was
simply to localize—to convert the pun to a joke that would
work in English, frequently leaving no trace of what was
there to begin with except the smirk effect. But things work
slightly differently in the world of literature. Which is not to
say that there's never a need to transpose a joke entirely, but
it's seen as more of a last resort, with the ideal being to get
across at least some of the joke's content if possible. In particular, this is a book I adore by an author I respect, and I
would prefer to cleave more closely to what the Japanese says

unless I'm left with no option, in part because I don't feel wholly confident to judge whether or not the content of the joke is resonating or linking up with something else in the book in a way I can't see.

One of the adverts I have to translate is for an estate agency, and ends with the line: "The gorilla on our billboard sure is glad he stopped by!" followed by the sound "uho-uho." The first time I encountered this section I felt puzzlement, which faded when I looked up uho-uho in the dictionary and found it defined as 1) the state of being satisfied or full of glee and 2) the noise that a gorilla makes. Great, I thought. What the hell am I going to do about this? And so I did what I always do when I'm on my first draft: I put in a very literal translation as a placeholder, and highlighted it. As I go through for the second time, I aim to get rid of these highlighted sections; by the third pass, there are only a few remaining.

But now, here I am on my final go-through, and the crappy placeholder translation is still there: *joyful roar*. I'm aware that this is no good for a number of reasons: a) it doesn't sound very simian, b) it's not the sort of thing I can imagine appearing in a real ad, and c) it's not remotely funny. In short, it's a terrible translation, but I feel at a bit of a loss as to how to make it better. I try various searches like "gorilla sound english," but don't have much luck, and since I'm a bit bored, and since it feels like a novelty to have someone around to consult, I go to the top of the stairs and look down at my mother, checking her emails at her desk in the hall.

"Can I ask you something?" I say. "What noise do you think of gorillas as making? Like, in English."

My mother looks up at me blankly. I explain my problem to her more fully, including what I've got in there at the moment.

"Hmm," she says. "Definitely not a roar, I don't think."

"Really?"

"I don't really think of gorillas as making any noise, but definitely not roaring. Don't they grunt, more?"

"I was wondering that," I say. "But then 'joyful grunt' sounds weird, doesn't it? Like too sexual or something."

"I think roar is misleading, though. It sounds like a big cat."

Maybe she's right, I think, and then it strikes me that I don't have a clear image of what noise gorillas *do* actually make. I thank my mother, go back up to my room, put on some YouTube videos, thinking that I'm a bad translator, that this should have been my first port of call, back when I was doing my first draft. Not long after there's a knock on my door: my mother's come to tell me she's going out.

"About the gorillas, I definitely think roar is wrong," she adds. "I think grunt is better."

"Okay, got it. I was just listening to some live recordings of them, and it's pretty indefinable as a sound. But I'll go with grunt for now, I guess. I feel like there has to be something better, though. It just doesn't feel very funny. Maybe I'll write a note to my editor about it."

"Right," she says. "Well, I'm off, I'll see you later."

"See you later."

My mother opens the door, and as she makes to leave the room, she pauses by the doorframe and throws a look back in my direction.

"Is this, um—is this how you spend your days?"

I look at her straight-faced. "Yes," I say and nod. "It really is."

"Hah!" says my mother. Then her eyes grow very wide and her face falls slack, taking on a look of faint horror. "Oh," she says.

————

If I look beyond my own situation for a second, I feel I can easily understand my mother's reaction. To the unaccustomed eye, it would seem a crazy way to spend one's time: almost profligate in its attention to apparently random detail. Registering this to myself, I have a faint memory of an era before all this became my reality, when the process of literary translation had seemed similar to me: enviable and important, sure, but also frivolous in what it actually involved, like spending all day selecting the precise patterns and shades of floor tiles.

It would be untrue to say that I am untouched these days by concerns about whether what I do is indulgent, but now the worries take a different form. Looking at other literary translators translating important texts that wouldn't otherwise make it to the attention of the world outside their nations, I feel convinced that literary translation is, as often stated, a form of activism, but as regards myself, there are frequently days when, as the world burns and crumbles, I wonder if sitting around adding to the pile of texts people feel obliged to read is where it is at—if this is comfortable inaction dressed up as virtue. This is not just a dark-night-of-the-soul fear but a genuine concern, and I increasingly feel that as translators we need to be activists in far more than simply our choices of texts and processes. And yet these days, when it comes to the everyday process of translating, the strange avenues of research it leads me down and the endless pondering, not only do I not feel that what I do is indulgent, but I find myself strangely full of conviction. I've never been a parent, but I can imagine that this is a similar sort of feeling to the one I might have if someone were to ask me, on seeing me playing some hare-brained game with my child, if this was what I did all day. This sense that, even if it wasn't what I did all day, I would turn and reply without shame, yes, it is, and the reply would come out of a direct understanding that this indulgent attention is the birthplace of all the good stuff. That the big things people are keen to heap glory on, be they people or books, are built up out of an accumulation of the tiny little indulgences that people are inclined to look down on and find silly or profligate. Obviously, not every book or every person can become a good one, but without that sort of effort invested, there's really no hope.

It feels odd to me to realize, now, in this moment, exactly how stable I am in what I do, how impervious I feel to aspersions cast on the role of the translator. I can remember looking at the people around me in school who wanted to be doctors or engineers (it was always those professions which kids started talking about with gravitas from the age of eleven), and finding that sense of calling utterly alien. It would probably be an exaggeration to say that I think of what I do now as a calling, but what I can say is that sometimes when I'm doing it, I can feel this umbilical rope leading all the way back. To being in Japan, of course—to learning, and to speaking; to hanging on the words of another person and finding them magical; to dreaming about one day being able to read real adult books, and then when I'd managed that, to dreaming about translating those books. But the rope leads even further back than that, to my own childhood. To the struggles and the miracles of learning to express myself then, too. To putting your ear up close to another person, and trying to tune in to their world. To the kind of playfulness with words that I was brought up ingesting, the immense joy to be taken in silliness and in language which I think my mother helped me find—even if at this precise moment she's slightly taken aback that her daughter gets paid (for a certain value of "gets paid") to listen to gorillas on YouTube. Connected up with all of this, even though I might not always or almost ever be aware of such connections on a moment-by-moment basis, what I feel is groundedness.

It's strange, really, that such groundedness can exist here, in what seems objectively like an implausible place to find certainty: this in-between place which is translation, this space where you hover spectral between one language and another, where ideas routinely swim, and give way underfoot, and where there aren't any right answers. It's not the sort of place that you're supposed to draw security from, or which is supposed to make you happy or prosperous. As the parable tells us, success is reserved for the man who builds his house on the rock. Nowadays I think that maybe I've known always somewhere deep down that I couldn't live for long on any rock. What took me longer to figure out was that living on the sand didn't have to be just a running away or an experience of permanent overwhelm. That the topsy-turvy place between languages and cultures, which has been a site of humility and triangulation and self-knowledge, of absurdity and inanity and the best sort of creative fertility, can also offer, paradoxically, a kind of safety. It comes to me that I have built a kind of dwelling here, where I can google gorilla noises all day long, and not worry too much about my productivity; a big, small, crazy dwelling, in which I don't just work but also live.

Sitting on my brother's chair, I open my mouth and let out a joyful sound.

.

FIFTY SOUNDS:
A MULTIMEDIA MIXTAPE

Compiled roughly in order of appearance

PREFACE

Parmy Olson, "Crowdsourcing Capitalists: How Duolingo's Founders Offered Free Education to Millions," *Forbes*, 10 February 2014.

Yoko Hasegawa (ed.), *The Cambridge Handbook of Japanese Linguistics* (Cambridge: Cambridge University Press, 2018).

Bjarke Frellesvig, *A History of the Japanese Language* (Cambridge: Cambridge University Press, 2010).

Hugh Bredin, "Onomatopoeia as a Figure and Linguistic Principle," *New Literary History*, 27, no. 3, Literary Subjects (Summer 1996).

Roman Jakobson, "Linguistics and Poetics," in *Language in Literature* (Cambridge, MA: Belknap Press of Harvard University Press, 1987).

Ferdinand de Saussure, *Course in General Linguistics*, tr. Roy Harris (Chicago: Open Court, 1983).

Lawrence Schourup, "Nichi-ei onomatope no taishōkenkyū" [A Comparative Study of Japanese and English Onomatopoeia], *Gengo*, 1993.

Sotarō Kita, "Two-Dimensional Semantic Analysis of Japanese Mimetics," originally in *Linguistics* 35 (1997), http://wrap.warwick.ac.uk/106489/.

Imai, Mutsumi, and Sotarō Kita, "The Sound Symbolism Bootstrapping Hypothesis for Language Acquisition and Language Evolution," *Philosophical Transactions of the Royal Society* 369, no. 1651 (19 September 2014).

V. S. Ramachandran and E. M. Hubbard, "Synaesthesia—A Window into Perception, Thought, and Language," *Journal of Consciousness Studies* 8 (2001).

Gergana Ivanova, "Sound-Symbolic Approach to Japanese Mimetic Words," *Toronto Working Papers in Linguistics* 26 (2006).

Rie Hasada, "The Semantic Aspects of Onomatopoeia; Focusing on Japanese Psychomimes," Master's Thesis, Australian National University, 1994.

Mattho Mandersloot, "Korean Onomatopoeia in Translation: Negotiating between Meaning and Feeling," Master's Thesis, University of Oxford, 2019.

Joshua Marrinor Caldwell, "Iconic Semantics in Phonology: A Corpus Study of Japanese Mimetics," Master's Thesis, Brigham Young University, 2010.

Hiroshi Nara, "Onomatopoeia," https://www.japanpitt.pitt.edu/essays-and-articles/language/onomatopoeia.

Nakami Yamaguchi (ed.), *Giongo Gitaigo Jisho* [Dictionary of Japanese Onomatopoeia] (Tokyo: Kodansha, 2015).

Tomoyuki Makita, Chie Morimoto, and Ichio Ōtsuka, *Giongo Gitaigo Jisho* [Dictionary of Japanese Onomatopoeia] (Tokyo: Robot Communications Inc., Pie Books, 2004).

Hisao Kakehi, Ikuhiro Tamori, and Lawrence Schourup, *Dictionary of Iconic Expressions in Japanese* (Berlin: De Gruyter Mouton, 1996).

Susan Sontag, "Against Interpretation," *Against Interpretation and Other Essays* (London: Penguin, 2002).

¶ GIRO'

W. G. Sebald, *Austerlitz*, tr. Anthea Bell (London: Penguin, 2001).

Ludwig Wittgenstein, *Philosophical Investigations*, tr. G. E. M. Anscombe (Oxford: Blackwell, 2001).

Ray Monk, "Looking for Wittgenstein," review of *Ludwig Wittgenstein: Ein biographisches Album*, ed. Michael Nedo, *The New York Review of Books*, 6 June 2013.

¶ GIZA-GIZA

Helen Gilhooly, *Teach Yourself Japanese Language, Life & Culture* (London: Teach Yourself, 2002).

Brandon Labelle, *Lexicon of the Mouth: Poetics and Politics of Voice and the Oral Imaginary* (London: Bloomsbury, 2014).

Yukio Mishima, *Confessions of a Mask*, tr. Meredith Weatherby (London: Panther, 1972).

Kenzaburō Ōe, *Teach Us to Outgrow Our Madness,* tr. John Nathan
    (London: Serpent's Tail, 1994).
Haruki Murakami, *Sputnik Sweetheart*, tr. Philip Gabriel (New York:
    Knopf, 2001).

¶ ZARA-ZARA
Ray Monk, *Ludwig Wittgenstein: The Duty of Genius* (London: Vin-
    tage, 1991).
Brian McGuinness, *Wittgenstein: A Life; Young Ludwig, 1889–1921*
    (London: Duckworth, 1988).
Ludwig Wittgenstein, *Letters to Russell, Keynes and Moore,*
    ed. G. H. von Wright (Oxford: Basil Blackwell, 1974).
Gottlob Frege, *The Basic Laws of Arithmetic I*, 1893. As quoted
    in P. M. S. Hacker, *Wittgenstein's Place in Twentieth-Century Ana-
    lytic Philosophy* (Oxford: Blackwell, 1996).
Ludwig Wittgenstein, *Tractatus Logico-Philosophicus*, tr. D. F. Pears
    and B. F. McGuinness (London: Routledge Classics, 2001).
Ludwig Wittgenstein, *Zettel*, tr. G. E. M. Anscombe (Oxford: Blackwell,
    1967).
Ludwig Wittgenstein, *The Blue and Brown Books: Preliminary Studies
    for the "Philosophical Investigations"* (Oxford: Blackwell, 2008).

¶ NOBI-NOBI
The Velvet Underground, "Ride into the Sun," *Another View*, Verve
    Records, 1986.
Rachel Cusk, "In Praise of the Creative Writing Course," *Guardian*, 18
    January 2013.
Roland Barthes, *Empire of Signs,* tr. Richard Howard (New York: Hill
    and Wang, 1983).
bell hooks, *All About Love: New Visions* (New York: William Morrow,
    2001).

¶ MOJA-MOJA
Heinrich Hoffmann, *Struwwelpeter, or, Pretty stories and funny pictures*
    (London: Pavilion, 2010).

¶ YOCHI-YOCHI
Anne Fernald and Hiromi Morikawa, "Common Themes and Cultural Variations in Japanese and American Mothers' Speech to Infants," *Child Development* 64, no. 3 (June 1993).

¶ ZU'
Toni Morrison, *Beloved* (London: Vintage, 2019).

¶ MECHA-KUCHA
House, dir. Nobuhiko Ohbayashi, 1977.
Timothy J. Vance, "What Students of Japanese Can Learn from Akkadian Cuneiform," *Japanese Language and Literature* 48, no. 2 (October 2014).

¶ CHIRA-CHIRA
The Yellow Monkey, "Miteinai yō de miteiru" [Pretending Not to Look at You], *Sicks*, Ariola Japan, 1997.
Love Exposure, dir. Sion Sono, 2008.

¶ JIN-JIN
Jun Togawa, "Virgin Blues," *Shōwa Kyōnen*, Teichiku Entertainment, 1990.
Anne Carson, *Eros the Bittersweet* (Champaign, IL: Dalkey Archive, 1988).
Roland Barthes, *A Lover's Discourse: Fragments,* tr. Richard Howard (London: Vintage, 2002).
Slime Forest Adventure (Fight Slimes, Save a Princess, Learn Japanese!), Project LRNJ. http://lrnj.com.

¶ BARE-BARE
Iris Murdoch, *The Sandcastle* (London: Chatto & Windus, 1957).
Vladimir Nabokov, *Lectures on Literature*, ed. Fredson Bowers (Boston: Houghton Mifflin Harcourt, 2017).

¶ JARA-JARA
Yeah Yeah Yeahs, *Fever to Tell*, Interscope, 2003.
Arcade Fire, "Neighbourhood #1 (Tunnels)," *Funeral*, Me´rge, 2004.
Kō Machida, *Kokuhaku* [Confessions] (Tokyo: Chuokoronsha, 2008).

¶ KORO-KORO

Susan Ervin-Tripp, "An Analysis of the Interaction of Language, Topic, and Listener," *American Anthropologist* 66, no. 6 (December 1964).

Alice Robb, "Multilinguals have Multiple Personalities," *New Republic*, 23 April 2014, https://newrepublic.com/article/117485/multilinguals -have-multiple-personalities.

¶ KIRA-KIRA

aiko, "Kira Kira," *Kanojo*, Pony Canyon, 2006.

¶ SHOBO-SHOBO

Nicholas Bornoff, *Pink Samurai: The Pursuit and Politics of Sex in Japan* (London: Grafton Books, 1992).

Garth Greenwell, " 'I Wanted Something 100% Pornographic and 100% High Art': The Joy of Writing About Sex," *Guardian*, 8 May 2020.

¶ KIRI-KIRI

Audition, dir. Takashi Miike, 1999.

David Howe, *Attachment Across the Lifecourse: A Brief Introduction* (London: Palgrave Macmillan, 2011).

Keiko Takahashi, "Examining the Strange-Situation Procedure with Japanese Mothers and 12-Month-Old Infants," *Developmental Psychology* 22, no. 2 (1986).

Antonia Dodge and Joel Mark Witt, hosts; Bruce Muzik, guest, "Attachment Theory in Relationships," *Personality Hacker* (podcast), episode 0125, 16 May 2016.

Spitz, "Kaede," *Fake Fur*, Polydor, 1998.

¶ SHI'KURI

Misumi Kubo, *So We Look to the Sky*, tr. Polly Barton (New York: Arcade Publishing, 2021).

¶ HI'SORI

Tadaaki Imaizumi (ed.), *Wakeatte shinimashita* [Died for a Reason] (Tokyo: DIAMOND, Inc., 2018).

Leopold von Sacher-Masoch and Gilles Deleuze, *Masochism: Coldness and Cruelty & Venus in Furs*, tr. Jean McNeil (New York: Zone Books, 1999).

¶ UWAA

List of SFX at http://japan-and-me.com/japanese-sfx/.

Tadahiro Ōtsu et al., "Blue Monday Phenomenon among Men: Suicide
Deaths in Japan," *Acta Medica Okayama* 63, no. 5 (2009).

¶ UDA-UDA

Takashi Murakami (ed.), *Little Boy: The Arts of Japan's Exploding Sub-
culture* (New Haven, CT: Yale University Press, 2005).

¶ DON

"Kabedon," Wikipedia, accessed 5 May 2020.

Tom Hanaway, "It's Time to Talk about 'Terrace House' and Consent,"
Japan Times, 10 May 2020.

¶ BORO-BORO

Devo, *Q: Are We Not Men? A: We Are Devo!* Warner Bros, 1978.

¶ SARA-SARA

Roald Dahl, *The Witches* (London: Jonathan Cape, 1983).

Nanae Aoyama, "Kakera" [Fragments], tr. Polly Barton, *The White
Review*, no. 23 (October 2018).

Kakera: A Piece of Our Life, dir. Momoko Ando, 2009.

¶ GU'TARI

Jun Togawa, "Teinen Pushiganga" ['Laughing, Dancing and Drinking
Song of Resignation'], *Tamahime-sama*, Yen Records, 1984.

Talk Talk, "Time It's Time," *The Colour of Spring*, EMI Records, 1986.

Yura Yura Teikoku, *Hollow Me/Beautiful*, DFA Records, 2009.

¶ UHO-UHO

Kikuko Tsumura, *Kono yo ni tayasui shigoto wa nai* [There's No Such
Thing as an Easy Job], tr. Polly Barton (London: Bloomsbury, 2020).

Tenniscoats, "Oetsu to Kanki No Nanoriuta (Given Song by Sob and
Joy)," *Tan-Tan Therapy*, HEADZ, 2007.

ACKNOWLEDGMENTS

THIS BOOK HAS GROWN OUT of tens of thousands of conversations and meetings and textual encounters, and I'm grateful to everyone who and everything which has helped to shape the ideas in here, in some way. Special thanks go:

To Kimihiro Tomioka, for always being there and always making me feel like I'm worth something; to Geraint Howells, for Matsusaka, and for trying with me; to Rose O'Gallivan, for being a perpetual source of books, talks, and joy across so many years; to Michael Troy Judd, an inspiration and an ally; to Asa Yoneda, for helping me understand myself and the world better; to Bernice Birleson, whose wisdom, calm, and optimism I still carry with me; to the earlyish readers of this book, Jozef van der Voort and Daniel Joseph; to Hiromitsu Koiso for tolerating my crazy questions at all times of the day.

To the other people whose friendship and support helped me get through my times in Japan: Caroline and Cameron Archibald, Daniel Demarse, Reiko Ogawa, Ellie Smith, Mila Zviarovich, Masumi Jōmura, and Yuji Nishino.

To people who have helped connect me with ideas and sources which have helped in writing this book: Katherine Finkelstein, Mattho Mandersloot, and Michiyo Miyake. And to all the people at the Spike Island Art Writing Group, especially Leah Reynolds and Eleanor Duffin.

To Jacques Testard, for believing I could do this damn thing when I still didn't, and for his transformative edits; and to Tamara, Joely, and Clare at Fitzcarraldo.

To Guy Robertson, for bringing about one of the most magical summers ever, and to everyone whom I shared my time in Spoleto with.

To the people whose names I can't say here, but who have shaped this book.

To George, for your invaluable help and interlibrary loans, and for being a true friend.

To my mum, for so much, but particularly for showing me the joy of words. To my dad, for always being on my side, and for the Sunday phone calls in Japan. And to both of you, for all the stories.

This book is for Y. Thank you for everything, and for not being scared.

ABOUT THE AUTHOR

POLLY BARTON IS A JAPANESE literary translator. Her translations include *Where the Wild Ladies Are* by Aoko Matsuda, *There's No Such Thing as an Easy Job* by Kikuko Tsumura, and *Spring Garden* by Tomoka Shibasaki. She won the 2019 Fitzcarraldo Editions Essay Prize for *Fifty Sounds*. She lives in Bristol, England.